AFRICAN
COUNTERTERRORISM
COOPERATION

Related Titles from Potomac Books

AFRICAN
COUNTERTERRORISM
COOPERATION

Assessing Regional and Subregional Initiatives

Edited by
Andre Le Sage

Foreword by
General Carlton W. Fulford, Jr.,
USMC (ret.)

Africa Center
for Strategic
Studies

National
Defense
University
Press

Potomac
Books,
Inc.

Washington, D.C.

Library of Congress Cataloging-in-Publication Data
African counterterrorism cooperation : assessing regional and subregional initiatives / edited by Andre Le Sage ; foreword by General Carlton W. Fulford, Jr.— 1st ed.
     p. cm.
Includes bibliographical references and index.
ISBN-13: 978-1-59797-176-8 (hardcover : alk. paper)
ISBN-13: 978-1-59797-177-5 (pbk. : alk. paper)
1. Terrorism—Africa—Prevention. 2. Terrorism—Africa. I. Sage,
     Andre Le.
HV6433.A35A36 2007
363.325'17096—dc22
2007022316

Printed in the United States of America on acid-free paper that meets the American National Standards Institute Z39-48 Standard.

Available from:

Potomac Books, Inc.
22841 Quicksilver Drive
Dulles, Virginia 20166
800-775-2518

First Edition

10 9 8 7 6 5 4 3 2 1

CONTENTS

ILLUSTRATIONS

FOREWORD

Representatives from the African Union (AU), five African regional economic communities (RECs), the U.S. State Department, the Kenya National Counter-Terrorism Center, the United Nations Office on Drugs and Crime, and the South African Institute of International Affairs addressed important issues concerning counterterrorism (CT) in Africa. This volume brings together five of the papers presented by scholars representing the five African regional economic communities; the first and final chapters, written by Andre Le Sage of the Africa Center for Strategic Studies, offer an overview of terrorism threats and vulnerabilities in Africa and a review of U.S. support for African CT efforts.

This workshop series aims to build CT capacity in Africa by evaluating terrorist threats and strategies for countering these challenges through close partnership with the AU. The first workshop for African subregional organizations took place in September 2004 in Washington, DC. Participants discussed the history of terrorism and its evolution, as well as international CT efforts as undertaken by the United Nations. The second workshop focused on the role of the AU and RECs in fighting terrorism and explored specific avenues for building CT capacity throughout the continent.

The workshop addressed three key areas concerning the formulation and execution of CT strategy in Africa. Participants heard presentations concerning the nature and scope of the threats facing the five African regions and discussed the domestic and international factors that render African states vulnerable to terrorist attacks and exploitation. An assessment of African responses to terrorism and discussion of strategies to advance the CT agenda on the continent followed these presentations. In this discussion, participants identified insufficient political will as one of the most important challenges to successful CT strategies.

The workshop closed with the designation of concrete steps that

African RECs would take in order to implement the AU CT Plan of Action. The plan developed at the workshop focused on expanding the capacity of the AU, RECs, and individual states. The workshop furthers the interests of the AU and the U.S. Government through two key goals: universal ratification of the 1999 Organization of African Unity Convention on the Prevention and Combating of Terrorism and designation of CT focal points by all member states and RECs. The Africa Center nonattribution policy fostered frank, vibrant, and informative discussions.

The Africa Center appreciates the great purpose and dedication the participants demonstrated in grappling with the challenges posed by terrorism. Furthermore, their determination to cooperate on many levels to combat terrorist threats bodes well for ongoing efforts to work with African leaders and governments in confronting those challenges.

General Carlton W. Fulford, Jr., USMC (ret.)
Director, Africa Center for Strategic Studies
Washington, DC, October 2005

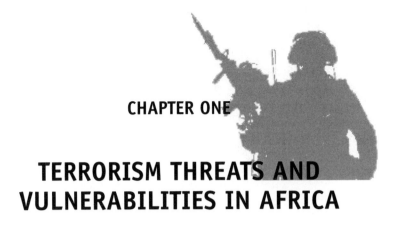

CHAPTER ONE

TERRORISM THREATS AND VULNERABILITIES IN AFRICA

Andre Le Sage

Africa is a continent of growing strategic importance in the global war on terrorism. Over the past decade, a significant number of terrorist attacks and operations have taken place in Africa, both north and south of the Sahara. Many of these attacks have been led by, coordinated with, or purported to be in support of al Qaeda, but others have been launched by African organizations without significant external support. Some of the most prominent attacks and operations over the past decade are mentioned here.

- Al Qaeda's first spectacular attack in Africa was the simultaneous bombing of the U.S. Embassies in Nairobi, Kenya, and Dar es Salaam, Tanzania, in August 1998, killing 224 people and wounding more than 5,000.
- Al Qaeda continued its global terrorist campaign by bombing the USS *Cole* in Yemen in October 2000, killing 17 U.S. Sailors.
- Two different al Qaeda–linked attacks took place in Africa in 2002: a suicide car bomb attack on a synagogue in the popular resort area of Djerba Island, Tunisia, and simultaneous attacks by al Qaeda in Mombasa, Kenya, on a hotel and an airline popular with Jewish tourists.
- In 2003, al Qaeda conducted attacks on Jewish and foreign interests in Casablanca, Morocco, and a violent local uprising occurred by a group in northern Nigeria known as either Takfir wal Hijra or the "Taliban Gang."
- Tourist destinations in Egypt were targeted extensively between 2004 and 2006. In October 2004, attacks in Taba and

1

Ras Shitan killed 34 people. Cairo and Sharm el Sheikh were attacked in April and July 2005, respectively, and bombings in Dahab took place in April 2006.

- The Salafist Group for Preaching and Combat (*Groupe Salafiste pour la Predication et le Combat*, or GSPC) has undertaken regular attacks in Algeria and across the Sahel. In addition to regular raids against government officials and civilian transportation, 32 European tourists were taken hostage in 2003, a Mauritanian border post was attacked in 2005, and GSPC networks were exposed in Mali, Niger, and Chad.

- Attacks in 2006 in Algeria and confrontations with heavily armed militants by security forces in Tunisia confirmed the GSPC's announcement of its subordination to Osama bin Laden and the formation of a unified subregional terrorist group known as al Qaeda in the Land of the Islamic Maghreb (AQIM).

- From June to December 2006, the Supreme Council of Islamic Courts (SCIC) seized control of southern and central Somalia. The SCIC includes former leaders of the al Ittihad al Islami (AIAI) who provide protection for the al Qaeda East Africa cell and are associated with a network of jihadi militants known as Al Shebab.

- From 1996 through 2001, South Africa's Western Cape province witnessed over 100 attacks by the anticrime vigilante movement known as People Against Gangsterism and Drugs (PAGAD). In August 1998, extremists connected to PAGAD conducted their most notorious attack: the bombing of the Planet Hollywood restaurant in Cape Town, which took one life and injured two dozen.

- Lastly, North African extremists—particularly those from Algeria, Morocco, and Tunisia—are well represented in al Qaeda, GSPC, and other terrorist group networks in both Iraq and Europe.

The threat of terrorism is not always the first security concern that comes to mind when discussing Africa. The continent is not a base for any senior al Qaeda leaders, and it is no longer a haven for significant al Qaeda training camps. Moreover, while Africa is endowed with exceptional natural and human resources, it has been plagued for decades by military coups, civil wars, and ethnic conflict. From a broader, human security perspective, poverty, the absence of essential social services, and the devastation wrought by diseases such as malaria, tuberculosis, dysentery, and the HIV/AIDS pandemic are all far greater threats to lives and livelihoods of Africans than terrorism has ever been.[1] This helps explain why African citizens have only been partially receptive to the maxim that the war on terrorism is a global responsibility.

This does not mean, however, that counterterrorism efforts have been ignored in Africa. In fact, even when one excludes the atrocities committed by African rebel and insurgency movements, terrorism was already a factor in African security prior to the events of September 11, 2001, with incidents in Kenya, Tanzania, Tunisia, Egypt, and many other countries. As a result, African governments and regional organizations had taken specific steps—including the adoption of the 1999 Organization of African Unity (OAU) Convention on the Prevention and Combating of Terrorism—to counter the terrorist threat well before the September 11 attacks in the United States.

Terrorists seek to exploit and exacerbate ethnic and religious tensions, leading to increased social tensions and undermining fragile institutional structures. Poverty, the scale of the territories requiring protection, porous borders, ongoing conflicts, and the difficulty of effective international cooperation are all challenges. Institutional weakness, governance problems,[2] and economic marginality have all provided an environment that is highly conducive to the spread of extremism and terrorism. Just as critically, governments have sometimes coopted the rhetoric of counterterrorism to legitimize internal security measures that suppress expressions of political opposition. When this happens, it weakens democratic standards of governance and respect for human rights—factors that can fuel the cycle of conflict.

This chapter begins with an overview of counterterrorism as an African challenge. It argues that the long and bloody history of terrorist attacks in Africa and the wide range of vulnerabilities to terrorist penetration, recruitment, and operation in Africa make counterterrorism a key security priority for both Western and African governments. The second section focuses on the main terrorist threats, including al Qaeda and its associated movements, as well as more local groups that now operate on the continent. It covers the different subregions in turn, including the Horn of Africa, the Trans-Sahara area of North and West Africa, and Southern Africa and the Indian Ocean. Before concluding with an overall assessment of terrorism threats and vulnerabilities across Africa, the third section briefly reviews the wider political implications associated with the "war on terrorism," particularly the concomitant rise of political Islamic sentiment and movements.

Definitional Challenges

Terrorism is widely recognized when it occurs but difficult to define in the abstract. Attempting to arrive at a single definition is fraught with difficulties and has become an inevitably political process. Terrorism is widely viewed as a manifestation of political violence that is distinct from other types of substate violence such as guerrilla warfare, organized crime, and mass civil conflict. It is characterized by premeditation with the aim of creating a climate of extreme fear, the targeting of a wider audience beyond the immediate victims, and the symbolism of its targets, and is generally used to influence broader political behavior and advance a particular set of political and social objectives.[3]

However, efforts to arrive at a common definition of terrorism have also been stymied on a number of fronts. Some assert that terrorism is a tactic employed by a wide range of armed actors and that the line between being treated as a terrorist group rather than a rebel group is not clear. For instance, one of the most vexing dilemmas in the definitional debates surrounds the maxim that "one man's terrorist is another man's freedom fighter." This statement, although now very much a cliché, reflects the difficulty of arriving at a universally accepted definition of terrorism. It is a particularly important point in the African context, given that many countries considered groups such as the African National Congress (ANC) and South West Africa People's Organization (SWAPO)—both of which are now ruling parties in their countries' democratically elected governments—to be terrorist organizations.

Additional definitional problems have emerged during attempts at the United Nations (UN) to draft a Comprehensive Anti-Terrorism Treaty.[4] In particular, the question of "state terrorism"—the use of armed force by a state against civilians during times of war or to repress internal dissent—has been raised. While many see this as sufficiently dealt with by other bodies of law, such as the Geneva Conventions and international human rights instruments, it has remained a sticking point in negotiations. Compounding this problem is the potential for some governments to abuse the terrorism label to justify crackdowns against political opponents and stifle domestic criticism.

In lieu of an agreed definition, many international organizations have opted to criminalize various actions that constitute the most common and egregious forms of terrorist behavior. For instance, the United Nations, in the absence of a single comprehensive treaty, holds 13 different conventions outlawing common terrorist actions ranging from hostage taking and bombings to financing of terrorism and attacks on airports, airplanes, and maritime vessels. Similarly, as detailed in the section on African counterterrorism responses below, the 1999 OAU Convention on the Preventing and Combating of Terrorism defined and outlawed "terrorist acts."[5]

In this chapter, the problem of terrorism is not defined in the abstract but rather addressed from the perspective of individual countries through assessments of what militant and extremist groups are operational across the continent. As a baseline, the chapter begins by investigating the presence of organizations that have been designated as terrorist groups by the U.S. Government and then considers the adequacy of this list through comparison with the present level of threats and vulnerabilities in each African subregion. The three main lists of terrorist groups and operatives used by the U.S. Government include the Foreign Terrorist Organizations (FTO) List (see table 1–1),[6] the Terrorist Exclusion List (TEL),[7] and the list of entities and individuals annexed to Executive Order 13224.[8]

TABLE 1–1 **Groups in Africa on the U.S. Foreign Terrorist Organizations List**
1. Armed Islamic Group
2. Egyptian Islamic Group
3. HAMAS
4. Hezbollah
5. Egyptian Islamic Jihad
6. Libyan Islamic Fighting Group
7. Moroccan Islamic Combatant Group
8. al Qaeda
9. Salafist Group for Preaching and Combat

In addition, the U.S. Secretary of State, as authorized by Section 411 of the USA PATRIOT Act of 2001, has placed a number of Africa-based groups on the TEL (see table 1–2), which has not been officially updated since 2004.

TABLE 1–2 **Groups in Africa on the U.S. Terrorist Exclusion List**
1. al Ittihad al Islami
2. Army for the Liberation of Rwanda
3. Libyan Islamic Fighting Group
4. Moroccan Islamic Combatant Group
5. People Against Gangsterism and Drugs
6. Revolutionary United Front
7. Salafist Group for Preaching and Combat
8. Allied Democratic Forces
9. Lord's Resistance Army
10. Tunisian Combatant Group

Other than commercial operations (such as the Al Barakaat group of companies), nonprofit organizations (such as the Al Haramein Islamic Foundation), and individuals associated with groups named above, the annex to Executive Order 13224 does not name any further terrorist entities known to be present or operating in Africa. Thus, according to the three main U.S. terrorist designation lists, there is a total of 16 terrorist entities, both transnational and domestic, on the continent. This includes 9 Foreign Terrorist Organizations and 10 African groups (including 3 groups already listed as FTOs) on the Terrorist Exclusion List.

However, while the threat posed by terrorists in Africa is very real, the Foreign Terrorist Organizations and Terrorist Exclusion lists do not completely describe that threat. These lists are products of complex and time-consuming bureaucratic deliberations and have not always been able to keep pace with the dynamic evolution of the terrorist threat on the continent. As a result, not all currently active terrorist groups are listed, and some groups that are listed are no longer active. In order to clarify this situation, the conclusion of this chapter will return to the question of which terrorist groups are active in Africa after reviewing the present terrorist threats and vulnerabilities across the continent in the following sections.

Africa's Counterterrorism Challenge

The threat of terrorism is not static and continues to evolve in response to both global political dynamics and specific counterterrorism strategies. In past years, many of the major terrorist groups have been secular, such as the Red Brigades in Italy, or have focused on specific territorial issues, such as the Basques in Spain or the Irish Republican Army in Northern Ireland. Since the 1990s, we have seen the emergence of groups such as al Qaeda and, even more recently, various affiliates in Africa, Southeast Asia, and elsewhere.

Since the war on terror began, the dynamics of terrorism have continued to change at a remarkably fast pace. Internationally coordinated actions to defeat al Qaeda have resulted in the ousting of the Taliban regime that sheltered the group, the capture or killing of the majority of the network's top leadership, and the seizure of millions of dollars in money used to finance terrorism. Most remaining al Qaeda organizers, including Osama bin Laden and Ayman al-Zawahiri, are in hiding, and their abilities to command and control terrorist operations have been severely curtailed.

Nonetheless, terrorist attacks have continued across the globe from Bali and Mombasa to Casablanca, Sharm El Sheikh, Madrid, and London. A number of changes in the ways that terrorists organize and operate have led to their resiliency:

- the transformation of al Qaeda from a centralized organization in a few locations into a loose network of Islamist insurgents and affiliated terrorist operatives around the world, with al Qaeda leaders playing the role of strategists and propagandists and not commanders
- the ability of global terrorist networks to appropriate local grievances and conflicts around the globe into their ideology and political tactics to justify their actions and garner public support
- the planning of low-cost terrorist attacks that do not require the transfer of large sums of money around the world and the use of new mechanisms, including cash smuggling and local criminal activities, to finance terrorist activities
- the use of the ongoing insurgency in Iraq and other continuing conflicts not only as a tool for recruiting a new generation of terrorists, but also as an opportunity to train those recruits and then position them around the globe.

The changing nature of the global terrorist threat in response to post–September 11 security measures has actually come to favor al Qaeda's focus on Africa. Consistent with the evolution of terrorist target selection, attacks have become generally less spectacular than those of September 11. However, they are now less costly in their organization and occur more frequently around the globe. Africa may become a favored destination because of the wide range of "soft" Western targets, ranging from tourist destinations to expatriate hubs to embassies. While concerted efforts have been made to secure these potential targets, the wide range of African countries' vulnerabilities to terrorist penetration (as will be explored below) leaves them exposed.

Realizing that Africa is often the venue for attacks against Western interests rather than African interests, some African leaders have stated that terrorism is primarily a Western problem rather than their own. Others believe their countries' close political ties to the United States or other Western countries make them possible targets. Yet such arguments flounder in the face of the evidence when one considers the wider impact of terrorist incidents. First, one needs to consider the human costs of terrorist attacks. Although Western interests and sites may be targeted when attacks occur in Africa, more Africans are killed than foreigners. This was certainly the case in the U.S. Embassy bombings in Kenya and Tanzania.

Second, terrorism undermines the core African pursuits of democratization and development. In the aftermath of an attack, African governments are forced to undertake aggressive security efforts that often exacerbate preexisting national, regional, ethnic, religious, and class cleavages. The resulting increase in local political tensions serves to forestall continued democratic reform and may, in fact, lead to the resumption of dictatorial or authoritarian governance. Similarly, terrorism exacerbates the difficulties of economic development. Attacks or even the threat of attacks discourage trade, investment, and tourism; destroy national infrastructure; deplete national income; and displace African communities.

There is no indication that the targeting of Africa by al Qaeda or al Qaeda–associated movements is going to decrease in the foreseeable future. Rather, there is growing evidence that al Qaeda is building further capacities and alliances on the continent. Despite the absence of another spectacular terrorist attack in sub-Saharan Africa since the 1998 and 2002 attacks in East Africa, al Qaeda has continued to express interest in the continent. This has come in four related objectives promulgated by Osama bin Laden, Ayman al-Zawahiri, and their followers. First, al Qaeda has made clear its desire to "liberate" African Muslim populations from the rule of "apostate" regimes,[9] which include predominantly Muslim nations in North and West Africa, particularly those with cooperative ties to Western governments and Israel. Second, in mid-2006, al Qaeda made two separate statements encouraging its followers to undertake a jihad against any international peacekeeping operations that take place in Sudan to resolve the Darfur crisis[10] and in Somalia to support the nascent Transitional Federal Government established at a peace conference in 2004.[11] The call to arms was both an indictment by al Qaeda of the United Nations as a pro-Western, anti-Islamic grouping and a warning even to Muslim states such as Tunisia not to partake in any planned peacekeeping deployments.

Third, al Qaeda has referred to countries such as Nigeria as being "ripe" for infiltration.[12] Since Nigeria is a major oil-producing state, this assertion fits with al Qaeda's stated interest to disrupt natural resource exploitation as a means to disrupt the global economy and weaken Western states. Fourth, al Qaeda has long pursued a strategy of connecting with and uniting militant Islamist movements across the globe into an expanded jihadi network. To this end, al Qaeda has sought to spread some of its key operational leaders across Africa through cooperation with al Qaeda–associated movements, such as al Ittihad al Islami in the Horn of Africa and the GSPC in the Trans-Sahara area.

African Vulnerabilities to Terrorism

African countries remain vulnerable to terrorist activities within their borders for a wide range of reasons. When discussing vulnerabilities to terrorism in Africa or other parts of the world, it is necessary to distinguish between the possible root causes or drivers that encourage individuals to lead, join, or support terrorist enterprises and permissive factors that allow existing terrorist movements to undertake operations in a given country. These root causes and permissive factors are very closely related, but the distinction is important. While permissive factors can be addressed by building African capacities, root causes and drivers are far more complicated to mitigate.

Permissive factors include physical, economic, institutional, and political weaknesses in African states' ability to prevent terrorists from entering and operating in their territories. Although every country in Africa is unique, the majority of the following factors apply to each nation.

Physical Safe Havens. Also referred to as "ungoverned spaces," this is a primary lens or "threat paradigm" through which the U.S. Government has come to view terrorist vulnerabilities across Africa.[13] A physical safe haven is an area where the responsible national government is either unable or unwilling to exercise control, and thus it becomes an actual or possible location for terrorists to train, mobilize, and operate. Across the African continent, ungoverned spaces come in four primary forms: dense urban areas (particularly "slums"), rural desert areas, maritime zones, and sections of "weak" or "failing" states that fall outside governments' controls.

Legal Safe Havens. Some African countries lack a suitable legal framework to outlaw terrorism, the provision of material and financial support to terrorists, and incitement to commit terrorist acts. In response to UN Security Council Resolution 1373 (2001) requiring all countries in the world to implement the 13 international conventions and protocols related to terrorism, only 2 countries (Kenya and Togo) have acceded to or ratified all of the documents; only 27 have acceded to or ratified 10 or more; and 13 have acceded to or ratified fewer than 6. Even within the African Union (AU), only 45 African countries (excluding Western Sahara, which is an AU member) have signed the 1999 OAU Convention on the Prevention and Combating of Terrorism, and only 35 of these countries have ratified it.

Financial Safe Havens. African countries are also vulnerable to terrorist efforts to mobilize and transfer funds for their operational purposes. An estimated $125 billion moves through the remittance, or *hawala*, economy each year, and many countries are highly dependent on remittances for their financial well-being.[14] Remittance systems are largely unregulated arrangements for money transfers based on trust. They are particularly popular among diaspora communities to send relatively small amounts of money to family abroad in a way that helps avoid taxes and fees and reaches locations where traditional banks are not present. International pressure has induced larger remittance companies to adopt some minimum standards of information collection regarding customers. However, efforts that overregulate or close remittance companies do not stop the practice of *hawala*, but rather they push it further underground and out of sight. There is also the special case of South Africa, as described below, which has sophisticated financial systems that are not yet adequately monitored or regulated and may be subject to abuse.

Organized Crime and Smuggling Networks. Criminal and smuggling networks (for illegal immigration, money, drugs, weapons, and other commodities) provide opportunities for terrorists and militants to mobilize funds, move operatives, and build networks with other armed groups. There is no evidence that terrorist groups are merging with criminal syndicates in Africa. Rather, terrorists are emulating criminals through their involvement in a wide range of illegal activities, including kidnappings; smuggling of weapons, people, drugs, cigarettes, car parts, and bootleg music and films; credit card fraud; counterfeiting; and protection racketeering. Increased terrorist reliance on criminal means is particularly alarming since those activities are hard to monitor and stop. Additionally, the involvement of corrupt local officials in illicit activities in some locations compromises states' abilities to act.

Competing Domestic Interests. Terrorism is only one of numerous security challenges facing Africans today. Efforts to respond to terrorist threats and vulnerabilities inevitably compete with demands posed by poverty, weak public institutions, corruption, efforts to promote democratic reform, protracted insurgencies and civil conflicts, tense regional relations, and the scourge of HIV/AIDS, to name only a few. Counterterrorism cooperation with Western countries, particularly the United States, is also a political football in many African countries.

Tense Regional Relations. Despite many positive efforts, interstate cooperation, information sharing, and combined operations are in some cases made difficult or impossible by lingering national and foreign policy disputes and the fallout from continuing civil conflicts. This is the case, for instance, between Ethiopia and Eritrea over the demarcation of their border, between Morocco and Algeria over the status of Western Sahara and the Polisario Front, between many Sahelian countries and Libya and Burkina Faso for support given to Tuareg movements, and between countries across West Africa given the spillover from recent conflicts in Côte d'Ivoire, Sierra Leone, and Liberia.

Weapons Availability. Decades of civil wars, fueled in part by military support from world powers during the Cold War and continued access to black market arms dealers, have left North and West African countries awash with small arms and ammunition. In addition, rocket-propelled grenades, mortars, antipersonnel and antitank landmines, and other explosive materials are not difficult to acquire, while some conflicts have involved the use of truck-mounted artillery, indicating that it too is available in the region. Despite the incorrect assertions in the run-up to the Iraq war regarding yellowcake uranium from Niger, some African states remain in possession of mines or nuclear processing facilities, where extremists could obtain dangerous materials, possibly to use in a "dirty bomb."

Weak Border, Port, and Customs Controls. Africa's long and remote borders are largely unmonitored and uncontrolled, making terrorist transit a serious potential problem. Illegal immigration, refugee flows, and human smuggling networks are a significant part of the problem. In addition, false documentation and fraudulent passports, the limited number of trained and motivated border guards and customs officials, and the prevalence of corruption across Africa leave even official points of entry vulnerable.

Lack of Public Information and Support. As noted earlier, Africa has been plagued for decades by military coups, civil wars, and ethnic conflict. From a broader, human security perspective, poverty, the absence of essential social services, and the devastation wrought by diseases such as malaria, tuberculosis, dysentery, and the HIV/AIDS pandemic are all far greater threats to lives and livelihoods of Africans than terrorism has ever been. This helps to explain why some African citizens have only been partially receptive to the idea that the war on terrorism is a global responsibility. Further, a lack of clear public information about the threat of terrorism in Africa and its implications for Africans has not helped to overcome such beliefs.

Grievances and Ideological Support for Extremism

There is no firm answer to the question of what drives or causes terrorism. Two common notions are that terrorism is fueled by either the lack of democracy or the desperation associated with extreme poverty. On the one hand, repressive and unrepresentative governance, combined with popular anger toward a government's inability to effect positive change, is thought to preclude options for peaceful resistance and lead to violent efforts to delegitimize and overthrow a country's leaders.[15]

On the other hand, high rates of poverty, unemployment, and other factors leading to marginalization of entire social groups may be seen as a condition that may create a pool of potential terrorist recruits.[16] Urbanization has concentrated the poor in slums that compound both the pressures that they face and the challenge of effective security monitoring. Desertification and environmental degradation have been exacerbating factors, undermining the livelihoods of agricultural and pastoralist populations alike and resulting in pauperization and population movements that spark conflicts over access to land and water supplies.

There are, however, two different problems with these arguments. First, with regard to the poverty thesis, Africa is home to some of the poorest and most globally marginalized populations in the world. If increased poverty levels are directly associated with increased terrorism, then Africa would be a hotbed of terrorist groups and attacks. Further, a review of the socioeconomic profile of the leaders and operatives of the al Qaeda movement indicates that many—including Osama bin Laden and Ayman al-Zawahiri as well as the leaders of associated movements in Africa—are actually well-educated and hail from financially well-off families. In other words, the evidence does not support a strong correlation between poverty and terrorism, especially with regard to terrorist leaders. At most, poverty can explain the terrorist leaders' abilities to recruit and pay for support from foot soldiers.

The democracy thesis is equally complicated. Terrorism is sometimes associated with violent protest against unrepresentative governments. However, protests against dictatorship also take many other forms, ranging from peaceful demonstrations to grassroots insurgencies. Terrorism is not the only option available to "freedom fighters," nor is it the most readily chosen. In fact, studies of the use of suicide bombings in terrorism around the world have found correlation not with local authoritarian governance but with foreign military occupation.[17] Further, the reverse argument that increased levels of democracy lead to decreasing terrorism is not straightforward. In the long term, this may be the case. However, in the short run, democratic change that destabilizes existing governance structures may reduce the capacities of national security services to prevent violence, increase violent political competition between local groups, and even bring to power militant movements that support terrorist actions amongst their allies in other countries.

In addition to issues of poverty and democratization, complicated domestic politics and rising anger toward the United States and other Western governments must be considered. First, the ability of local governments in Africa to promote reform is limited by overlapping national, regional, ethnic, religious, and class cleavages. These domestic conflicts make governments feel insecure and, at the same time, make many groups suspicious of any government security activities, including counterterrorism efforts. It is distinctly possible that these overlapping cleavages can create sufficient tension for some local groups to find common cause with extremists and militants against the government and their international partners.

Second, even where local populations do not support terrorist and extremist movements, they often hold antipathy toward Western governments, particularly the United States.[18] Muslim populations are particularly sensitive to the U.S. occupation of Iraq, the perceived lack of U.S. effort to resolve the Israeli-Palestinian crisis, and the controversies surrounding Abu Ghraib, Guantanamo Bay, and Central Intelligence Agency (CIA) renditions of terrorism suspects. Both Muslim and non-Muslim public opinion has also turned against U.S. policy, which is perceived as imperialistic, bombastic, and/or unconcerned with local poverty, the local impacts of globalization, and bad governance.

In short, no single factor is sufficient to understand the root causes of terrorism. Many factors lead to the feelings of alienation and antagonism that make terrorist recruitment possible. It must be recognized that in addition to poverty and unrepresentative governance, anger at unpopular policies of foreign governments—for instance, the U.S. decision to invade and occupy Iraq—is associated with increased ideological support for terror. In the African context, sympathy for the plight of Palestinians among African Muslim communities is also a critical factor. Finally, terrorism does not begin as a popular movement or uprising. In Africa, terrorist groups tend to be small, organized networks, involving leaders (often well-educated, middle-class men) and cliques of committed individuals who invent, adopt, and propagate specific ideologies that justify their recourse to violence.[19]

Terrorist Threats in Africa

This section summarizes the threats posed by terrorist groups in the five different subregions of Africa (see figure 1–1) as well as reviews specific vulnerabilities faced in each area. While nearly all African countries can be viewed as highly vulnerable to terrorist operations owing to the factors described in the previous sections, the determination of the threat posed to each country is based on the presence, intentions, and capacities of terrorist groups.

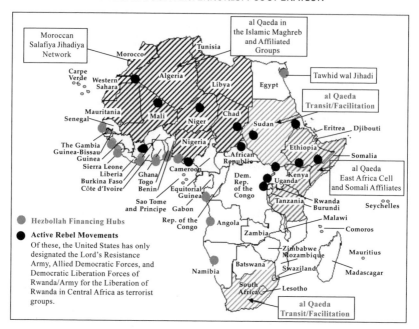

FIGURE 1–1. Map of Major Terrorist Groups in Africa

It should be noted that the terrorist group with the widest ranging presence in Africa is Hezbollah. The group's presence in Africa is directly linked to that of expatriate Lebanese business communities, primarily in West Africa but also in parts of Central and Southern Africa. In nearly a dozen countries, it is generally accepted that some members of this community contribute funds to Hezbollah, though the exact extent is unknown. That said, in the tables presented in this section, Hezbollah is not explicitly listed as a terrorist threat since the group does not maintain an operational capacity or intention to launch terrorist attacks on the African continent.

The Horn of Africa and East Africa

The Horn and East African subregion is a source of primary terrorist threats and vulnerabilities on the continent. The current terrorist presence and level of threat for each country in Southern Africa are summarized in table 1–3.

The particular dynamics of concern in the Horn and East African subregion are detailed below.

Somalia. This is the primary hub of terrorist activity in the Horn and East African subregion. Somalia's vulnerability to terrorism is significant. The country is a base for both al Qaeda's East Africa cell and Islamist militants associated with the AIAI terrorist

TABLE 1–3 Terrorist Presence in Horn of Africa and East Africa		
Country	Level of Threat	Terrorist Presence
Djibouti	Significant	al Ittihad al Islami (AIAI)
Eritrea	Low	Eritrean Islamic Jihad Movement
Ethiopia	Significant	AIAI
Kenya	Significant	al Qaeda and AIAI
Somalia	Significant	al Qaeda and AIAI
Tanzania	Moderate	Possibly al Qaeda and AIAI

group. On multiple occasions, al Qaeda has used Somalia to prepare for operations and seek safe haven after launching successful attacks in neighboring countries—notably the 1998 bombing of the U.S. Embassies in Kenya and Tanzania and the 2002 simultaneous attacks near Mombasa, Kenya, that targeted the Paradise Hotel and an Israeli commercial jet. In addition, a number of other attacks have been planned from Somalia but were then disrupted, including an effort to fly an explosives-laden aircraft into the new U.S. Embassy in Nairobi, Kenya, in August 2003,[20] and the September–October 2003 reconnaissance of the Combined Joint Task Force–Horn of Africa military base in Djibouti for targeting with a suicide truck-bombing attack.[21]

Al Qaeda's East Africa cell includes key individuals such as Abu Talha al-Sudani, Fazul Abdullah Mohammed (also known as "Harun"), Salah Ali Salah "Nabhan," and Isse Osman Isse, among others.[22] They receive support from a network of Somali Islamist militants connected with the AIAI terrorist group. Designated AIAI leaders, including Hassan Dahir Aweis and Hassan Abdullah Hersi "al Turki," operate across southern Somalia and maintain operational ties with jihadi supporters across Somalia, as well as Ethiopia, Djibouti, Kenya, and possibly other Horn and East African countries. AIAI is considered by many analysts to be a defunct organization, but its leaders took on new roles in the Supreme Council of Islamic Courts that controlled Mogadishu and much of southern Somalia from June through December 2006.[23]

Young foreign jihadis were attracted to Somalia by fighting with U.S.-backed warlords in the same year, leading to the emergence of an extremist militant arm of the SCIC known as Al Shebab ("The Youth").[24] Shebab militants, led by Ibrahim Haji al-Afghani, Aden Hashi Ayro, and Ahmed Abdi Godane, have been responsible for over a dozen assassinations in Somalia, targeting Western aid workers and journalists, Somali politicians and peace activists, and Somali security personnel supporting counterterrorism efforts. Despite an Ethiopian military incursion in late 2006 and early 2007 that successfully dislodged the SCIC from power, none of these high-value targets are known to have been captured or killed, and they appear to be reorganizing as urban insurgents in Mogadishu. Their targets include the Transitional Federal Government and foreign peacekeeping forces from the African Union.

Other Countries in East Africa. The threat posed by terrorist groups in East Africa outside of Somalia is much more difficult to detail. It remains an ongoing challenge for U.S. intelligence collection operations to provide more specific details of the terrorist threats in the subregion. Without a single, identifiable network through which terrorists organize their efforts, such as the old AIAI network in Somalia and their current manifestation as the "hard-liners" and jihadis within the SCIC, terrorist threats in other countries in East Africa can only be detailed at the micro level, involving the personal support network and activities of individual terrorist operatives and their facilitators.

Despite intensive African and international counterterrorism efforts in the subregion, al Qaeda has maintained a limited operational presence and is able to organize, resource, and launch cross-border attacks from southern Somalia.

- Kenya has been unable to successfully prosecute local affiliates of al Qaeda, including Aboud Rogo, leaving terrorist suspects free to organize and mobilize support.[25]
- In Djibouti, al Qaeda's East Africa cell and AIAI cooperated in sending an operative, Gouled Hassan Dourad, to Djibouti from September to October 2003 to conduct reconnaissance for a suicide truck-bombing attack against Camp Lemonier.[26]
- In Ethiopia, AIAI militants have been implicated in numerous attacks over the past 15 years, including the targeting of state-owned hotels and private businesses in both Addis Ababa and other towns in eastern Ethiopia with explosives and hand grenades.[27]
- In response to the continuing border crisis between Ethiopia and Eritrea, the latter's government has provided support, including military trainers and military supplies, to the Somali Islamic Courts. Some of this is likely to fall into the hands of al Qaeda and AIAI elements connected to the SCIC.[28]

- In addition, Eritrea has supported the operations of Ethiopian rebel movements, including the Oromo National Liberation Front and Ogadeni Liberation Front, to enter Ethiopia from Somalia.[29]
- Eritrean Islamic Jihad Movement (EIJM) is a militant Islamist splinter group of the Eritrean independence movement and is opposed to the current Eritrean government. Based in Eritrea's western provinces on the border with Sudan, EIJM is not a U.S.-designated terrorist group, although it has been responsible for numerous guerrilla attacks.[30]

Ideological support for terrorism amongst Somalis in the subregion exists only in a small cadre of Islamist militants associated with al Qaeda, AIAI, and a limited number of Wahabist or Salafi mosques. However, much of the Somali public supports prominent roles for Islamist leaders and the implementation of shari'a law as the basis for reconstructing the Somali state. This is because of a number of factors, including anger toward the country's clan-based warlords and militia factions for failing to negotiate peace; confidence in the ability of Mogadishu's shari'a courts to deliver security; and desire to use the pan-Somali nature of Islam as a force for national unity.[31]

In northern Kenya and coastal areas of both Kenya[32] and Tanzania,[33] support for Islamic extremism is also limited. However, it may grow in response to local lawlessness, criminality, corruption, poverty, and public antipathy toward the poor performance of the local governments. Favorable public opinion toward Western countries, particularly the United States, has been affected by controversies surrounding compensation for Kenyan victims of the 1998 U.S. Embassy bombings, the issuance of terrorism-related travel warnings, efforts to promote antiterrorism legislation that is considered discriminatory or liable to abuse, and concerns about U.S. foreign policy with particular regard to the war in Iraq.

Finally, all countries in the subregion provide easy access for weapons procurement, movement of funds, and transit of terrorist operatives, although ideological support for terrorist activities has not gained substantial influence beyond a small cadre of Islamist militants.

North Africa and the Sahel

The North African subregion is a second area of significant terrorism threats and vulnerabilities on the continent. In addition to occasional actions by al Qaeda operatives, the region is home to a large number of al Qaeda–affiliated groups. The current terrorist presence and level of threat for each country in North Africa and the Sahel are summarized in table 1–4.

Despite efforts by governments across North Africa to enhance border security to prevent the movement of terrorist operatives and limit their access to weapons or funds, the potential of corruption, lack of resources, and limited numbers of trained, equipped, and motivated personnel mean that borders remain porous. Thus far, support for terrorist groups has been primarily motivated by desires to establish Islamic states and to join al Qaeda in opposing Western foreign policies, particularly with regard to the U.S.-led war on terrorism, the Israeli-Palestinian conflict, and the war in Iraq.[34] However, there is a real danger that radicals who seek dramatic political changes may increasingly pursue violent forms of opposition. Although North African governments have been able to maintain order and prevent further attacks through the deployment of their security services, governments in the subregion may eventually prove unable to suppress political opposition. At the same time, any rapid shift toward political liberalization would be met with the reestablishment of Islamic political parties with significant public support.

While the entire region shares many of the same vulnerabilities to terrorism, threats are specific to each of the countries.

Morocco. In addition to the Moroccan Islamic Combatant Group (GICM) and the possible presence of al Qaeda itself, an unknown number of unnamed clandestine terrorist cells is present in the country, often referred to under the banner of Salafiya Jihadiya (SJ).[35] In May 2003, terrorists connected with these groups launched a series of coordinated mass-casualty attacks against Western and Jewish interests in the country, specifically in Casablanca. Following widespread arrests of suspected terrorists in Morocco, much of the known leadership and membership of GICM moved to Western Europe.[36]

Although the precise number and identity of SJ networks and cells are unknown, they appear to be growing. The March 2004 train bombings in Madrid were linked in part to Moroccan militants, including the SJ network known as Al Oussououd Al Khalidine, or "The Eternal Lions."[37] Most recently, in July and August 2006, over 50 people suspected of collusion in a network named Jama'at Ansar al Mehdi were arrested for plotting attacks that would rival, if not exceed, the scale of the Casablanca bombings.[38]

Despite the continued guerrilla operations of the Polisario Front to achieve independence for Western Sahara, there are no indications that this three-decade-long conflict has drawn in terrorist elements. However, the possibility of future ties between militant Polisario splinter groups and either al Qaeda or Moroccan terrorists cannot

TABLE 1–4
Terrorist Presence in North Africa and the Sahel

Country	Level of Threat	Terrorist Presence
Algeria	Significant	Salafist Group for Preaching and Combat (GSPC)/ al Qaeda in the Land of the Islamic Maghreb (AQIM), Armed Islamic Group, and Djamaat Houmet Dawa Salafiya
Chad	Low	GSPC transit
Egypt	Significant	Tawhid wal Jihad and likely dormant al Qaeda cells
Libya	Moderate	Libyan Islamic Fighting Group (LIFG) and al Qaeda transit
Mali	Moderate	GSPC
Mauritania	Moderate	GSPC and Mauritanian Group for Preaching and Jihad
Morocco	Significant	Moroccan Islamic Combat Group and Salafiya Jihadiya networks with al Qaeda support
Niger	Low	GSPC transit
Sudan	Moderate	al Qaeda, al Ittihad al Islami, Lord's Resistance Army, Allied Democratic Forces, HAMAS, LIFG, and other non-operational groups
Tunisia	Moderate	GSPC/AQIM, Tunisian Combatant Group, and al Qaeda transit

be entirely discounted.[39] In addition, tensions between the Moroccan and Algerian governments resulting from the Western Sahara conflict continue to undermine diplomatic relations required for regional cooperation against terrorism.

Algeria and the Sahel. A number of transnational and domestic terrorist groups are present in Algeria, including the GSPC, the Armed Islamic Group (GIA), and smaller movements such as the Djamaat Houmet Dawa Salafiya (DHDS). The GIA is largely a spent and inactive force with less than 100 militia members, while groups such as DHDS are essentially small networks of clandestine cells. Neither has any substantial base of public support. However, the GSPC has emerged as one of the most significant al Qaeda–associated movements in Africa and has spread its area of operation from its base in northeast Algeria across the Sahara into Mali and other Sahelian countries.[40] The GSPC's transnational focus and its attempt to cooperate with, if not coordinate, militants from across the subregion are symbolized in its merger with al Qaeda in 2006 and its subsequent adoption of the new name al Qaeda in the Land of the Islamic Maghreb (AQIM) in January 2007.

Elements of the Algeria-based GSPC led by Mokhtar Belmokhtar (also known as Mokhtar Bin Mokhtar) are increasingly present in northern Mali. GSPC elements in northeast Algeria have come under intensifying pressure from Algerian security services. A small number of GSPC units initially moved south of the Sahara in order to access funds for their compatriots in Algeria through involvement in smuggling and protection racketeering. However, the area of the Sahel from northern Mali across to Mauritania has effectively become a second theater of operations for the GSPC.

GSPC units in northern Mali and Niger operate with support from a segment of the Tuareg community. While some local supporters may believe in the GSPC cause, the main motivation of Tuareg facilitation of the GSPC is likely much more parochial. In particular, GSPC operatives have cultivated Tuareg loyalty by offering money and participation in cross-border smuggling rackets and by marrying into prominent Tuareg families. Tuareg motivation stems from longstanding tensions between Tuareg rebels and the Malian government and the limited implementation of the Pact Nationale that ended the civil conflict between them in 1992.

The most significant source of funds for the GSPC is widely reported to be protection racketeering for regional smuggling networks, including drugs, weapons, and human trafficking, as well as the trade in contraband cigarettes and petrol. Terrorist groups also receive additional funds remitted from supporters in Europe.[41]

Until 2003, there was no indication that operatives of GSPC,

GIA, or other groups were targeting U.S. or other foreign interests in Algeria. However, GSPC commander Amari Saifi (also known as Abdirizak or "Al Para") led the 2003 kidnapping and ransoming of 32 Western tourists in southern Algeria. In 2004, Al Para was captured in Chad by the Movement for Democracy and Justice in Chad and eventually turned over to the Algerian government.[42] The GSPC also plays a critical role in facilitating al Qaeda operations in Europe, particularly the recruitment and transit of North African operatives to and from terrorist cells in Iraq and other Middle Eastern countries.[43] In addition, the recent alliance between GSPC and al Qaeda, formalized in September 2006, is likely to retarget GSPC attacks toward Western interests.[44]

Subsequently, in January 2007, the GSPC changed its name to al Qaeda in the Land of the Islamic Maghreb. Two recent events have demonstrated the seriousness of this transformation of the GSPC into the AQIM. Three GSPC attacks using improvised explosive devices in October and December 2006 were the first GSPC activities inside the Algerian capital in years. In addition, the December explosion targeted U.S. and other foreign oil workers. As described below, there is also the possibility that, under the AQIM banner, the GSPC is attempting to synchronize operations with jihadi militants in Morocco and Tunisia.[45]

Tunisia. Tunisia's vulnerability to terrorism is moderate. In April 2002, al Qaeda demonstrated its capacity and intentions to attack Tunisia by exploding a truck laden with flammable liquid in front of a Jewish synagogue at the popular tourist resort of Djerba Island.[46] From that time until late 2006, the Tunisian security services effectively clamped down on Islamist organizations, including both militant activity associated with the Tunisian Combatant Group (TCG) and political activity associated with the Al Nahda movement. This forced most Tunisian Islamists to seek refuge abroad, particularly in Europe. It was assumed that some residual jihadi capacity continued to exist in Tunisia, focused on terrorist recruitment and facilitation of travel to fight with al Qaeda in Iraq or elsewhere. However, it was also believed that Tunisian security efforts effectively kept the problem under control. This assessment began to change in December 2006, when Tunisian forces engaged heavily armed militants in the suburbs of Tunis. The militants, apparently in cooperation with the GSPC and possibly part of the evolving AQIM network, had detailed plans of Western embassies and a significant cache of weapons and explosives.[47]

Mauritania. The GSPC elements led by Mokhtar Bin Mokhtar are also operational in northern Mauritania and attacked an eastern

Mauritanian border post in June 2005.[48] Another terrorist group, the Mauritanian Group for Preaching and Jihad (GMPJ), has also emerged locally and is concentrated in Nouakchott and other urban centers. GMPJ, which appears to be inspired by al Qaeda and associated movements in North Africa, aspires to establish a fundamentalist Islamic state in the country. Other small, clandestine Islamist terrorist networks may exist in the country as well, as evidenced by Internet postings in May 2006 under the name of the Islamic Front for Jihad in Mauritania.[49]

Libya. Libya's vulnerability to terrorism is moderate. While Libya was considered a state sponsor of terrorism and it provided safe haven and material support for a wide range of terrorist groups—including the terrorists who executed the 1988 bombing of Pan Am Flight 103, and others such as the Popular Front for the Liberation of Palestine and the Abu Nidal Organization—the country has renounced terrorism, and its cooperation in the global war on terrorism has increased significantly. As a result, the United States restored full diplomatic ties with Libya in 2006. The Libyan Islamic Fighting Group (LIFG), some members of which are also associated with al Qaeda, is present in the country. Libyan security services have effectively suppressed LIFG activities within the country, forcing most operatives to seek refuge abroad, particularly in Europe. Nonetheless, LIFG does maintain enough of a presence and capacity in Libya to support the recruitment and travel of fighters to other jihadi insurgencies.[50]

Egypt. While Egypt was home to numerous Islamist terrorist groups that emerged from the Muslim Brotherhood network, including the Egyptian Islamic Group (EIG) and Egyptian Islamic Jihad (EIJ), the majority of leaders of this first generation of Egyptian terrorists has either been arrested, killed, or fled the country. While EIG has respected the ceasefire its leaders declared in March 1999, EIJ is now defunct since its members, including Osama bin Laden's deputy Ayman al-Zawahiri, joined the core al Qaeda group. These events led to a drastic reduction in the terrorist threat to Egypt for nearly 5 years.[51]

A new wave of terrorist attacks—including attacks in October 2004 in Taba and Ras Shitan, in Cairo in April 2005, in Sharm al Sheikh in July 2005, and in Dahab in April 2006—were inspired by and may have been facilitated by al Qaeda. However, the terrorists who perpetrated these acts were drawn from Bedouin tribal groups living in the northern Sinai Peninsula and were motivated by a mix of anger at enduring poverty and political marginalization and of rising ideological support among young militants for global jihad. The primary terrorist group drawn from the Bedouin community is Tawhid wal Jihad, which was led by Nasser Khamis al Mallahi and Mohamed Abdullah Abu Grair until they were respectively killed and captured by Egyptian authorities. Despite these successes, Tawhid and other groups may continue to operate clandestinely.[52]

Sudan. Sudan's vulnerability to terrorism is moderate. Sudan has long been listed by the U.S. Government as a state sponsor of terrorism. The country provided safe haven and material support for a range of terrorist groups—including, inter alia, al Qaeda, the Egyptian Islamic Group, HAMAS, Palestinian Islamic Jihad, and the Libyan Islamic Fighting Group, as well as sub-Saharan African groups such as al Ittihad al Islami (AIAI), the Lord's Resistance Army, and the Allied Democratic Forces. Under international pressure, al Qaeda was forced to leave Sudan in 1996, at which time it relocated to Afghanistan. However, only following internal political changes and the events of September 11 has the Sudanese government made substantial efforts to curtail its support for these groups, and its cooperation in the global war on terrorism has increased significantly.[53]

As a result, Sudan is no longer a substantial base for terrorist leaders or the planning and resourcing of terrorist attacks. The country does, however, remain an important hub for Sudanese and foreign extremists who support terrorist groups with extremist proselytism, ideological mobilization, recruitment, funding, and possibly logistical support. It remains possible that a small number of terrorist training camps and businesses and Islamic charities dedicated to financing terrorist activities continue to operate in the country under the protection of Islamist hard-liners in the government, particularly in the state security forces.[54]

Although the Comprehensive Peace Agreement is being implemented to end the long-running conflict between northern and southern Sudan, the continuation of the civil war in the western Darfur regions has implications for terrorism. In particular, al Qaeda has expressly condemned plans to replace AU peacekeepers with a United Nations force and has appealed for al Qaeda supporters to launch a jihad against any foreign troops participating in such an operation. In addition, individuals associated with the Arab Gathering (a network promoting the power of extreme nationalists from Sudan's northern Arab tribes) and the Sudanese Muslim Brotherhood (led by Hassan al Turabi) have both made use of the Darfur conflict to mobilize support.

West Africa

The West African subregion has experienced far less terrorist activity than either North or East Africa. With the exception of Nigeria and Senegal, all countries in the subregion face few terrorist threats, although each is highly vulnerable to terrorist penetration and operations should the attentions of terrorist groups shift. Although the Revolutionary United Front (RUF) in Sierra Leone has been placed on the U.S. Terrorist Exclusion List, that group no longer represents a military or terrorist threat following the end of hostilities in 2002, and it continues to exist only as a marginal political party.

The current terrorist presence and level of threat for each country in West Africa are summarized in table 1–5.

Nigeria. Nigeria's vulnerability to terrorism is moderate, owing to the presence of extremist groups in the country and the stated intention of terrorists to attack both Nigerian and foreign interests there.[55] There are significant concerns that al Qaeda is seeking to penetrate Nigeria after a video statement issued by Osama bin Laden targeting the country because of its close ties to the United States, its critical role as an oil supplier to the global economy, and the significant size of the country's Muslim population.[56]

TABLE 1–5
Terrorist Presence in West Africa

Country	Level of Threat	Terrorist Presence
Benin	Low	None
Burkina Faso	Low	None
Cape Verde	Low	None
Côte d'Ivoire	Low	None
Senegal	Moderate	None
Gambia	Low	None
Ghana	Low	None
Guinea	Low	None
Guinea-Bissau	Low	None
Liberia	Low	None
Nigeria	Moderate	Salafist Group for Preaching and Combat and possibly al Qaeda
Sierra Leone	Low	None
Togo	Low	None

The Algeria-based GSPC has spread its operations across the Sahel and established ties as far south as Nigeria. The group does not maintain an operational capacity in the country but is known to have recruited a limited number of Nigerian nationals. Some of these individuals likely emerged from Takfir wal Hijra, which is also referred to as the "Taliban Gang." Takfir was a hierarchical and well-organized movement counting 200 to 300 members based in northeastern Nigeria in 2003. After a series of attacks in 2004, government security services succeeded in arresting and dispersing the majority of Takfir militants. Nigerian security services fear the possibility that the group could either merge with the GSPC, provide assistance to al Qaeda to enter into Nigeria, or transform into a criminal/rebel group.

Finally, Nigeria's delta region remains unstable as armed groups regularly attack Nigerian and foreign oil production interests and take hostage employees of oil companies. The Movement for the Emancipation of the Niger Delta is a particular threat; however, the group is not known to have any ties to al Qaeda or other transnational terrorist groups, and it has not been designated a terrorist entity by the United States.[57]

Senegal. Senegal's current vulnerability to terrorism is moderate, although the evolution of political Islamist movements in the country and their ties to al Qaeda or other terrorist groups must be monitored closely.[58] Two local Islamist movements—Jama'at Ibadu Rahmane (JIR) and Moustarchidine wal Moustarchidates (MWM)—receive support from radical clerics, some Senegalese intellectuals and businessmen, and a growing number of students. These movements oppose traditional Sufist Islamic practices and may seek to transform Senegal into an Islamic state.[59] Both JIR's and MWM's politics remain focused on overt opposition to Senegalese government policies; however, ideological extremism and militancy could develop among splinter groups. Nonetheless, there is no indication that Senegal's Muslim community, which comprises over 90 percent of the country's population, has been receptive to extremist ideologies. This is despite the growing presence of foreign fundamentalist groups, such as Jama'at al Tabliq and Islamic charities associated in other countries with terrorist groups.

Across the West African subregion, although individuals within the Lebanese community may divert a portion of revenues from licit and illicit business activities to support Hezbollah, the group does not maintain a substantial presence and has never used the area as a base for terrorist operations.[60] Regional instability and civil wars in West African countries provide easy access to small arms and light weapons. In addition, weak border control, corruption, and limited government capacity make it possible for terrorists to use the subregion for transit, financial, or logistical purposes.

Southern Africa

The situation in Southern Africa is dramatically different from the subregions discussed above. There is no indication that terrorist groups are present in Southern Africa in any significant number. There are no known terrorist leaders in the subregion, although an unknown number of foot soldiers who are primarily focused on facilitating funding, transit, and hiding for terrorist groups, particularly al Qaeda, have been active.[61] The current terrorist presence and level of threat for each country in Southern Africa are summarized in table 1–6.

However, the subregion's relatively high levels of development and political stability have made Southern Africa an attractive venue for terrorist operational planning and safe haven for a variety of reasons.

- Porous borders, corruption, and easy access to travel documents—combined with excellent port, road, and airport infrastructure—make transit possible.
- Modern banking systems and criminal syndicates make money laundering and resource mobilization possible.
- High crime rates and regional weapons smuggling make access to small arms and explosives possible.

TABLE 1–6
Terrorist Presence in Southern Africa

Country	Level of Threat	Terrorist Presence
Angola	Low	None
Botswana	Low	None
Lesotho	Low	None
Malawi	Low	None
Mozambique	Moderate	Transit by al Qaeda and possibly al Ittihad al Islami
Namibia	Low	None
South Africa	Moderate	al Qaeda and People Against Gangsterism and Drugs
Swaziland	Low	None
Zambia	Low	Past al Qaeda transit
Zimbabwe	Low	None

- The operating environment is secure so long as terrorist supporters and transient operatives do not break local laws or otherwise attract the attention of local police.
- Muslim populations are peaceful but are increasingly targeted for extremist indoctrination by foreign charities and preachers.[62]

Numerous al Qaeda operatives have been arrested in the subregion or captured after transiting it, including:

- Khalid Rashid, who was allegedly rendered from South Africa in November 2005 for al Qaeda connections in Pakistan
- Haroon Rashid Aswat in Zambia (after leaving South Africa) in July 2005 for his connections to the London bombings
- Ahmed Khalfan Ghailani, a key al Qaeda member involved in the 1998 embassy bombings, and two South African supporters in Pakistan, where Ghailani moved via South Africa
- Khalfan Khamis Mohamed in Cape Town in 1999 (after transiting Tanzania and Mozambique) for plotting the U.S. Embassy bombings
- Fazul Mohamed Harun of the al Qaeda East Africa cell, who lived in Zimbabwe as the U.S. Embassy bombings were being planned.[63]

Although there are no countries in Southern Africa with a significant vulnerability to terrorism, two countries have a moderate vulnerability.

South Africa. South Africa's vulnerability to terrorism results from the presence of three different types of terrorist groups within the country. First, as detailed above, a number of al Qaeda operatives and affiliates have maintained a presence in South Africa for unspecified durations before being detained either locally or abroad. In addition, al Qaeda must maintain a network of supporters to facilitate these operatives' entry into and stay in the country. In January 2007, the United States moved to designate two South African businessmen and religious leaders from the Dockrat Family as terrorist facilitators supporting al Qaeda with funding and recruitment.[64] Second, Hezbollah and HAMAS maintain ties with individuals in South Africa in order to raise and launder funds. Third, the domestic terrorist group People Against Gangsterism and Drugs, a vigilante group drawn from parts of South Africa's urbanized Muslim community, and its associated movements are a lingering cause for concern, despite their successful disruption by South African security services.[65]

Since the end of apartheid rule, terrorist activity in South Africa has primarily been associated with extremist Islamic movements. Although less than 3 percent of the overall South African population is Muslim, that proportion rises to approximately 30 percent in some specific regions, such as the Western Cape. There and in other major urban centers, a minority of the Muslim community view religiously inspired vigilante movements and terrorist attacks as an effective means of combating rampant crime and non-Islamic practices, including drug dealing, prostitution, and the prevalence of bars, nightclubs, and discos.

Mozambique. Mozambique's vulnerability to terrorism is moderate, although no terrorist groups maintain a lasting presence in the country. Mozambique has been a transit point for terrorist operatives, including those affiliated with al Qaeda and possibly AIAI. For instance, it is reported that al Qaeda's East Africa operative, Khalfan Kahmis Mohammed, transited from Tanzania via Mozambique to South Africa (and eventually to Pakistan) following his participation in the bombings of the U.S. Embassies in Kenya and Tanzania.[66] In addition, local Islamic movements and foreign-led Islamic charities and schools are of growing importance.[67]

In addition, Southern African Muslims (and much of the wider non-Muslim population as well) are opposed to U.S. foreign policies in the Middle East, the conduct of the war on terrorism, and the war in Iraq. In this context, Southern Africa has become a hub for foreign fundamentalist groups, including Jama'at al Tabliq and a number of Islamic charities associated with terrorism in other countries. All of these factors combine to make extremist and terrorist indoctrination, recruitment, and training highly possible.

Central Africa

In contrast to the previously reviewed subregions, Central Africa is an area of low terrorist threats but high vulnerabilities. The current terrorist presence and level of threat for each country in Central Africa are summarized in table 1–7.

While financial supporters of Hezbollah—mostly drawn from a small number of Lebanese business communities—are present in two countries in Central Africa, there is no indication that Hezbollah has any operational presence in the subregion or that the group intends to launch attacks there against local or foreign targets.

Although there are no countries in Central Africa confronted by the presence of active terrorist organizations, Uganda's vulnerability

TABLE 1–7
Terrorist Presence in Central Africa

Country	Level of Threat	Terrorist Presence
Burundi	Low	None
Cameroon	Low	None
Central African Republic	Low	None
Democratic Republic of Congo	Low	Democratic Liberation Forces of Rwanda (FDLR) and Lord's Resistance Army (LRA) safe haven
Equatorial Guinea	Low	None
Gabon	Low	None
Republic of Congo	Low	None
Rwanda	Low	FDLR
São Tomé and Principe	Low	None
Uganda	Moderate	LRA, Allied Democratic Forces, FDLR, and possible transit by al Ittihad al Islami

is considered moderate, and Rwanda and the Democratic Republic of Congo (DRC) continue to struggle with ethnic rebel groups that are designated as terrorists by the United States.

Uganda. At present, no transnational terrorist groups are present and the country has not been the target of any transnational terrorist attacks. However, a number of different groups included on the U.S. Terrorist Exclusion List are present in Uganda, including the Lord's Resistance Army (LRA) and the Allied Democratic Forces (ADF). The LRA operates in northern Uganda and across the border into southern Sudan; the ADF has largely been defeated but used to operate in western Uganda. While LRA and ADF members have intended to establish theocratic governments in Uganda (Christian and Muslim, respectively), they have not succeeded in controlling or administering any Ugandan territory and have resorted primarily to guerrilla attacks against the Ugandan government and civilians as well as foreign aid workers.

Support for the LRA is primarily derived from lingering ethnic tensions between the northern Ugandan Acholi community and the southern-dominated government. This has antecedents in previous civil wars in Uganda before the National Resistance Movement (NRM) of President Yoweri Museveni came to power. Further peacebuilding and power sharing in the context of Ugandan democratization efforts and negotiations with the LRA would be required to decrease the level of ethnic-based ideological support for extremism.[68]

There is no evidence of significant support for transnational terrorist groups or extremist ideologies in Uganda. There is, however, a growing political consciousness within the country's Muslim community, which represents 16 percent of the population. Foreign fundamentalist missionary groups and Islamic charities and schools have gained a growing foothold in Uganda. Leaders and followers of the ADF, in particular, have demonstrated associations to Jama'at al Tabliq and that group's austere vision of proper Islamic practice.[69]

Rwanda and the Democratic Republic of Congo. No transnational terrorist groups are present in Rwanda or the DRC, and the countries have not been the target of any transnational terrorist attacks. However, the Democratic Liberation Forces of Rwanda (FDLR), an ethnic Hutu rebel movement operating across the border from the DRC and associated with the perpetrators of the 1994 Rwandan genocide, is a designated terrorist group.

The FDLR primarily conducts guerrilla warfare against the Rwandan government and Rwandan civilians with the intention of returning ethnic Hutu political leaders to power. The FDLR has not taken a specifically anti-U.S. stance and does not cooperate with transnational terrorist groups such as al Qaeda. However, FDLR forces were responsible for the March 1999 massacre of eight Western tourists in Bwindi National Park in southern Uganda. Approximately 14 percent of Rwandans are Muslim, and they have been targeted by foreign fundamentalist groups such as Jama'at al Tabliq for proselytism. Insecure borders, corruption, and access to weapons make Rwanda a possible, although not likely, venue for transit or access to materiel by transnational terrorist operatives and their facilitators.[70]

Although al Qaeda and its affiliated movements are not known to have been active in Central Africa, insecure borders, corruption, and access to weapons and Western targets make the subregion a possible, although not likely, venue for transnational terrorist attacks.

The Indian Ocean Area
Finally, while vulnerabilities to terrorism in the Indian Ocean area are rife, there is no indication that terrorist groups are present

in the subregion.[71] The current terrorist presence and level of vulnerability for each country in the Indian Ocean area are summarized in table 1–8.

The primary concern facing the subregion is the potential for terrorist operatives to transit the Indian Ocean area as a means of moving between Southern or East Africa and either the Middle East's Gulf States or South Asia. This owes to weak coordination of maritime security efforts and the prevalence of illegal immigration flows, problems with port security, and lack of maritime surveillance and interdiction capacities. In addition, while al Qaeda is not present in any Indian Ocean country, there are concerns regarding the personal ties of some individuals. In particular, Fazul Mohamed Harun of the al Qaeda East Africa cell is a native and national of Comoros. Finally, the subregion may be vulnerable to terrorist efforts to acquire weapons or funds.

The Rise of Political Islam

Terrorism is a dynamic phenomenon, and it is not necessarily associated with any one national, ethnic, religious, or ideological group. However, as demonstrated by the African subregional and country cases described above, terrorism in the current era is closely associated with militant Islamist groups such as al Qaeda, AIAI, the GSPC, and others. While these groups have focused the world's attention on "Salafism" and "Wahabism" as the extremist ideological interpretations of Islam that justify militancy, there also exists a panoply of political Islamic beliefs that range from "nonviolent fundamentalism" to "reformist" and "modernist" interpretations.[72]

Political Islam—a term coined in the 1970s—may best be defined as the belief that Islam provides the most appropriate basis for a community and its political, economic, legal, and social arrangements.[73] Islamist movements are those that seek to promote the realization of that situation. Over the past decade, political Islamic movements have made great strides in Africa in building their base of public support among Muslim communities. More so than secular government leaders or even traditional Sufist Muslim leaders,

TABLE 1–8
Terrorist Presence in Indian Ocean Countries

Country	Level of Threat	Terrorist Presence
Comoros	Low	None
Madagascar	Low	None
Mauritius	Low	None
Seychelles	Low	None

these groups are seen to offer a vision for achieving a more moral society in response to endemic African problems such as poverty, bad governance, political marginalization, social alienation, high levels of corruption, and pervasive insecurity. In addition, political Islamic beliefs have been fueled by unpopular policy decisions at both national and foreign levels. With regard to the United States, for instance, many in the Islamic world have come to view the "war on terror" as a "war on Islam."[74]

All of the above impulses have translated into the growing appeal of political Islamic ideologies and movements as an offensive force to promote domestic political opposition and/or a defensive force to resist Western influence and the effects of political and economic change. In Muslim communities from Nigeria to South Africa to Somalia, even dogmatic calls for the implementation of Islamic shari'a law have resonated with some local populations as offering the potential for grassroots responses to rampant crime and corruption and to rein in other forms of illicit behavior, ranging from gambling to prostitution to drinking.[75]

Overall, very few political Islamic movements are violent or lead their followers to engage in terrorism. Most engage in little more than preaching and providing charitable services to needy members of their community. However, there is concern that increased mobilization of Muslim communities against these perceived injustices could increase receptivity to extremist ideologies. Moreover, in some instances across the globe and in Africa in particular, there is significant concern that political Islamic groups have been instrumentalized by terrorist supporters and facilitators, and there are concerns that future generations of African militants are being developed through the growth of political Islam.

African Islamist Movements

A growing number of political Islamic movements in Africa are starting to make their presence felt by challenging the agendas of secular state authorities and traditional Sufist imams. Such movements include SCIC in Somalia, Izala in Niger and Nigeria, JIR and MWM in Senegal, and Qibla in South Africa. While each group is different, all articulate a need to rid Islam of syncretist practices and to infuse a strong religious dimension into national politics. Some of these groups go so far as to mobilize support for the establishment of theocratic states in place of existing authorities. In this sense, they are promoting a political vision and mobilizing public support for an agenda that, although nonviolent, is similar to that of many Islamist terrorist groups.

In North Africa, particularly in Algeria, Egypt, Tunisia, Libya, Mauritania, and Morocco, overt and clandestine Islamist movements have become the basis for opposition to governments that have limited democratic political competition. In the Sahel, countries such as Senegal, Mali, and Niger are now seeing significant strains emerge in their traditional modes of cooperation between secular state authorities and Sufist religious brotherhoods.[76] In Nigeria, Sudan, and Chad, the activism of Islamist movements is a potential factor exacerbating north-south political tensions. In those three countries and in Somalia, support for political Islam has developed into campaigns to establish strict Islamic shari'a courts to take action against criminality and other social problems where state authorities have not done so. Even in East and Southern Africa, there has been increased mobilization of Muslim communities against perceived political marginalization by central government authorities.

Islamic Charities

There are often dozens of Islamic charities operating in any one country in Africa, mostly in capital cities and rural areas where Muslim communities predominate, that collectively inject millions of dollars per year into the continent. The practice of *zakat* (tithing) is a fundamental tenet of Islam and has resulted in some highly successful humanitarian and development efforts in Africa. The most common Islamic charity projects focus on key sectors of education, orphanages, and health care.[77]

However, the work of Islamic charities in Africa (similar to the work of other nonprofit groups) is often unregulated. Individual donors are hard to identify, and funding for Islamic charity projects is rarely made transparent for government scrutiny. In addition, a wide range of charities that have been affiliated with terrorist activities around the world are present in Africa. These include the Muslim World League, the International Islamic Relief Organization, African Muslims Agency, World Association of Muslim Youth, and Munazzamat al Dawa. The Al Harameyn Foundation in particular managed projects in several African countries until being listed as a terrorist operation under U.S. Executive Order 13224.

In Africa, such groups with terrorist ties are of particular concern as they may provide extremist indoctrination to African youth through schools and mosques, supply logistical support for the transit of terrorist operatives and materiel, and act as financial fronts for terrorist groups through the fraudulent solicitation of donations, diversion of branch offices' funds, or the corruption of individual staff members.[78]

Foreign Fundamentalist Groups

Foreign preachers associated with extremism and terrorism are another concern. Al Tabliq is noteworthy for its substantial presence across Africa. The movement professes to be nonviolent but has nonetheless attracted the attention of counterterrorism authorities for the particularly conservative brand of Islamist ideology that it espouses. Tabliq mosques and schools are known to be used by al Qaeda as recruiting grounds, a fact evidenced by John Walker Lindh—the so-called American Taliban—who was recruited to fight in Afghanistan from a Tabliq institution in Pakistan.[79]

In Africa, Tabliq is a relatively recent phenomenon but has grown to become the largest fundamentalist Islamist movement on the continent.[80] Tabliq leaders believe that Muslims across the world continue to suffer oppression and live in poverty when they do not follow the exact path laid down by God. They use the notion of "following" in two different senses: both metaphorically and in practice. Metaphorically, new Tabliq members are expected to follow and adopt the teachings of an established Tabliq preacher for approximately 4 years before joining the ranks of the religious group as a full member. In practice, Tabliq members break into small groups (usually 10-man teams) to travel through African countries to proselytize. In addition, the group now manages some of the largest mosques in Muslim cities ranging from Mogadishu in Somalia to Kidal in northern Mali.

Finally, it should be noted that the rise of political Islam in Africa has been paralleled by the growth of extremely conservative, evangelical Christian movements. There is a distinct possibility that these two religious movements may come into conflict, particularly in Nigeria but also in countries such as Kenya. While it bears repeating that there is no inherent tendency of any religion toward violence or terrorism, the rapid growth and political nature of both Muslim and Christian groups in Africa raise legitimate concerns.[81]

Conclusion

From the subregional summaries presented above, it is possible to provide a breakdown of the terrorist groups currently present in Africa and their history of attacks over the past decade in four main categories:

- transnational terrorism: attacks by al Qaeda and al Qaeda–associated movements, including the GSPC/AQIM, AIAI, and North African groups, on African governments and Western targets
- domestic terrorism: attacks by domestic terrorist groups such as PAGAD and the ADF on African governments and Western targets
- rebels using terrorist tactics: attacks on African governments, African civilians, Western aid efforts, and tourists

by African rebel movements and insurgent groups such as the LRA, FDLR, and RUF as part of a wider ethno-regional guerrilla struggle
- terrorist financing and facilitation: funding and political support provided to Hezbollah and, to a far lesser extent, HAMAS by businessmen and other supporters.

These findings represent a best-case and a worst-case scenario at the same time. On the one hand, it is reassuring to understand that Africa is not currently a major bastion of terrorist operations or ideological support for terrorists. As stated at the beginning of this study, the three main U.S. terrorist designation lists, including the FTO, TEL, and Annex to Executive Order 13224, identify a total of 16 terrorist groups on the African continent. However, if one assesses the operational status of these 16 groups, the threat of terrorism in Africa appears even more specific. A number of those groups were listed for terrorist activities in the past and do not represent a present terrorist threat. The GIA in Algeria, PAGAD in South Africa, and ADF in Uganda have all been defeated by a combination of military force, law enforcement efforts, and their own internal schisms. In Egypt, the EIG has declared and respected a ceasefire since 1999, and EIJ ceased to exist as an independent entity when its leaders and militants merged into al Qaeda and left the African continent. Finally, the RUF has transitioned from a vicious rebel movement to a recognized, although marginal, political party in Sierra Leone.

Additionally, the various terrorist groups that have been listed from across North Africa—including GICM, DHDS, LIFG, and TCG, but not yet including the GMPJ in Mauritania—are only examples of cells that function as part of larger terrorist networks that, in Morocco at least, have been termed *Salafiya Jihadiya* for lack of more specific and comprehensive information on the organization of their terrorist enterprise. Further, the vast majority of known operatives affiliated with these groups are either in African custody or living abroad in Europe to escape local security service efforts.

Other groups on the Foreign Terrorist Organization and Terrorist Exclusion lists, even if they are present in Africa, maintain no operational capacity on the continent. This includes Hezbollah and HAMAS, for which Africa only functions as home to a limited number of financial supporters. The LRA in Uganda and FDLR/Army for the Liberation of Rwanda in Rwanda are predominantly ethnic-based rebel movements that have utilized terrorist attacks as a means of asymmetric or guerrilla warfare but are more like other African rebel groups than transnational terrorist groups such as al Qaeda. Further, both of these movements are engaged in peace negotiations with the governments that they oppose and may be offered amnesty for their terrorist actions in exchange for the end of their guerrilla campaigns.

Finally, the presence of al Qaeda terrorists remains limited. According to the country studies presented above, al Qaeda is not known to have any senior leaders on the continent and consistently has foot soldiers in only 3 countries (Somalia, Kenya, and South Africa). This does not include any senior al Qaeda leaders, and the group does not operate any large-scale terrorist camps or bases. Although al Qaeda has established connections with the GSPC and has likely conducted reconnaissance in Nigeria or other countries, these activities have yet to coalesce into a direct threat. Further, the fear that al Qaeda and other terrorist operatives may flee to Africa from war zones has not yet been realized.

If one then reconsiders the terrorist threat in Africa with this information in mind, there are 4 main groups on the continent of substantial counterterrorism concern to the United States at the present time (see table 1–9).

This analysis is not intended to downplay the very real threat posed by terrorists in Africa. Rather, it is intended to demonstrate that the U.S. Government's system of lists does not adequately describe that threat.

Durable Vulnerabilities to Terrorism

On the other hand, these findings represent a serious challenge for African governments, the United States, and other countries engaged in the war on terrorism worldwide. Despite the limited scale of transnational terrorist operations in Africa, the risk that they pose is very significant. Even a small number of al Qaeda operatives—such as those involved in the 1998 bombings of the U.S. Embassies and the 2002 attacks near Mombasa, Kenya—can launch deadly attacks, the implications of which will resonate for many years. Such small networks of terrorists have been very dynamic and effective in Africa.

TABLE 1–9 Operational Terrorist Groups in Africa
al Qaeda
al Ittihad al Islami
Salafist Group for Preaching and Combat/al Qaeda in the Land of the Islamic Maghreb
North African Salafiya Jihadiya

In the Horn and East Africa, although AIAI is widely reported to have been disbanded or at least broken into different groups and renamed as early as 1998, its former members have established new initiatives and continue to play important political and military roles in Somalia. This includes espousing jihad against neighboring countries and providing support for al Qaeda's East Africa cell under the banners of the Supreme Council of Islamic Courts, Al Shebab, and other entities that are tied genealogically to AIAI but that represent fundamentally new and different threats.

Similarly, as previously mentioned, the full array of militant Islamist cells inspired by al Qaeda and operating in North Africa has yet to be identified, let alone targeted. Surely new groups will continue to be named and added to this list, but only as they are identified before or after launching and claiming responsibility for new attacks.

Second, these terrorist groups have been successful in appropriating local African grievances as synonymous with their own agenda and integrating themselves into African communities by establishing family, business, and/or criminal ties. This has been the case in the Sahel, where the GSPC has developed support from a small but important segment of the local Tuareg ethnic community, and in Somalia, where AIAI leaders have wrapped themselves in the veil of shari'a courts. Both of these avenues of penetrating and operating on the continent make it extremely difficult for African governments and foreign counterterrorism efforts to identify, isolate, and remove terrorist elements.

Third, there appear to be four main areas of terrorist activity that may not be full-blown "safe havens" for terrorist operations but that have certainly proven amenable to continued terrorist activity. They include densely populated urban areas; vast rural, desert spaces; unpatrolled maritime zones; and areas of "weak" and "failing" states outside of any government's control. Despite efforts by the United States and other countries to train and equip African governments and their security services, terrorist groups have continued to operate in these areas. This activity is facilitated by uncoordinated police and military efforts; weak border, port, and customs controls; corruption and smuggling networks; access to financing through legal businesses, unregulated remittances, and the diversion of charity funds; and the widespread availability of weapons and explosives. While terrorists have yet to seize the opportunity to operate in Africa's maritime domain, this area suffers equally from these vulnerabilities and may prove an inviting target for terrorist operations in the future.

Fourth, the political, social, and economic grievances that can be considered the root causes or drivers of terrorism in Africa remain unresolved. Despite efforts to encourage economic development and promote democratization, Africa remains the poorest continent on earth; authoritarian, corrupt, and ineffective governments remain common; and it is understandable for Africans to be less concerned about the potential for a terrorist attack in their country than they are about the immediate problems of poverty, unemployment, civil war, disease, corruption, and a lack of social services such as education and health care. As a result, the African public's understanding of and support for the war on terrorism are limited.

In addition, many African political parties and political Islamic movements have seized on unpopular policy decisions at both national and foreign levels and turned their countries' counterterrorism cooperation into a political football. With regard to the United States, for instance, many in the Islamic world have come to view the "war on terror" as a "war on Islam," and there are widespread concerns regarding the U.S. occupation in Iraq, the continuation of the Israeli-Palestinian conflict, public perceptions of U.S. practices at Guantanamo Bay and Abu Ghraib prison, the creation of CIA "black prisons," and, most recently, the Israeli invasion of Lebanon. In some countries, this has been reinforced by the abuse of the notion of a "threat of terrorism" as a potential justification for governments in the region to exploit citizens—both to garner increased international support (for money, weapons, or recognition) and to repress potential domestic opposition forces.

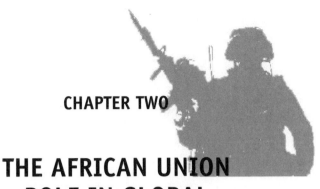

CHAPTER TWO

THE AFRICAN UNION ROLE IN GLOBAL COUNTERTERRORISM

Ibrahim J. Wani

The role of regional organizations such as the African Union (AU) in the campaign against terrorism has been uneven at best. Immediately following the terrorist attacks in the United States on September 11, 2001, the first reaction was for the United States and other countries to brace for their own national defense. The United Nations (UN) was then drawn in as both a symbol of global solidarity and a mechanism to galvanize a cooperative global response. Thus, UN Security Council Resolution 1373 was swiftly adopted to establish a framework to coordinate international efforts under the aegis of the United Nations Security Council.[1]

The particular role of regional and subregional organizations was recognized at a subsequent meeting of the UN Security Council in March 2003. It was noted that these organizations have vested interests in and sensitivities to regional situations, can help to instill a sense of responsibility in their member states and strengthen their will to deal with regional problems, and can teach and learn from each other. In short, with respect to terrorism, they can work toward achieving full implementation of UN Security Council Resolution 1373. The United Nations must combat terrorism on a regional basis as well as work with individual nation states.[2]

However, the regional dimension of counterterrorism cooperation has received far less attention in the development of counterterrorism strategies, partly because the potential roles of regional organizations are not immediately apparent and partly because these organizations are viewed as ineffectual in (or, in a few instances, possibly hostile to) the counterterrorism agenda. In the case of the African Union, the fact that the continent is replete with regional or subregional organizations with rather checkered

This chapter argues in favor of involving the African Union more substantively and consistently in the counterterrorism campaign. The organization's own initiatives, weak as they may be at this time, provide some guidance and direction about where it might play a role. That role might not be massive, but it will be substantial enough to complement other global and national initiatives and make a difference. The AU has demonstrated that it can serve as a forum for developing regional consensus and raising awareness about terrorism, and it can provide much-needed legitimacy to the actions of member states. The AU can also provide a useful linkage with other regions and regional organizations and facilitate the exchange of information, experiences, and expertise. The Organization of African Unity (OAU) Convention on the Prevention and Combating of Terrorism (1999), the AU Plan of Action on the Prevention and Combating of Terrorism (2002), and the convention's subsequent protocol (2004)—all discussed in more detail below—also contain important legal frameworks on extradition, the exchange of information, capacity building, and other forms of cooperation that have the potential to enhance the counterterrorism campaign.

For the moment, many of these and other potential areas of contribution from the African Union remain largely as promises because of a lack of resources and the absence of mechanisms to ensure implementation. To realize the AU's full potential requires stronger faith in the organization and, equally important, continuous investment and engagement in its institutions and capacities. It also requires a reexamination of some the assumptions as well as the strategies and tools of the global counterterrorism campaign. For the United States, that means striking a more conscious balance between the security and military orientations of its current counterterrorism programs and other economic, social, and political aspects, including the increased foreign involvement of organs of the U.S. Government other than the Department of Defense.[3]

This chapter is organized in four parts. It starts with a brief overview of the phenomenon of terrorism in Africa to try to establish why the region and its preeminent regional organization, the African Union, should be of interest in the counterterrorism debate. The second part looks at some recent AU initiatives to highlight what one might describe as an African perspective on counterterrorism, at least from the official points of view of governments, and the potential role of the organization. The third part compares the main elements of the African response and other global responses, primarily the approach adopted by the United States, to determine possible points of convergence as well as areas where divergences in assumptions and approaches might pose obstacles to collaboration. The last section of the paper discusses specific areas where the AU could complement global counterterrorism efforts and how that potential can be realized.

Terrorism in Africa

To fully appreciate the role that the African Union can play in counterterrorism, it is important to understand how Africa is affected by terrorism. The question of the extent, if at all, to which terrorism is relevant in Africa is important from a strategic and policy perspective because it, among other things, determines whether one should invest in the AU. In other words, it would not be cost effective to invest in the AU if Africa's connection with terrorism is very limited and does not go beyond a generalized global concern.

In the immediate period after September 11, Africa was considered a marginal region at best in the global counterterrorism campaign. Analysts and policymakers alike initially viewed sub-Saharan Africa as a minor stage because of the perception of its limited relationship to the attacks that took place in the United States.[4] By the end of 2001, however, this perception began to change as U.S. security officials focused on the history of al Qaeda in Africa, the presence of local terrorist groups such as al Ittihad al Islami in Somalia and the Salafist Group for Preaching and Combat in the Sahel, and the chance that terrorists fleeing from Afghanistan or other countries may transit to Africa.

Although there are still those who believe that the "emergence of a genuinely African type of international terrorism is rather improbable," there is no doubt that today Africa is considered an important theater in the ever-growing threat of international terrorism. The prevailing wisdom is that terrorism could spread in Africa for several reasons, notable among them the growth of radical Islam in several parts of the continent;[5] the existence of so-called failed states in the Democratic Republic of Congo, Liberia, Sierra Leone, and Somalia;[6] proximity to the Middle East and the Arab world, where many terrorist groups thrive; the general inability of states in Africa to sufficiently secure their vast borders; and the movement across the continent of potential terrorists from other regions. Also of concern are the abject poverty and repressive political environments that leave many young Africans desperate, frustrated, and potentially vulnerable to recruitment by terrorist elements.

Indeed, there is plenty of evidence to support the recent description of Africa as the "soft underbelly" of international terrorism.[7] After all, the bombings of the U.S. Embassies in Nairobi and

Dar es Salaam in August 1998 and the attack on the Paradise Hotel and an Israeli airliner in Mombasa in November 2002 were carried out by young Muslim men— many of whom originate from Africa and have connections to al Qaeda.[8] Likewise, many of those involved in the July 2005 bombings in London had connections with Eastern Africa and the Horn of Africa. Before the London bombings, there were also purported connections between al Qaeda and African countries such as Sudan, Algeria, Malawi, and South Africa. Africa's rich ethnic and racial mixtures, the prevalence of huge and diverse refugee populations, the absence of the state in places such as Somalia, and the ability of people and weapons to move freely across largely uncontrolled and perhaps uncontrollable terrain form a volatile mixture that undoubtedly can aid terrorism. This is part of the intricate web of terrorist linkages that span from America, Britain, and other European countries to Pakistan and the Middle East.[9]

Yet it would be a mistake to portray the analysis of Africa's relationship to terrorism with such a broad brush; rather, it is quite complex and goes beyond these apparent symptoms. In order to formulate a constructive and comprehensive counterterrorism strategy involving the African Union, it is important to understand in detail the nuances of the terrorist phenomenon in Africa. Analysts have categorized the relationship of Africa to terrorism into several interrelated phenomena.

Domestic Terrorist Attacks on African Interests

These usually involve domestic insurgents—such as the Lord's Resistance Army (LRA) in Uganda, the Revolutionary United Front (RUF) in Sierra Leone, and the Army for the Liberation of Rwanda— who are driven by local political, social, and economic grievances and use terrorist tactics against domestic targets, typically those related to the state and its supporters. This has been the most typical form of terrorism in Africa both before and after September 11, although it has never motivated the same concerted global or regional reaction as has transnational terrorism of the type associated with al Qaeda.

Transnational Terrorist Attacks on Western Interests

This form of transnational terrorism is best illustrated in the case of the 1998 bombings of the U.S. Embassies in Kenya and Tanzania and the subsequent attacks in Mombasa, Tunisia, Morocco, and Egypt. Western nationals, property, and interests are targeted in Africa because, among other things, they constitute soft targets and are vulnerable. The ease of movement and perhaps the ability to transport weapons and other items needed to execute the plans are enhanced by a better than average chance to escape apprehension.

These attacks are certainly what motivated the response to terrorism in Africa by the Organization of African Unity, the institutional predecessor to the African Union, and led to the adoption of the OAU Convention.

Use of African Territory as a Safe Haven

There are numerous instances of terrorists associated with al Qaeda seeking temporary safe haven in Southern Africa either before or after an attack takes place. In addition to the controversial capture of terrorist suspects in South Africa and Malawi, there are allegations of Zimbabwean and Libyan connections with al Qaeda's second-in-command, Ayman al-Zawahiri,[10] and the reported presence in Zambia of one of the alleged coconspirators in the London subway bombing.

Africa as a Terrorist Breeding Ground and Source of Recruits

The presence of unemployed young men and the sizable population of Muslim youth experiencing feelings of alienation, marginalization, desperation, and anger at what they see as the Western domination of the world, fueled by the ideology of radical Islam, are some factors that make Africa a location in which al Qaeda or other terrorist groups could find sympathizers and new recruits. In this regard, a number of the members of the al Qaeda cell that launched attacks in Kenya in 1998 and 2002 are nationals from African countries, including Kenya, Tanzania, and the Comoros Islands.

Africa as a Transit Point

It is argued that vast areas of Africa such as the Horn and Sahel subregions, which are historical crossing points between Africa and the Middle East, are largely uncontrolled by African governments and allow for the free movement of potential terrorists. These ungoverned spaces also provide possible training grounds. According to former U.S. Assistant Secretary of State for African Affairs Susan Rice, terrorist organizations take advantage of Africa's porous borders and weak law enforcement, judicial institutions, and security services to move men, weapons, and money around the globe.[11] However, there is also a contrary view that holds that Africa is clearly not a hotbed of terrorist activity. Extremist ideologies, including fundamentalist Islam, have been present in various parts of the continent for many decades without generating a wide base of public support.[12]

Several important points emerge from this simple analysis. First, African governments themselves have seldom been the target of transnational terrorist attacks, although they have inevitably suffered loss of lives and property damage. The major attacks on African soil—in Dar es Salaam, Mombasa, Nairobi, and elsewhere—primarily have been directed at Western interests and those of its allies. Despite attempts by countries such as Uganda to label violence by domestic insurgents such as the LRA as terrorism, this inclusiveness would seem to stretch the concept of terrorism and complicate the use of peacebuilding and political negotiations strategies to end civil wars.[13] Second, only a few African countries have actually been involved either as countries from which terrorist acts have been launched or as safe havens, and these have generally been countries that have a sizable Muslim population or are geographically close to other Muslim countries.

These trends in the post–September 11 period have not gone unnoticed by African leaders and citizens and have influenced their receptiveness to global counterterrorism policy and strategies. For instance, despite the refrain from leaders and policymakers that counterterrorism must be a common global effort,[14] the reality is that the key features of the prevailing counterterrorism strategy are premised on the most obvious, outward face of the counterterrorism struggle—notably, that it is a fight against largely radical Muslim perpetrators who are targeting primarily American and Western interests. This certainly explains the focus of U.S. counterterrorism efforts on the African continent in particular locations of East Africa, the Horn, and the Sahel, all areas perceived to have sizable Muslim populations or that are proximate to other countries with large Muslim populations and the Middle East. However, at the same time, this reality does not necessarily motivate countries from other parts of the continent to prioritize counterterrorism cooperation over other priorities such as domestic security or economic development.

While one cannot escape the fact that the terrorist attacks of the last 4 years have targeted the United States and have been orchestrated by radical Islamists, a unifying and long-term counterter-rorism strategy must go beyond these current instances of violence. Otherwise, short-term counterterrorism efforts will reinforce the growing view that the struggle is primarily an American campaign, designed to pursue and protect American interests and uncritically target Muslims. This would clearly undermine unanimity in the African Union and miss the opportunity to probe the deeper reasons why otherwise mainstream youth seem to harbor so much anger against the United States and its allies and, through that, engender the broad consensus needed to stamp out terrorism as a global threat. This is presumably what Tony Blair had in mind shortly after the July 2005 London bombings when he said that governments should enlist the cooperation of Muslim leaders to "take this common fight forward."[15]

AU Counterterror Response

The scope of the counterterrorism initiatives and programs established by the African Union, and before that by the Organization of African Unity,[16] reveals much about the organization's potential contribution to the global campaign. It also reveals the organization's limitations. Africa's concern with terrorism in one form or another predates the September 11 attacks in the United States.[17] At the continental level, at least, terrorism was first broached as an African regional security issue in 1992, when the OAU Assembly of Heads of State and Government Summit in Dakar, Senegal, adopted a decision to enhance regional cooperation to fight extremism in Africa.[18] Terrorism remained on the OAU agenda in subsequent meetings from 1994 through 1999 when, following the al Qaeda attacks on the U.S. Embassies in Kenya and Tanzania, the summit occurred in Algiers, Algeria, and adopted the OAU Convention on the Prevention and Combating of Terrorism.

Despite adoption of the OAU Convention, however, implementation was left entirely up to individual AU member states. Those that acted most concretely were the same countries that had been affected by the 1998 attacks or other forms of extremist violence. This laissez-faire attitude changed with the September 11 attacks, which coincided with the beginning of the transition from the OAU to the AU. This event introduced a renewed sense of concern and urgency and, in significant ways, changed the orientation of the thinking about terrorism in Africa. Terrorism was immediately on the agenda of the new organization as a regional, as well as global, security concern. Back-to-back AU summits in Dakar and Algiers took up the issue and sought to adapt the OAU's counterterrorism instruments and framework to the realities of both the new AU structure and the post–September 11 environment.[19]

As a result, the AU counterterrorism framework is today captured in three primary instruments: the OAU Convention on the Prevention and Combating of Terrorism (also referred to as the Algiers Convention),[20] adopted in 1999; the AU Plan of Action on the Prevention and Combating of Terrorism in Africa, adopted by the High-Level Intergovernmental Meeting on the Prevention and Combating of Terrorism in Africa in September 2002; and the Protocol to the OAU Convention on the Prevention and Combating of Terrorism, adopted in 2004. These regional instruments are supplemented by various decisions and declarations of AU summits[21] and AU subsidiary bodies.[22] Together these instruments and decisions spell out the normative and legal framework for African counterterrorism cooperation and develop institutional mechanisms to monitor their implementation. Overall, they represent a fairly impressive baseline that parallels and seeks to regionalize some of the global standards and rules, although the institutional framework for implementation is rather weak.

Despite some initial misgivings that September 11 and the war on terrorism would lead to the strategic marginalization of Africa,[23] the AU has sought to carve a niche for itself in the global counterterrorism campaign. As detailed in the following sections, these efforts reveal numerous points of convergence between the African Union and other global approaches to counterterrorism, but they also disclose subtle but profound points of departure that are critical in delineating the appropriate role of the regional organization.

The OAU Convention

The Algiers Convention, which predates September 11, represents the continent's earliest attempt to deal with a phenomenon that in 1999 was not yet considered a major global strategic issue. Perhaps its greatest value lies in articulating the common concern of OAU member states about terrorism. The convention covers a wide range of issues. It identifies a number of critical areas, such as the exchange of information and technical assistance, in which member states would cooperate to stem terrorism. It also attempts to extend national jurisdiction over acts of terrorism committed elsewhere, and it lays a framework for the extradition of perpetrators of terrorism.

Among its substantive provisions, the convention provides a definition of a "terrorist act" (article 1, section 3) and makes it a criminal offense:

> (a) any act which is a violation of the criminal laws of a State Party and which may endanger the life, physical integrity, or freedom of, or cause serious injury or death to, any person, any number or group of persons or causes or may cause damage to public or private property, natural resources, environmental or cultural heritage and is calculated or intended to:
>
> (i) intimidate, put in fear, force, coerce, or induce any government, body, institution, the general public or any segment thereof, to do or abstain from doing any act, or to adopt or abandon a particular standpoint, or to act according to certain principles; or
>
> (ii) disrupt any public service, the delivery of any essential service to the public or to create a public emergency; or

(iii) create general insurrection in a State.

(b) any promotion, sponsoring, contribution to, command, aid, incitement, encouragement, attempt, threat, conspiracy, organizing, or procurement of any person, with the intent to commit any act referred to in paragraph (a) (i) to (iii).[24]

Furthermore, state parties to the convention agree to take measures to prevent the establishment of terrorist support networks, including actions to suppress the financing of terrorism (article 4[f]). The convention then provides mechanisms for controlling terrorism, identifies specific measures to be taken by member states, and defines wide areas of cooperation among member states,[25] including mutual police and judicial assistance for any investigation, criminal prosecution, or extradition proceedings relating to terrorist acts,[26] and the determination of national jurisdiction over acts of terrorism.[27] From a practical, operational standpoint, the convention's provisions on mutual legal assistance, including extraterritorial investigations, are among its most useful.[28]

The convention's provisions on extradition and national jurisdiction are also, in principle, among the farthest reaching. State parties to the convention agree to include terrorist acts as extraditable offenses and to extradite any person charged with or convicted of any terrorist act carried out on the territory of another state and whose extradition is requested by one of the state parties. In articles 6 and 7, member states defined the parameters of national jurisdiction over terrorist acts including those committed on board an aircraft, on board a vessel, or in the territory of another state. The concept of extradition is expanded in article 13, which requests state parties to seize and transmit all funds and related materials or assets purportedly used in the commission of the terrorist act(s), including all relevant incriminating evidence, to the requesting state.

In contrast to the rather detailed substantive provisions, the convention does not provide any mechanisms for enforcement or implementation. That is part of the reason why it was thought necessary to adopt additional instruments in the aftermath of September 11.

AU Plan of Action

In the search for a more effective regional regime, in September 2002, the Commission of the African Union convened a High-Level Intergovernmental Meeting on the Prevention and Combating of Terrorism in Africa to discuss how to strengthen African counterterrorism efforts and, more specifically, how to implement the OAU Convention. This was an attempt to respond to the transition from the OAU to the AU as well as to respond to the requirements of UN

Security Council Resolution 1373 and other new international instruments. The meeting adopted the "Plan of Action on the Prevention and Combating of Terrorism in Africa," intended to give concrete expression to the commitments and obligations of African countries and to provide guidelines for specific actions against terrorism. Overall, it sought to strengthen the AU's legal framework and address the weaknesses of existing implementation mechanisms.

The plan parallels the key provisions of UN Resolution 1373 and establishes a complex network of cooperation and information exchange among AU member states. It also outlines the parameters for pursuing common counterterrorism objectives, particularly with respect to the exchange of information on the activities and movement of terrorist groups in Africa, mutual legal assistance, exchange of research expertise, mobilization of technical assistance and cooperation, and upgrading of the scientific and technical operational capacity of member states.

On the more operational aspect, the plan of action commits member states to implement a range of measures and best practices to enhance their border security and passport control, including the provision of "regular training to immigration officials with regard to the profiling of travelers and the verification of authenticity of documents." It takes the imperative of suppressing terrorist financing further, building on Security Council Resolution 1373, and provides a wide range of authorities to seize terrorist assets and disrupt the links or sources used to finance terrorist activities. For instance, it proscribes anonymous accounts; provides for the confiscation of movable and immovable assets intended for financing of terrorism; establishes the need for financial intelligence units in member states; and calls for training of personnel in charge of preventing and combating money laundering.

The plan of action also outlines specific legislative and judicial measures for member states to take to combat terrorism, including amending national laws relating to bail and other criminal procedural issues; harmonizing the standards and procedures regarding the burden and standard of proof for terrorism-related crimes; promoting specialized training to reinforce the capacity of the judiciary; concluding extradition and mutual legal assistance agreements; and making provision in national laws to establish jurisdiction over persons accused of terrorist acts.

The plan of action provides for member states to conclude bilateral and multilateral extradition and mutual legal assistance agreements and to identify the national authorities responsible for processing extradition and mutual legal assistance requests. In addition, it argues for finalization and adoption of a Convention on Extradition and a Convention on Mutual Legal Assistance. With respect to research and collection of data on terrorism and terrorist organizations, the plan of action buttresses the general provision in the convention. For example, it calls for the establishment of a common Terrorism Activity Reporting schedule as a data collection instrument for names of identified terrorist organizations, persons, places, and resources.

Finally, the plan of action established the African Center for the Study and Research on Terrorism, based in Algiers, Algeria. The center, which was launched in 2004 as part of the AU, was envisaged to carry out research, facilitate the sharing of information, provide training to member states in measures to combat terrorism in Africa, and otherwise assist in implementing the plan of action. The center is expected to provide a centralized database with information and analyses on terrorist groups and their activities and to organize training symposia and conferences to discuss terrorism.

Protocol to the Convention

The protocol was intended to update the convention in view of the evolving forms of terrorism such as the use of sophisticated technology[29] and to clarify internal bureaucratic mandates with regard to the implementation of the OAU Convention and AU Plan of Action. Thus, in articles 4, 5, and 6, the protocol establishes the Peace and Security Council,[30] the AU Commission, and Regional Mechanisms (AU parlance for African subregional organizations), respectively, as the responsible instruments for implementation.

At the apex of the implementation mechanism, the AU Commission was given the general mandate to provide needs-based advice and recommendations to member states on how to secure technical and financial assistance in the implementation of continental and international measures against terrorism. More specifically, it is mandated to:

- provide technical assistance on legal and law enforcement matters, including combating the financing of terrorism and the preparation of model laws and guidelines
- follow up with member states and with regional mechanisms on the implementation of decisions taken by the Peace and Security Council and other organs of the union on terrorism-related matters
- maintain a database on terrorism-related issues, including experts and available technical assistance and contacts with regional and international organizations and other entities dealing with issues of terrorism.

The AU Protocol relating to the establishment of the Peace and Security Council likewise, in article 16, describes African subregional organizations as part of the overall security architecture of the African Union. Regional mechanisms are seen as important political and economic actors of their respective regions. The fact that they are closer to their member states and are more attuned to subregional political cultures gives them a comparative advantage over the AU when it comes to mobilizing member states to take action.

Assessing the AU's Role

From this rough sketch of the AU counterterrorism framework, it is clear that the organization has expended a great deal of effort to harmonize its programs and activities with global counterterrorism programs since September 11. It has adopted what at first blush appears to be a comprehensive set of legal instruments and norms on counterterrorism.[31] Nevertheless, this masks some significant gaps and issues. Indeed, the AU views itself as part of a larger global effort, with a role to facilitate and promote the implementation of UN Resolution 1373 as well as other international legal instruments. It seems to perceive its niche very judiciously between the global level, where the UN has taken the lead in developing global consensus, and the national level, where most operational activities related to counterterrorism are required. It also seems to resolve the position of subregional organizations such as the Inter-Governmental Authority on Development (IGAD) and the Economic Community of West African States (ECOWAS), which, according to the AU framework, are viewed as complementary and perhaps even subsidiary to the continental organization.[32]

Despite this comprehensive framework, however, fairly serious gaps and shortcomings remain. It is unclear if the framework represents a broad-based, regional consensus on the best approach to counterterrorism or if there is sufficient buy-in to translate it into concrete actions. AU member states have been slow to ratify the OAU Convention and, in what is evolving as a typical AU modus operandi, the legislative history behind the drafting of the convention is rather scanty because there was little critical debate before its adoption. Thus, one cannot judge the extent to which there is support for the framework. Part of the problem of implementation emanates from this lack of critical dialogue and reflection.

Related to this is the fact that the counterterrorism effort is led by a few countries, Algeria perhaps more than any other. For example, the AU's African Center for the Study and Research on Terrorism is located in Algiers. This has raised some questions about the scope of regional support for the new institution. Until 2006, the center had been almost exclusively supported by the government of Algeria, which provided the venue for the office, seconded all of the staff members, and also paid for costs of running the center. These circumstances raise questions about the level of commitment to AU initiatives and the extent to which member states can be depended upon to provide information and other critical support.

Africa's preoccupation with colonialism and self-determination, a dominant theme in the initial creation of the OAU, has a strong imprint that creates ambivalence in the AU's normative framework on counterterrorism. The Algiers Convention defines terrorism very broadly, yet its preamble and other provisions exempt the use of force in the cause of self-determination from this definition. Article 3 of the convention exempts the use of force by so-called freedom fighters for their liberation or self-determination, including armed struggles against colonialism, occupation, aggression, and domination by foreign forces, from the definition.[33] At the same time, it denies the legitimacy of using political, philosophical, ideological, racial, ethnic, religious, or other motives to justify terrorism.

More positively, the AU also adopts a much broader perspective on counterterrorism that takes into account the root causes and drivers of terrorist violence. For example, the AU Plan of Action calls for member states to promote policies aimed at addressing poverty, deprivation, and marginalization, all of which can promote alienation and be used by militants to justify their violent actions.[34] However, at the same time, the AU does not elaborate on how member states can act against these root causes in a manner that will be any more successful than the countries' long history of checkered attempts at economic development and social reform.

These ambiguities seem to be deliberate and appear to be designed to mask fairly fundamental differences of opinion within the organization. They also put the AU on a potential collision course with the United Nations, where there is a growing consensus toward an absolute prohibition on the use of force,[35] and an apparent north-south rift over the status of partisan warriors or freedom fighters and whether official forces of a state can be viewed as committing terrorist offenses.[36] To sidestep the problem of a general definition, the UN has historically approached the topic by prohibiting specific aspects of terrorism, such as the taking of hostages, hijacking, sabotage, crimes against internationally protected persons including diplomats, violence at airports, the making or use of plastic explosives, use of explosive bombs, and financing of terrorism.[37]

Perhaps more importantly, the gap between aspirations and reality is immense. Many of the AU provisions remain at the level of ideas, and, as discussed earlier, their implementation is hampered by a lack of resources and other constraints. The example of the Algiers-based African Center for the Study and Research on Terrorism has already been given. Further, the AU Commission has also designated limited human capacity for the counterterrorism agenda and lacks a clear institutional structure to fulfill the role designated for the commission.[38] Nor can the absence of a political will, which needs to be understood in terms of its full impact in limiting the AU's institutional ability to act independently, be ruled out. These and other challenges raise serious questions about the scope of the AU's commitment to counterterrorism and will definitely have implications in determining the union's role in the global campaign.

Convergence with Global Counterterrorism

The conscious effort by the AU to harmonize its interventions with global developments in counterterrorism, particularly with respect to the implementation of UN Security Council Resolution 1373 and other international instruments, clearly delineates the role of the AU from a global perspective. In fact, the AU has tailored most of its efforts toward assisting member states that meet the requirements of the United Nations as expressed in Resolution 1373 and other decisions. Yet there are also some serious points of divergence between the AU and global trends that can potentially hamper this role.

In reality, UN initiatives constitute only a small component of the overall global counterterrorism effort. Most concrete initiatives have come from the United States or other governments, and these are the ones that will have a major impact on how the war on terrorism is perceived and prosecuted in Africa and around the world.[39] These are also the practical initiatives that pose the greatest potential challenges to a full role for the AU, since nearly all of them will take place on a bilateral basis outside the aegis of AU monitoring. The AU must find some way to engage with such initiatives as they take place in Africa but must first resolve several challenges and divergences.

In the first place, there is a subtle but significant difference in the conception of terrorism between the AU and key global actors, particularly the United States. Shaped by the horror of September 11 and subsequent terrorist episodes, the United States increasingly perceives terrorism from a fairly narrow perspective as involving an attack on the United States, its interests, and its allies by militants espousing radical Islamic ideologies. While justifiable given the typical profile of groups responsible for contemporary terrorist acts over the past decade, the U.S. viewpoint has nonetheless led to a perception that the United States is engaged in a clash of civilizations or, worse, a war with Islam. The U.S. framing of the need to combat terrorism is thus having a negative policy impact.

An immediate implication of this difference in perspective is the belief that U.S. counterterrorism policies and initiatives only view Africa as important when the continent is a source of terrorist threats and vulnerabilities.[40] The main U.S. efforts in Africa—such as the creation of the Combined Joint Task Force–Horn of Africa in Djibouti, the East Africa Counter-Terrorism Initiative, Kenya's National Counter-Terrorism Centre, the Pan-Sahel Initiative, and now the Trans-Sahara Counterterrorism Initiative—are focused on small areas perceived as the greatest threat. While this focus may be prudent and practical in the short term, it undermines any efforts to cultivate a continent-wide response and diminishes the potential role of regional and subregional organizations. In addition, the demographics of these areas, which include a large number of Muslims, reinforce the perception that America's preoccupation is with Islam as the primary threat. This might be a perfectly legitimate reaction to the reality of threats emanating from Africa, but it has the unfortunate consequence of creating a rift and undermining the development of a common position with Africa on counterterrorism strategies.

U.S. counterterrorism strategy has also been criticized at times for overemphasizing the military and security dimensions almost to the exclusion of other tools and opportunities, particularly economic and political ones. Although the United States has conceded that poverty, repression, denial of human rights, and other socioeconomic factors fuel terrorism,[41] too little has been done to emphasize nonmilitary tools aimed at state building; enhancing democracy, good governance, and respect for the rule of law; broadening benefits from trade and investment; and dealing with the scourge of HIV/AIDS.

As Princeton Lyman, a former U.S. Assistant Secretary of State for African Affairs, has argued, this focus on the military can undermine the democracy progress in Africa and further compound political discontent and alienation, "thus increasing the threat of terrorism. . . . A response overly balanced to the military side will push too close to the line of oppressive regimes, too insensitive to political dynamics of anti-terrorism strategy, too limited in our response to the problems of poverty that underlie every African security problem."[42] The AU, on the other hand, has stressed the importance of an appropriate focus on the social, economic, and political dimensions, even though its own strategy does not seem to integrate any explicit and concrete linkages.

Conclusion

The African Union poses a dilemma for those hoping to craft a coherent, global counterterrorism agenda. On the one hand, the AU's own initiatives suggest a great potential role for the organization in controlling terrorism within Africa. The AU has defined a niche as an intermediary between the global and the national levels and has put together what appears to be a solid foundation for a region-wide counterterrorism strategy and plan of action. These clearly provide opportunities to integrate the AU more explicitly into the global campaign.

On the other hand, however, the positive nature of this readiness and apparent commitment are tempered by well-placed doubts about the organization's ability to deliver on its promises. These doubts derive from questions about the depth of commitment from the AU's member states, the lack of resources, and the gaps in institutional capacity. Beyond these internal problems, there are also key national differences among member states' perceptions of the terrorist threat and their desired approaches and strategies to counter that threat, which can hamper the development of a more integral role for the AU.

If these areas of doubt and concern can be addressed, the AU's possible role in counterterrorism emerges clearly. The AU Plan of Action, in particular, outlines critical areas where the union can complement counterterrorism efforts. These include its role as a facilitator and coordinator,[43] liaising with and playing an advocacy role for member states with the United Nations and obtaining access to technical assistance from institutions such as the International Maritime Organization. The AU can also help member states act directly and in unison to strengthen the capacity of border control initiatives, facilitate the exchange of expertise and personnel and the sharing of intelligence equipment, identify and share best practices, develop common policies, and build consensus behind the development and implementation of model counterterrorism legislation. The AU is potentially an important entry point for dealing with the socioeconomic and political issues that have been acknowledged as key factors in Africa's vulnerability to terrorism.

In a purely security dimension, the AU is unlikely to play a stronger role than subregional organizations such as IGAD or ECOWAS. In principle, the AU's counterterrorism efforts have been consciously linked with its wider peace and security architecture. The AU Peace and Security Council is mandated to monitor the implementation of the counterterrorism strategy. Thus, it is conceivable that other AU security initiatives such as the African Standby Force could be deployed in the counterterrorism campaign. This could be useful for training purposes and to develop common approaches and protocols for the use of military resources in responding to crises. However, the potential for the Standby Force to be deployed requires further time, resources, and clarity of political will from the AU member states before any counterterrorism role can be seriously considered.

Contemporary terrorism is increasingly global in nature. Therefore, any effective counterterrorism strategy must necessarily be comprehensive in geographical terms. This is the strongest case for the involvement of regional organizations such as the African Union in the post–September 11 counterterrorism campaign. Clearly, counterterrorism efforts that focus at the national and global levels, while ignoring the regional, will not be sufficient. Regional organizations are more closely linked to their member states than even the United Nations and are therefore best placed to influence and work with them. The national level is effective for operational initiatives, but even then there is a need for more harmonized policies and strategies that might best be developed regionally.

Through the counterterrorism instruments that it has adopted, particularly the convention, the plan of action, and the protocol, the AU has demonstrated that it can play an important role in encouraging member states to implement the international obligations in the global conventions and treaties related to terrorism; serving as a sounding board for regional concerns and issues; developing region-wide consensus and initiatives to tackle the increasingly global dimension of terrorism; facilitating the sharing of experiences and expertise among its member states; promoting common norms and standards; encouraging the sharing of crucial information about the movements of individuals and instruments that might aid terrorism; facilitating the apprehension and prosecution of terrorists as it is already doing; and promoting a broad-based regional approach that can focus on issues of human rights, democracy, and poverty and development, which have been recognized as important facilitators of terrorism in Africa.

The reality, however, is that the AU currently lacks the capacity to implement many of these initiatives, and so they remain at the level of ideas. The question, then, is whether that capacity can be built in a manner that can justify the cost of the investment and make it worthwhile, both for Africa and for key nations such as the United States. The only real option is to try to engage the AU. By all estimates, Africa is an important theater for international terrorism and probably will assume an even more significant role because all the factors that fuel terrorism are present and are most likely to get even more attractive. No other international organization can hone regionally specific strategies like the AU can, and a purely national or bilateral counterterrorism strategy is unlikely to offer the kind of comprehensive solution that can tackle the increasingly regional and global manifestations of contemporary terrorism. The international community, especially the United States, needs to forge stronger links with the AU to encourage it to play a more substantial role in the areas outlined above. It will also be necessary to bolster the AU's resource base and capacity to play that role.

For the African Union to fully embrace a more central role in global counterterrorism, it will also be necessary to resolve the points of divergence discussed earlier, especially regarding the conception and definition of terrorism, the issues related to the root causes of terrorism, and the factors that make Africa an attractive destination and arena for terrorism. The United States and other Western countries would also need to critically review their policies and relationships with Africa, in particular to address the apparent alienation and anger that some have argued are responsible for attracting Muslim youth to terrorist acts. This underscores the need for a truly global, not just U.S.-led, counterterrorism strategy—one that projects the terrorism challenge as an issue of common concern, not just one of American security, and one that emphasizes the need for more balance between the military, social, economic, and political responses to terrorism. Without such a consensus, it will be difficult to cultivate the sincere cooperation of the African Union and its member states in the war on terrorism.

CHAPTER THREE

THE ROLE OF THE INTER-GOVERNMENTAL AUTHORITY ON DEVELOPMENT IN PREVENTING AND COMBATING TERRORISM

Monica Juma

The global war on terrorism has catapulted the Horn of Africa onto the global stage. As in the Cold War era, when the Horn was central to the geostrategic calculus of the superpowers, this region has again become a front line in the confrontation between Western and militant Islamist forces. Today, the seven countries that form the Inter-Governmental Authority on Development (IGAD)— Djibouti, Ethiopia, Eritrea, Kenya, Somalia, Sudan, and Uganda— are under immense pressure to support the U.S.-led war against terrorism. While the region has cooperated with this initiative, glaring strategic and structural weaknesses at regional and national levels slow the pace at which capacity is being created to combat and prevent terrorism.

The involvement of IGAD member countries in the global war against terrorism is set against a background of a region emerging from conflicts of varying intensity. Until recently, Sudan's government was prosecuting a civil war with elements in the country's southern regions that spanned more than four decades, resulting in a humanitarian crisis marked by death, displacement, destruction of property, and loss of livelihoods.[1] In Somalia, after the fall of President Said Barre in 1991, the country imploded, and the majority of its population was displaced either inside or outside of Somalia's borders. Somalia has evaded more than a dozen attempts to create peace and remained without state authority until 2005, when a weak Transitional Federal Government (TFG) was created at IGAD-sponsored peace talks.[2] Between 1998 and 2000, Ethiopia and Eritrea fought a vicious cross-border war from which tensions are still simmering.[3] Internally, both countries confront the challenge posed by aggrieved political and ethnic groups.[4] Since 1986, northern Uganda has been embroiled in an insurgency marked by unthinkable abuses on civilian populations that has resulted in the displacement and destitution of more than 1.5 million people.[5] In the early 1990s, Djibouti also experienced tensions and sporadic violence as various groups challenged the legitimacy of the incumbent government. Meanwhile, parts of Kenya are intermittently rocked by ethnic and tribal clashes.[6] The result of these conflicts has been the weakening of the potential for collective action at the regional level, as each government has struggled to maintain law and order domestically.

Together, these conflicts presented major challenges for IGAD. Created in 1986, the authority was given a restricted mandate: to promote coordinated approaches between its member states to address the region's primary development problems, minimally defined as drought and desertification.[7] This limited mandate initially constrained IGAD from dealing with peace and security issues. Its capability was also impaired by limited national resources and tense regional political dynamics. Owing to its strategic location, the Horn of Africa was a main theater of superpower rivalry and competition, splitting countries into protégés and allies of either the East or the West at any given time and weakening the possibility of regional cohesiveness.[8]

IGAD has since expanded its mandate to encompass the search for peace and security—two essential prerequisites for development.[9] Currently, it is seeking to revitalize and consolidate its role as the primary regional player for the enhancement of state and human security.[10] However, IGAD remains fragile. It lacks appropriate structures, capacity, and resources to deal with so many conflicts, and it has been stifled by a glaring lack of political will and support from its principals. In fact, whether IGAD can broker and maintain sustainable peace in a region that many analysts argue is caught in numerous conflict traps is an open question.[11] However, since 2001, the institution has been strained further by pressures to participate in the global war on terrorism.

In terms of counterterrorism, IGAD has admittedly come a long way. It has developed a regional policy and a dual-pronged strategy to combat and prevent terrorism and has attained some important successes. However, the war against terrorism is far from won in this region of Africa. Threats of attack remain real in all countries, especially in Somalia, where acts of terror continue unabated. Recent conflicts between warlords and Islamic courts in Mogadishu, as well as the assassinations of peace activists, aid workers, and journalists, and continued abductions and hostage takings for ransom, suggest that the country remains a soft underbelly for terrorism. This reality—and the threat it poses across the region—calls for continuous review of IGAD's counterterrorism efforts to ensure that their intensification is well targeted.

This chapter explores the region's commitment to fight terrorism and the extent to which its member states have complied with relevant regional and international commitments. It sketches the background against which the region has engaged in the war against terrorism; outlines the process by which it has evolved a common position on the counterterrorist agenda; reviews the dual-pronged strategy that has emerged in an attempt to prevent and combat terrorism; highlights key challenges confronting the region and its member states; and makes recommendations on how their capacity can be enhanced in pursuit of effective counterterrorism.

The Horn of Africa and Terrorism

The focus on the Horn of Africa has stemmed from strong perceptions and consensus among various actors in the war against terror that the region was among the most vulnerable globally and, by extension, had the most potential for being used by terrorists. This view was given credence by the character of the region: weak states with minimally effective or nonexistent enforcement mechanisms, porous borders, vast areas of territory that fall outside state control, disputed authority and intense competition for political power, and international marginalization. Accentuating these weaknesses is endemic corruption that undermines state control over the flow of money, border controls, and migration, making these systems susceptible to people with terrorist intents. Furthermore, the region has a strong presence of Western interests including business establishments and pockets of American, European, and Israeli populations deemed as targets of choice by perpetrators of terrorism. As detailed above, the region is home to Somalia, a failed state that has become a fertile field for the proliferation of indigenous terrorist and extremist groups and networks with regional reach and international linkages.[12] In addition, Somalia lies proximate to the Arabian Peninsula, an area associated with key international terrorists group such as al Qaeda.[13] Arguably, a combination of these factors can facilitate money laundering, provide safe haven or safe passage for terrorists, and present an opportunity for terrorist organizations to hide, recruit, and train without interference.

The region's initial reaction to the global counterterrorism campaign was mixed. On the one hand, some governments, particularly Sudan, were fearful that the war on terror could provide an alibi for foreign governments to launch a war against their perceived enemies in the region.[14] Apprehension was enhanced by the Bush administration's renewal of the U.S. bilateral sanctions against Sudan in 2001, citing continued terrorist concerns. On the other hand, for countries such as Uganda and Ethiopia, the war on terrorism was viewed as a legitimization of their long-term struggles to defeat domestic insurgencies and provided them with an opportunity to seek international assistance in dealing with local threats. Overall, however, while the war against terrorism has been largely shaped and driven from outside, it has pushed IGAD member states to work together and catalyzed the emergence of a common position and evident political commitment to deal collectively with new security issues.

Embracing Counterterrorism in IGAD

Although all IGAD countries have suffered terrorist activities during their histories, either by foreign terrorist movements or by local rebels, and acknowledge their vulnerability to further attacks in the future,[15] the region did not conceive of terrorism as a common security threat prior to the 2001 attacks on America. This perception changed overnight after September 11, as attention turned to the region as a next logical sphere for the war against terrorism after the U.S. reprisal in Afghanistan. Memories of the attacks on the U.S. Embassies in Kenya and Tanzania in 1998, and the humiliation of American troops in Somalia in 1993, were still fresh. Nonetheless, Washington singled out Somalia and Sudan as hosting or supporting terrorist groups (a claim that both countries refuted)[16] and named Eritrea, Kenya, Uganda, Ethiopia, and Somalia as countries that unintentionally hosted al Qaeda cells or associated movements. Shortly thereafter, these countries admitted to the presence and operations of terrorist elements within their borders at various times.

In an effort to support the U.S.-led war on terror or to forestall the possibility of a war against some of its member states, IGAD met in October 2001 and collectively condemned terrorism. Since then, a consensus has evolved that terrorism constitutes a common security threat that requires cooperative action. The basis for common action in IGAD derives from the Organization of African Unity (OAU) Convention on the Prevention and Combating of Terrorism (Algiers, 1999), which defines terrorism in article 1 as:

> (a) any act which is a violation of the criminal laws of a State Party and which may endanger the life, physical integrity or freedom of, or cause serious injury or death to, any person, any number or group of persons or causes or may cause damage to public or private property,

natural resources, environmental or cultural heritage and is calculated or intended to:

> (i) intimidate, put in fear, force, coerce or induce any government, body, institution, the general public or any segment thereof, to do or abstain from doing any act, or to adopt or abandon a particular standpoint, or to act according to certain principles; or

> (ii) disrupt any public service, the delivery of any essential service to the public or to create a public emergency; or

> (iii) create general insurrection in a State;

> (b) any promotion, sponsoring, contribution to, command, aid, incitement, encouragement, attempt, threat, conspiracy, organizing, or procurement of any person, with the intent to commit any act referred to in paragraph (a) (i) to (iii).[17]

In line with other international instruments and obligations, the OAU Convention also reinforces the centrality of the general principles of international law (particularly those of international humanitarian law), as well as the African Charter of Human and Peoples' Rights, in interpreting and prosecuting the war on terrorism. In addition, article 3(1) excludes liberation struggles from the definition.[18]

The implementation of these commitments through IGAD is now being pursued through a dual-pronged strategy. First, at the national level, individual governments are the primary implementing agents, and across the region they are enhancing their capacities to execute various components of the regional plan and other international commitments. Second, to support action at the national level, the IGAD Secretariat in Djibouti provides strategic direction in the form of regional guidelines and plans of action, oversees implementation of the agreed positions, and ensures alignment, compliance, and coherence with continental and international commitments and obligations. IGAD is also mandated by its members to approach donors and research agencies that can assist them in mobilizing resources, building their capacity, and providing technical assistance.[19]

Regional Approach

IGAD's collective action is built on five pillars:

- a regional strategy that elaborates a common position, vision, and framework of engagement

- a regional plan of action for implementation
- alignment of existing IGAD mechanisms and structures to the imperative of combating and preventing terrorism
- consolidation of peace processes in the region
- the boosting of regional capacity through participation in internationally led initiatives.

Support of African Union and United Nations Efforts

Although IGAD does not have a well-articulated counterterrorist strategy, it commits itself to the eradication of the terrorist threat. In 2003, the organization drafted the Implementation Plan to Counter Terrorism in the IGAD Region.[20] Through such mechanisms and the deliberations of its member states, IGAD subscribes to the African Union (AU) and international commitments and obligations and has since 2001 evolved a common vision, position, and framework for preventing and combating terrorism. In doing so, the IGAD Secretariat is mandated to support member states in their efforts to undertake counterterrorism measures, oversee the implementation of the various aspects of the regional plan, and prepare an annual progress report to the IGAD Council of Ministers.[21] IGAD also participated in the process that finalized the continental strategy on counterterrorism. In October 2001, its member states took part in decisions to adopt an AU Declaration Against Terrorism (which reaffirmed commitment to the OAU Convention)[22] and an AU Plan of Action to support implementation of the convention. Through the AU, IGAD member states also resolved to establish an African Center for the Study and Research on Terrorism in Algiers to share information and build regional capacities, strongly supported the implementation of United Nations (UN) instruments on terrorism, and urged member states to adopt UN Security Council Resolution 1373.

Implementation Plan

Adopted in June 2003, the IGAD Implementation Plan to Counter Terrorism outlines six areas for action and provides benchmarks, standards, and indicators to measure performance in these areas and compliance with regional and international obligations.

First, the plan argues for a common regional policy framework, rooted in the broader international strategy that includes the ratification of regional and international instruments. IGAD members are expected to sign, ratify, and accede to all regional and international instruments that seek to prevent and combat terrorism, develop effective antiterrorism legislation, and regularly assess and combat new international and regional threats.[23]

Second, the plan encourages member states to develop measures to counter the financing of terrorism. Such measures include bolstering governmental capacity to identify individuals and organizations suspected of association with terrorism; facilitating information exchange between the private sector, financial institutions, and state structures on suspicious transactions; establishing specialized units to liaise with similar regional and international structures; and designing criteria to verify the activities of charitable organizations, including legislation that would set a minimum standard for registration for such organizations.

Third, the plan identifies the need to enhance operational capacity to counter illegal cross-border movement through tightening border controls, addressing the challenge of illegal immigration, and accepting dual responsibilities, including monitoring of shared borders. Enhancement of capacity would also involve upgrading information resources and harnessing border control procedures to curtail the use of forged documents, corruption at borders, infiltration by transnational criminals or suspected individuals, as well as deny sanctuary to terrorists or groups engaged in subversive activities. To bolster existing operational capacity, the plan recommits members to ongoing initiatives that have relevance to the terrorist agenda, particularly those on the proliferation of small arms and light weapons.[24]

Fourth, the plan envisages the establishment of a regional database and terrorism center to explore the scope, causes, and nature of organized crime and financial support networks that facilitate transnational crime, including money laundering and terrorism. It also underscores the need to promote cooperation and the exchange of information and mutual legal assistance, including harmonization of national legislation, coordinated training of relevant agencies, and enhanced international cooperation through participation in international meetings and interaction with relevant international organizations such as the United Nations Counter-Terrorism Committee.

Fifth, the plan upholds the primacy of the respect for human rights and the rule of law in undertaking counterterrorism actions in line with UN conventions and the African Charter of Human and People's Rights. For a region with a history of tyrannical and oppressive regimes, this provision is critical in addressing fears that the war on terrorism could be invoked to quash opposition groups and roll back democratic gains made in the 1980s and 1990s.

Finally, the plan hinges on cultivating public support through education and other social and economic programs as a basis for winning the confidence of the population and building its support in combating terrorism. An analysis of individual country performances in each of these areas is discussed later.

Adapting Other IGAD Mechanisms

The third pillar of the regional approach constitutes efforts to align existing IGAD organs, in particular its Conflict, Early Warning, and Response Mechanism (CEWARN), with the counterterrorist agenda. Created in 1992, CEWARN was mandated to facilitate the sharing of information on potential conflict areas. Since 2003, CEWARN has come under review owing to the centrality of information to counterterrorism, and suggestions have been made to expand its scope beyond pastoralist conflicts and to act as a regional database on terrorism. This has not happened, partly because of limited capacity but also because of the politicization of the issue and the reluctance of governments to allow an institution outside their direct control to deal with issues concerning intelligence and security.[25]

In an attempt to strengthen its capacity, IGAD has also increased its interaction and collaboration with international organizations dealing with aspects relating to antiterrorism, such as the UN Office on Drugs and Crime. Together, these institutions hosted an international cooperation meeting on counterterrorism and the fight against transnational organized crime in 2004. This meeting encouraged member states to use the assistance of the International Criminal Police Organization (Interpol) in accessing and sharing sensitive security information.[26] IGAD has also held capacity-building and training activities in enforcement capabilities and collaboration, the exchange of information on the subregional and bilateral levels, and border control aimed principally at halting the illicit trafficking of arms and drugs. One such training exercise culminated in the signing of a memorandum of understanding where all participating countries agreed to open liaison offices to enhance the exchange of information related to terrorism.[27]

Consolidation of Regional Peace Processes

Acknowledging a link between instability and terrorism, IGAD has stepped up its efforts to stabilize the region. Presumably, peace will enhance stability and promote good governance and hence curb terrorism's ability to maintain a foothold in the region. The agreement between Eritrea and Ethiopia (2000), the signing of the Sudan Comprehensive Peace Agreement (2005), and the formation of the Transitional Federal Government in Somalia (2005) brought hope to an otherwise fragile region. While the reconstruction of Sudan commenced with the engagement of the international community,[28] the stabilization of Somalia poses particular challenges. The TFG has yet to establish itself in Mogadishu, and because the international community has remained largely aloof, the burden of nurturing a peaceful transition in Somalia rests squarely on IGAD.

So far, IGAD has demonstrated an unprecedented commitment to stabilize Somalia. In 2004, IGAD foreign ministers convened under the aegis of the UN Security Council in Nairobi and endorsed a proposal to participate in the reconstruction of Somalia. This was followed by a summit decision to provide security support to the TFG for its relocation to, and guaranteed sustenance in, Mogadishu, prompting five IGAD members (Uganda, Sudan, Kenya, Ethiopia, and Djibouti) to pledge contributions to a peace support mission. Aware of the organization's limited mandate for intervention, the summit requested the AU to issue a mandate for deployment as it awaited United Nations endorsement.[29] The deployment has yet to receive support from some key international partners, including the United States, that remain cautious and favor greater internal consensus/cohesion before any intervention. Both IGAD and the AU argue for the need to seize any opportunity to support peace in Somalia because they view it as a fulcrum to regional peace and counterterrorism efforts.[30] As some experts rightly suggest, the successful draining of the swamps of terrorism in the Horn depends on a skillful mixing of counterterrorist measures and peacebuilding.[31]

Participation in U.S. Initiatives

IGAD countries currently participate in a number of U.S.-led initiatives that provide assistance to boost their counterterrorism capacities. Many member states participate in the most visible of these initiatives, the Combined Joint Task Force–Horn of Africa (CJTF–HOA), whose mission is to detect, disrupt, and defeat transnational terrorist groups and to enhance long-term stability in the region. CJTF–HOA has undertaken training with allied forces and armies of Kenya, Ethiopia, and Djibouti and conducted civic action programs that refurbish schools and clinics and provide medical services to people and animals. It has also established a temporary training facility and commenced the training of three Ethiopian antiterrorism battalions. Although it is difficult to measure the extent of its success, a former CJTF–HOA commander indicated that by May 2004, they had captured "dozens of terrorists" and averted at least five terrorist attacks.[32]

In 2003, President George Bush announced the East Africa Counterterrorism Initiative, for which the United States set aside $100 million to strengthen the capabilities and foster cooperation of partners in combating terrorism.[33] Priority capacities include conducting military training for border control and coastal security, strengthening control of the movement of people and goods across borders, combating terrorist financing, training police, monitoring aspects of aviation security, and instituting education programs to prevent extremist fundamentalist influences from gaining ground in targeted countries. Within this initiative, the U.S. Terrorist Finance Working Group is assisting East African countries to develop anti–money laundering/counterterrorism financing regimes. The State Department's Terrorist Interdiction Program commenced operations in 2003 at selected airports in Kenya, Tanzania, and Ethiopia. The program aims to identify terrorists when they try to enter or leave these countries. Meanwhile, the State Department's Anti-Terrorism Assistance Program provides courses to civilian law enforcement officials to boost their capacities on detection and rendering safe explosive devices, post-blast techniques of investigation, VIP protection, and senior leadership crisis management exercises, as well as hostage situation negotiations.

Combating and Preventing Terrorism at the National Level

Efforts at the regional level are meant to augment activities undertaken at the national level, which fall under three broad areas: the development of legal and policy frameworks, creation of administrative and coordination structures, and conduct of operational activities.

Development of Legal and Policy Frameworks

Prior to the current campaign, only Ethiopia had specific policies and programs on counterterrorism. Grounded in its penal code of 1957, this framework criminalized acts committed to serve terrorist objectives. Most IGAD countries were in a state of denial about . being potential sources of international terrorism, claiming instead to be victims.[34] Other than leading to failure, the lack of appreciation for the broader context of the terrorist threat slowed the evolution of policy and legal frameworks in the region. Fortunately, countries emerged from this inertia relatively quickly and embarked on creating national structures to counter terrorism.

Except for Somalia, whose peculiar challenges are detailed later in the chapter, other IGAD countries have signed and ratified regional and international counterterrorism instruments. By December 2004, Kenya, Sudan, and Djibouti had ratified all of the 12 relevant UN conventions; Uganda had ratified 11; Ethiopia, 7; and Eritrea, 1. Each of these countries is constantly improving its policy (legal and administrative) frameworks to ensure effectiveness in combating terrorism. Where no specific or weak counterterrorism laws existed, countries have drafted antiterrorist laws. Uganda passed an Anti-Terrorism Act in 2002, which allows for the death penalty in terrorism cases.

Where bills have been rejected, partly because of opposition and human rights concerns (as in Kenya), they have been revised for debate and possible adoption by parliament.[35] Measures have been taken to strengthen weak laws in conformity with international obligations. In Ethiopia, the Ministry of Justice prepared a legal memorandum aimed at facilitating the implementation of its international obligations, and the Ethiopian Justice and Legal System Research Institute is currently revising the Ethiopian penal code, including criminalizing the commission of a "terrorist act," which is expected to be promulgated by the parliament in the near future. In Sudan, the Minister of Justice created a Prosecuting Bureau for the Combating of Terrorism whose jurisdiction includes the implementation of the terrorism act and international conventions, treaties, and protocols to which Sudan is a party.

In spite of these efforts, there are constraints to the formulation and implementation of antiterrorist policies and laws. A glaring gap across the region is the lack of capabilities to uphold successful prosecutions, a shortcoming linked to the lack of investigative capabilities. In some cases, arrested suspects have been subjected to prosecution that would not qualify as due process, while in other instances, prosecution has been difficult to sustain. In one such case, two people suspected of supporting the attack on an Israeli passenger plane and hotel near Mombasa in 2002 were recently released from custody after Kenya's attorney general entered a *nolle prosequi* for lack of evidence to sustain the charges.[36] The launching of the AU's African Center for the Study and Research on Terrorism in Algiers provides an opportunity to support governments in crafting their national legislation and building their investigative and prosecution capacities.

Furthermore, the terrorist agenda is in competition with other national priorities, some of which are viewed as more critical and relevant to the needs of the country. In such circumstances, leaders have faced difficulties in seeking to secure resources for the antiterrorist agenda. To date, no IGAD country has allocated any substantial resources to counterterrorism, leaving this agenda almost totally dependent on international assistance and support.

Creating Operational and Coordination Mechanisms

Except for Somalia, all IGAD countries have established operational and coordination mechanisms, including national focal points that are mandated to facilitate and coordinate implementation of the various antiterror measures.

Djibouti has three government subcommittees that deal with legislative and judicial measures, the coordination of the security services, and the regulation of financial and banking systems. It has also set up a database for detecting and monitoring terrorist financing and has a crisis management unit that meets weekly under the Minister of the Interior to investigate individual suspects attempting to infiltrate the country.

Considered a lead state in East Africa, Kenya formulated a national counterterrorism strategy that encompasses all national security agencies and established a National Counter-Terrorism Center in 2004. The center is mandated to guide operations on the basis of integrated threat analysis, and it created a crack antiterrorism police unit. Sudan has a Coordinating National Technical Committee, comprising seven departments specialized in combating terrorism, and it also has a specialized counterterrorist unit. Uganda created a Joint Anti-Terrorism Task Force, comprising military intelligence, the police's criminal investigation department and special branch, the external security organization, and the internal security organization.

However, there are challenges arising from poor interdepartmental coordination. These mechanisms are heavily weighed in favor of security actors to the exclusion of other sectors that have a bearing on terrorism. The marginalization of agencies across and outside of government raises anxiety because security operatives have sometimes used harsh, even terrorist, measures against other actors, especially opponents of governments. In and of themselves, the security structures do not inspire public confidence.

Other Targeted Activities

In addition to the measures detailed above, each IGAD country is undertaking targeted activities in key areas. First among these is monitoring and tightening financial transactions to control money laundering and limit sponsorship of suspicious persons or organizations. Kenya has established a task force to review existing legislation and recommend a national policy on money laundering, and it is moving toward an act of parliament against laundering. The National Bank of Ethiopia has instructed all commercial banks and financial institutions to scrutinize the accounts and transactions of their clients. So far, the National Bank has blocked individual accounts detected at the Dashen Bank and the Commercial Bank of Ethiopia linked with the Al Barakaat group of companies, which the United States designated as involved in the financing of terrorist activities. Kenya, Eritrea, and Uganda have gone further and proscribed a number of religious "extremist" organizations and establishments, including charities.

A second area where countries are focusing is the tightening of border controls, including immigration rules and procedures and the documentation of persons entering and leaving through official borders. With foreign assistance, Kenya, Uganda, and Ethiopia have introduced a computerized system of travel documents[37] and enhanced border control and surveillance. Kenya has deployed two battalions to patrol its border with Somalia. These efforts have led to arrests of some suspicious individuals as well as illegal immigrants. However, the transborder movement of pastoralist communities poses a peculiar challenge to the IGAD region. Given the expansiveness of border areas and the prevalent cross-border raiding practices, the envisaged border control is likely to cost enormous resources.

IGAD countries have also carried out arrests and, in some cases, successfully prosecuted suspected individuals. Sudan, under pressure from the international community, expelled Osama bin Laden (in 1996) and extradited Ilich Ramírez Sánchez (Carlos the Jackal) to France (1994) and the hijackers of Ethiopian Airlines to Ethiopia (2001). It also has undertaken raids on alleged training camps of possible terrorists and has arrested and convicted suspects. Kenya has arrested and arraigned a number of suspects in court, and, while some of the cases have been terminated, the government is drawing lessons from these experiences.

Challenges and Gaps

Annual IGAD reviews indicate that terrorist threats to this region remain real and urge the commitment and collaboration of its member states and the international community in stemming them.[38] While the region has made great efforts, a number of challenges at the strategic and operational levels hinder its ability to fulfill its commitments.

Strategic Challenges

More than anything else, fledgling trust among IGAD countries remains a major obstacle to collective counterterrorism action. Although there is an understanding of the need for cooperation, the region is yet to embrace a shared vision that surpasses national interests. It is marked by political incoherence, distrust among political leaders, and lack of mutual comfort levels necessary to energize a collective antiterrorism agenda. Some countries are reluctant to cooperate fully with countries they consider their enemies. For instance, because of deep suspicion of each other, there has been no cooperation between Ethiopia and Eritrea. So far, Eritrea has declined to attend any meetings hosted by or in Ethiopia. There is also discomfort between Uganda and Sudan, as between Ethiopia and many leaders in Somalia, especially over the issue of foreign troop deployments to Somalia. Historically, IGAD dealt with political sensitivities through the creation of ad hoc mechanisms outside its secretariat, as evidenced by the Sudan and Somalia peace negotiations' structures. However, such structures would be insufficient for the pursuit of the counterterrorist agenda, where recommended action depends on a modicum of trust. Activities like sharing of information and intelligence, use of extraterritorial investigations, and provision of mutual legal assistance presuppose comfort levels not yet attained among IGAD member states.

Related to this uneasiness are concerns that some countries enjoy favored status from international partners and are accruing more benefits than their counterparts. Kenya, viewed as a key ally of the United States, hosts many counterterrorism activities and has received most of the financial and technical assistance earmarked for the region. Meanwhile, Eritrea feels slighted by what it perceives as a privileged position bestowed to Ethiopia, whose three battalions have been trained, and Djibouti, which hosts the CJTF–HOA. Feelings of inequity and loss do not bode well for regional cooperation and need to be addressed through approaches that pool resources and ensure their use for the benefit of the region.

Another strategic challenge arises from tensions between the counterterrorist activities and respect for human rights and rule of law. Structures used in the prosecution of the war on terror often lean toward extrajudicial mechanisms that include using emergency powers, prolonged detention, torture, and secrecy in dealing with suspects. In a region without countervailing forces or institutions to effectively check and balance the power of the executive, this could erode democratic gains achieved in IGAD member states. Governments have been accused of invoking this war on terrorism to suppress legitimate opposition. For instance, in Eritrea, the government of Issaias Afeworki has allegedly used the war on terrorism as an excuse to clamp down on opposition groups and Islamic associations.[39]

Tensions between human rights and counterterrorism are further complicated by two factors. First is the assumed and sometimes alleged link between Islam and terrorism. This perception generates a major challenge in a region where the majority of people are Muslim, distributed as follows: 100 percent in Somalia; 94 percent in Djibouti; 70 percent in Sudan; 50 percent in Ethiopia and in Eritrea; 16 percent in Uganda; and 10 percent in Kenya.[40] Where Muslims are in the minority or feel excluded from government, they are falling behind in terms of the social and political gains made in the past 10 years. On the East African coast, the social advancement of the Muslim minority has trailed that of the region's already low average. Such populations feel alienated and marginalized and have looked to Islamic charities from Arab countries to provide education, health, social welfare, and security.[41]

The involvement of the West in the wars in Iraq and Afghanistan has not helped the negative perception of the West as Christian crusaders seeking to counter Islam. These feelings translate into skepticism among a large proportion of the Muslim population about the intent of the counterterrorism campaign. Radical Muslims are particularly critical. They interpret the campaign as a possible "Western" invasion of Islamic lands and resent their governments' "acquiescing" behavior toward the "invaders." Although they are aware that this can accentuate their vulnerability, governments have not always tended toward restraint from strong measures that could alienate their Muslim populations.

The tension between counterterrorism and human rights is also linked to the domestic character of terrorism, which IGAD must address if its agenda is to bear relevance for the African region. While the global war on terrorism focuses almost primarily on international and Islamist terrorism, IGAD cannot ignore local manifestations of terrorism. As the number of militias, warlords, and rebels involved in violent activities multiplies,[42] even more worrying is their increasing adoption of terror tactics similar to those employed by international terrorist groups.[43] There is also evidence of Islamic terrorist networks and organizations supporting and funding fundamentalist groups of other forms. For instance, the Lord's Resistance Army reportedly depends heavily on the support of the Sudanese Islamist government. The failure of IGAD to address these emerging webs of terrorist activities would open it to accusations of complacency and being at the service of "foreign" interests and would erode its legitimacy in the region.

Regional Counterterrorism Capacities

The counterterrorism measures envisaged by IGAD presuppose that the organization has a range of capabilities to guide policy formulation and monitor implementation. This is simply not the case. Structurally, terrorism falls under the Division of Conflict Prevention, Management, and Resolution in IGAD's Department of Political and Humanitarian Affairs. Thinly staffed, this department lacks the requisite human and technical capacity to carry out the multiple roles that have been assigned to it, including oversight and alignment of action, monitoring of compliance, undertaking of assessments, supporting member states to adopt appropriate policies, and coordinating regional activities, obligations, and commitments.

To provide strategic leadership and capacity building across the region, IGAD would have to develop much greater legal and technical skills within its Secretariat to encourage, mobilize, and provide assistance to member states. Only then will IGAD be able to effectively develop and harmonize national legislation relating to terrorism, money laundering, organized crime, corruption, and drugs and arms trafficking; help to build the capacity of member states' judiciaries and law enforcement forces; conduct regular terrorism vulnerability and counterterrorism assessments; and establish a regional forum for information exchange.

Enhancing strategic cooperation—including project management, collaboration, and coordination; partnership agreements with other organizations; and coordination of regional efforts to avoid duplication of effort—means building key capacities that are weak or nonexistent within IGAD. Currently, it has no budget for capacity building at the secretariat level, nor is there a keenness among donors to strengthen its organizational and technical capacities. If IGAD remains incapacitated, governments may choose to pursue their own agenda, a path that may not encourage collective action.

National Counterterrorism Capacities

At the national level, IGAD countries exhibit degrees of fragility and inadequate capacity to effectively manage counterterrorism activities. Even in more stable countries such as Kenya and Ethiopia, the state neither has the monopoly of coercive power, nor does it control its entire territory. Border areas and slums of big cities are de facto outside state control. For years, the northeast region of Kenya that borders Somalia was essentially cut off from the rest of the country. Safer travel is only possible in military-protected convoys. Security forces have withdrawn to isolated forts, leaving control of the area to gangs and warlords, and many horrendous terrorist acts have occurred unchecked.[44]

Meanwhile, in the poverty-stricken areas of Nairobi, power rests in the hands of gangs and youth militias run by political parties, mafia bosses, religious sects, and ethnic leaders. Well supplied with weapons from conflict areas, these groups carry out gang robberies with impunity. Sometimes, police officers rent weapons and vehicles to criminal groups and occasionally participate in robberies. The government is currently incapable of controlling the trading of goods and movement of people across the Somali-Kenyan border even if it were determined to do so. Under these conditions, the Kenyan security forces would not have been able to prevent the attacks in Mombasa even if the government had been sufficiently informed of the danger and had taken the situation seriously.[45]

Limited state capacity is weakened further by ineffective interagency cooperation among government institutions dealing with terrorism. While countries have established coordinating structures, divergent operational cultures of different agencies persist, reducing the opportunity for complementarity, synergy, and interdepartmental optimization. Regular interdepartmental sessions that involve all primary national actors responsible for detecting, monitoring, and preventing terrorism have yet to evolve a common strategic culture.

Focusing on building state capacity is essential and should go beyond the reform of, and support for, the security sector alone. As argued elsewhere, the Horn will not help win the war on terrorism without a determined and sustained investment in state capacity building that enables governments to control their territories and borders and to protect potential targets of terrorist assault.

Inadequate Resources

The resources and attention devoted to counterterrorism in East Africa and the Horn are impressive but inadequate. As observed by David Shinn, the US$100 million East Africa Counterterrorism Initiative and several other modest programs do not measure up to the threat.[46] If any state with a combustible mix of a weak central government, widespread poverty, and an increasingly politicized Muslim population is at risk, then most of the Horn of Africa remains vulnerable to terrorism. Furthermore, the focus of current programs is primarily on short- and medium-term objectives, including capturing terrorists, providing training, and, to a limited extent, building up counterterrorism infrastructure.

Missing is a long-term program to reduce poverty and social alienation. The Africa Policy Advisory Panel, organized by the Center for Strategic and International Studies, recommended consideration of an annual US$200 million Muslim outreach initiative in Africa.[47] As one former U.S. Ambassador to Kenya put it, there is a need for focused assistance that serves the interests of the coalition against terrorism but also enhances the image of the United States and allied countries by boosting the continent's economic development and political stability. It is critical that Washington's relationship with various African states and leaders not be viewed narrowly or exclusively through the prism of the growing U.S. concern with combating terrorism.[48]

The Somalia Challenge

Somalia presents peculiar and difficult challenges to the war against terrorism. As a recent International Crisis Group report demonstrated, the country remains a theater of shadowy confrontation involving local jihadi extremists organized exclusively to conduct urban insurgency and terrorism, foreign al Qaeda operatives using Somalia as a platform for actions aimed at foreign interests, and intelligence services from a number of regional and Western countries that depend on the collaboration of local warlords and faction leaders. The lack of a functioning central government means there is no legitimate institution to direct counterterrorism activities. Somalia thus has no functioning institutions to fulfill the country's international obligations and seems to attract the germination of extremist elements of various shades.

So far, Western and regional governments conducting counterterrorism activities are dependent on the support of local faction leaders. However, this support base is under threat as some of these leaders increasingly feel that they are not receiving adequate support or recognition.[49] Local leaders also critique U.S. counterterrorism efforts as being ad hoc, a problem compounded by a rapid turnover of staff. The United States has been accused of violating airspace and territorial sovereignty, particularly by cooperating with partners such as the unrecognized Somaliland administration. Even more worrisome is the increasing resentment by ordinary Somalis of the opportunistic partnership between U.S. agents and Somali warlords. Most Somalis feel that the warlords are being further empowered at the expense of other sectors in society.[50] There is a need to engage ordinary Somali actors, without necessarily coopting them, and to build mutual understanding of both the threat and solution.

Principally, however, a successful counterterrorism strategy requires more attention in helping Somalia with the twin tasks of reconciliation and state building in ways that ensure the restoration of a legitimate, functional government.[51] If Somalia's protracted crisis is allowed to persist, its stateless territory will continue to attract criminal and extremist elements, and it will be only a matter of time before they succeed in carrying out new acts of terror against Somalis and their neighbors. The need to focus attention on Somalia is also critical to regional efforts. As long as Somalia is unstable and vulnerable, the region remains acutely vulnerable to terrorism and a wide range of other threats. For instance, Somali business tycoons, including Islamists, are becoming primary actors in the smuggling trade along both land and sea routes in East and Central Africa. These activities threaten the economy of countries across the region with a powerful black market economy. It is also linked to the threat that comes from the growing business of hostage taking and ransom demands.[52] In a recent event, the entire crew of a ship was taken hostage and ransom demanded for its release. This scenario calls for a concerted effort to address the challenges within Somalia as a basis for augmenting activities in the rest of IGAD countries.

While the nations of the Horn have an important part to play in Somalia, terrorism is an international security issue. The international community has an obligation to partner with the region in ways that boost the latter's capacity to deal with these threats. So far, assistance seems to be skewed to certain aspects, in particular financial mechanisms and border controls, that are viewed as high-priority areas by most donors. It is also imperative that action is grounded by sound research and regular assessment of threats. This requires investment in building multidisciplinary, intersectoral investigative and research capabilities across government departments and institutions in the region. So far, training has been carried out on an ad hoc basis, depending on the availability of a willing donor. This system clearly is not sustainable. If IGAD is to create a critical mass of counterterrorism capacity, it requires resources that guarantee ongoing understanding as well as training.

Conclusion

Generally, IGAD countries agree on the principles of cooperation to combat terrorism and have commenced activities toward enhancing individual country capabilities for dealing with terrorism rather than multilateral action. Fortunately, there is a great effort to align activities at the national level with regional, continental, and international commitments. However, the level of threat compared to capacity created indicates that the region remains a soft underbelly in Africa that is vulnerable to terrorist threats. This challenge entails building protective and preventive strategies that aim to deny terrorists opportunities to exploit current vulnerabilities and investing in changes that strengthen national institutions in ways that reduce the vulnerabilities being taken advantage of by people with terrorist intents.

Enormous resources have to be committed to strengthening local institutions and addressing the cross-border, refugee, and immigration issues that are central to an effective antiterrorist policy. This requires a greater and more nuanced coordination between security, development, and relief enterprises and programs. So far, the focus seems to lean in favor of security structures. Furthermore, strategies for combating terrorism in fragile democracies must be reconciled to the need for achieving and consolidating gains in democracy and economic stability and progress.[53] While increased foreign assistance to build effective capacity will encourage coherence across the region, that investment must be met with local material support and political will from within the region in order to succeed.

Any counterterrorism strategy in the Horn of Africa must also take into account the historical dimensions and character of the region. The lack of trust and a tendency toward the pursuit of national rather than common interests are weaknesses that can only be addressed through patient confidence-building measures at the political and technical levels across the region. For the war against terrorism to be won, it is critical that it be viewed as legitimate, owned and led by, and responding to the needs of the IGAD region and its peoples.

There is also a need to revisit the mandate of the IGAD agreement to reflect current threats and the imperative to deal with them. As it stands, the IGAD agreement of 1996 gives preference to the use of soft power in the form of negotiation and mediation in dealing with the insecurity in the region. The coordination of more robust action envisaged in the war on terrorism can only emerge from a precise and firm mandate. A current review process within IGAD may provide an important opportunity to initiate a restructuring of the organization's framework to promote security in ways that enable member states to act in concert and to respond rapidly and effectively to hard security issues and threats.

CHAPTER FOUR

COUNTERTERRORISM MEASURES IN THE EAST AFRICAN COMMUNITY

Wafula Okumu

East Africa has been a soft and direct target of international terrorism since the 1970s. Prior to August 1998, when U.S. Embassies were bombed simultaneously in Kenya and Tanzania, the countries of the region had no plans or strategies to counter terrorist tactics by local organizations and international terrorists. These bombings also demonstrated that security and intelligence services in East African countries were underfunded and ill equipped to prevent and combat terrorism.[1] Furthermore, it took time for these countries to realize that they were not only helpless and easy targets but also havens for terrorists with regional and international networks.[2] Since 2003, the countries in the region have been vigorously addressing institutional weaknesses that impede their ability to pursue terrorists and respond to threats while simultaneously harmonizing their measures and cooperation at the regional level.

Although all three East African countries—Kenya, Tanzania, and Uganda—have embarked individually on various strategies to address transnational and domestic terrorism, they are also gradually moving toward regional initiatives under the aegis of the East African Community (EAC). The EAC member states have made a commitment to take effective collective measures to preserve peace, security, and stability and to eliminate threats to regional cooperation and peace.

This chapter provides an overview of terrorism in East Africa and the reasons why the countries in this region have been targeted by international terrorists and then discusses the measures being taken to deal with transnational and domestic terrorism in the region. Particular attention is paid to counterterrorism measures that are in place or have been proposed in the region, the challenges to be faced in their implementation, and the role the EAC is playing or can play to facilitate their implementation. The chapter argues that these measures are short- and medium-term strategies aimed at building up counterterrorism infrastructure but that they fall short of addressing the reasons that the region is both a vulnerable target and a haven for domestic and international terrorism. While ascribing a role for the EAC to play in countering transnational and domestic terrorism, the chapter suggests that the most effective measures must be based on eradicating conditions that contribute to poverty and bad governance in the EAC member states and to instability and conflicts in the Eastern and Central Africa regions. Finally, proposals are offered on how the EAC can enhance counterterrorism measures in East Africa and strengthen regional and international partnerships in preventing and combating terrorism in the region.

Terrorism in East Africa

The most notable acts of international terrorism on the continent have taken place in East Africa. Of the three EAC countries, Kenya is the most frequent target of international terrorism. Whereas Kenya's and Tanzania's threats are mainly transnational, Uganda has been plagued by domestic terrorism for over 20 years. The first international terrorist attack in East Africa took place in Kenya on the eve of 1981, when a terrorist group linked to the Popular Front for the Liberation of Palestine planted a bomb in the historic Norfolk Hotel, then owned by a Jewish family. It was later claimed that this was a revenge attack on Kenya for assisting Israeli commandos in the successful July 1976 rescue of hostages from a hijacked Air France airbus that had been commandeered to Entebbe, Uganda. When Air France Flight 139 with 250 people on board was hijacked on June 28, 1976, it was diverted to Entebbe, where the 10 hijackers demanded the release of 53 militants held in jails in 5 countries, Kenya being among them.[3] Two years earlier, Kenya had arrested three Palestinians within the vicinity of Nairobi airport who were planning to shoot down an El Al plane with a surface-to-air missile. Instead of trying them in the Kenyan courts, the government handed them to the Israeli government.

However, the most devastating terrorist attack in East Africa took place in August 1998, when the U.S. Embassies in Nairobi and Dar es Salaam were simultaneously bombed. The embassy bombings killed 224 people—among them 12 Americans—and injured more than 5,000 others. Immediately after these bombings, Osama bin Laden and al Qaeda were identified as the primary suspects in the attacks. Before moving to Afghanistan, bin Laden had an East Africa connection when he was exiled in Sudan from 1991 to 1996.

Osama bin Laden's personal secretary, Wadi el-Hage, is credited with establishing the Kenya cell in 1994.[4] Bin Laden's followers were also linked to the terrorist attacks on the Paradise Hotel near Mombasa in which 15 people, mostly Kenyans, were killed and on an Israeli jetliner in Mombasa on November 28, 2002. The Paradise Hotel was targeted because it was frequented by Israeli tourists. At the same time, another group of terrorists also tried but failed to shoot down with shoulder-held surface-to-air missiles an Israeli Arkia plane, Flight 582, carrying 264 Israeli tourists. Terrorists then embarked on their next plan, to bomb the new American Embassy in Gigiri, Nairobi, in June 2003.

These terrorist activities have spurred regional governments to formulate strategies and undertake individual and joint measures to address transnational and domestic terrorism threats and vulnerabilities. In order to analyze and determine the effectiveness of these measures, we must first understand the reasons why East Africa has been targeted by international terrorists.[5] These reasons range from proximity to the failed state of Somalia to weak counterterrorism and police capabilities, porous borders, and bad governance. They, in turn, contribute to poverty and corruption, which are easily exploitable by those planning and carrying out terrorist activities.

Proximity to Somalia

In late 2001, Rudolf Scharping, Germany's defense minister, caused a stir when he announced that the United States had decided to make Somalia its next target in the war on terrorism. Although Washington vehemently denied this claim, State Department spokesman Richard Boucher reiterated that the U.S. goal was to "make sure Somalia does not become a location where [terrorists] could operate, or a safe haven for terrorists."[6] Press reports also said that the United States had been gathering information on suspected military training camps in southern Somalia, near the Kenyan border. These camps were mainly run by al Ittihad al Islami, a radical Somali Islamic group believed to have ties to Osama bin Laden and to members of Somalia's fledgling Transitional National Government. The suspicion that Somalia was being keenly watched by Washington was confirmed on December 6, 2001, when al Ittihad al Islami was added to the U.S. Foreign Terrorist Organizations List.

The U.S. concern was that al Ittihad al Islami could develop into a Taliban-like movement and take over the stateless and lawless Somalia. According to David Shinn, a former U.S. Ambassador to Ethiopia, al Qaeda operatives and sleepers in Somalia are few but dangerous and have regional links to cells in Kenya, Tanzania, and the Comoros.[7] International intelligence sources have established that the bombings of the U.S. Embassies in 1998 and the Paradise Hotel in 2002 were planned from southern Somalia, possibly in the Ras Kiamboni area, which was believed to be a stronghold and training base for foreign Arabs linked to al Qaeda.[8]

Intractable Conflicts in the Region

The East Africa region has been plagued by intractable and long-running armed conflicts that have littered the region with small and light weapons that, due to the permeable borders, are easily moved around. The refugees produced by these conflicts have crossed borders, carrying weapons with them. Likewise, a small number of terrorists have benefited from the Somali conflict by transiting regularly into Kenya and Tanzania and bringing with them radical Islamic ideas.

Aggrieved Muslim Populations

Although the general Muslim population in the region has not shown interest in Islamic fundamentalism, there are small, radicalized Islamic elements in Kenya and Tanzania that have "assisted outside terrorist groups."[9] These radical elements have easily hidden in the Muslim population, as in the case of Fazul Abdullah Mohammed (also known as "Harun"), the al Qaeda mastermind of the Paradise Hotel bombing. A Comoran citizen, Mohammed settled on a remote island off the coast of Kenya one hour away from Kiamboni on a speedboat. After moving to an impoverished, remote, and desolate ancient settlement of about 1,500 Muslim people, he married a local girl and founded three football teams, which he named Al Qaeda, Kandahar, and Kabul, for the local youth.[10] Like the other international terrorists who exploited Kenya's endemic corruption and open environment for terrorist activities, Mohammed obtained Kenyan citizenship, set up a small business, and did charity work in a Muslim community.

Radical Islamic Charities

At the New York trial of four men convicted of involvement in the Nairobi and Dar es Salaam Embassy attacks, a former al Qaeda member named several charities as fronts for the terrorist group, including the Mercy International Relief Organization. Documents were presented at the trial demonstrating that Mercy smuggled weapons from Somalia into Kenya, and Abdullah Muhammad, one of the Nairobi bombers, delivered to Mercy's Kenya office eight boxes of convicted al Qaeda operative Wadi el-Hage's belongings, including false documents and passports.[11] Intelligence sources have also confirmed that the branches of al-Haramain in Kenya and Tanzania have been used as conduits for financial, material, and logistical support to al Qaeda and other terrorist organizations.[12] The Somali branch of al-Haramain Islamic Foundation, an affiliate of the Saudi Muslim World League, has also been linked to al Qaeda and al Ittihad al Islami.[13]

Western Presence in East Africa

Although there reportedly are only about 200 Israelis in East Africa, some are very prominent in business and professional circles and lead a luxurious expatriate lifestyle.[14] Some prominent businesses and exclusive hotels are owned by Jewish businesspeople. Kenya has also maintained very close ties to Israel, even during the 1970s and 1980s, when many African countries severed relations with Israel over the Palestinian crisis.

It is notable that the African countries that supported the U.S.-led war to oust Saddam Hussein in March 2003 were all from Eastern Africa, particularly Uganda, Rwanda, Eritrea, and Ethiopia. The Kenyan government has also supported the U.S.-led war on terror by opening its military bases for use by American military units to patrol the region, particularly the neighboring Somalia area. Kenya allowed the American military to operate from its country in 1991 during the Persian Gulf War and in 1994 during the ill-fated 1994 Operation *Restore Hope* mission in Somalia.

Since its independence from Britain in 1963, Kenya has been closely linked to British interests in Africa and has over the years become one of Britain's most reliable allies within the region. Besides being a regional hub for British businesses, Kenya has also signed agreements giving the British military access to bases and training grounds. The closeness to the West and Israel has not endeared Kenya to Islamic extremists. Mohammed Sadeek Odeh, an al Qaeda operative who was arrested after the 1998 Nairobi blast, told interrogators that he was willing to carry out a terror attack in Kenya because he did not like Kenyans partly for this reason.[15]

Corruption, Weak Government Control, and Bad Governance

Corruption and lack of investment in the development of professional public services in the region have contributed to weak government structures and processes, particularly those related to law enforcement and protection of national interests from foreign threats such as international terrorism. Low pay and poor work conditions have made security personnel vulnerable to bribery. Weak government control of territories, laxity in control of border and immigration entry points, and poorly equipped, trained, and paid security personnel have enabled al

Qaeda operatives to move into the region, establish cells, and carry out terrorist attacks.

Bad governance has provided fertile ground for institutionalized corruption. Endemic corruption that is pervasive in the security sector and immigration and customs departments has in turn facilitated international terrorists' unimpeded entry and movement around the region. For instance, a 2002 survey carried out by Transparency International Kenya showed that the average urban Kenyan paid 16 bribes a month, amounting to US$104, yet the average monthly income among Kenyans was only US$331. The survey showed that public servants are the most corrupt, "accounting for 99 percent of all bribery transactions and 97 percent of the total value of bribes given."[16] The police were found to be the most corrupt government institution, while the immigration department was the third most corrupt institution.

Abject Poverty

According to David Shinn, abject poverty in the East Africa region has combined with bad governance, social injustice, and political alienation to create an environment that attracts "religious extremists to export their philosophy and of terrorists to find local support for their nefarious acts."[17] The East African Muslim community, particularly that residing along the Indian Ocean coastline and in the far-flung northeast bordering Somalia, has felt "alienated from the mainstream political establishment and . . . increasingly looked to Islamic agencies funded by Persian Gulf donors to provide education, health, social welfare, and security."[18]

As the case of Fazul Mohammed illustrates, terrorists have capitalized on poverty to gain access to communities that give them cover to plan and execute their illegal acts. Although Kenya is the most economically developed country in the region, the uneven distribution of wealth is most pronounced in Muslim settlements along its coast and in the area bordering Somalia. Similarly, Islamic radicalism on Zanzibar and Pemba has also been linked to the high levels of poverty on these islands. However, it must be pointed out that Islamic radicalism and poverty alone do not create terrorists. Other factors such as political alienation, the perceived loose morals of the West, and Muslim solidarity combine to create a fertile ground that terrorists can exploit.

EAC Counterterrorism Measures

The East African Community was formed in 1967 but collapsed in 1977 because of political differences between its three members—Kenya, Uganda, and Tanzania. Although the organization was formally dissolved in 1984, in a provision of the mediation agreement for the division of assets and liabilities, the three states agreed to explore areas of future cooperation and to make concrete arrangements for such cooperation. Following a series of meetings, the three heads of state signed the Agreement for the Establishment of the Permanent Tripartite Commission for East African Cooperation on November 30, 1993. However, full East African cooperation began on March 14, 1996, when the Secretariat of the Permanent Tripartite Commission was launched at EAC headquarters in Arusha, Tanzania. On April 29, 1997, the East African heads of state directed the Permanent Tripartite Commission to begin upgrading the cooperation agreement to a treaty.

While deciding on January 29, 1999, to establish the EAC, the heads of state also signed a memorandum of understanding on foreign policy coordination and agreed to set up a mechanism to deal with terrorism in the region. The treaty establishing the East African Community was signed in Arusha on November 30, 1999, and entered into force on July 7, 2000, following its ratification and deposit of the instruments of ratification with the Secretary-General by all three partner states. The EAC was inaugurated in January 2001 to promote cooperation among the three countries in the priority areas of transport and communication, trade and industry, security, immigration, and the promotion of investment in the East Africa region.[19]

To achieve these objectives, the EAC will seek to ease travel restrictions, harmonize tariffs, increase cooperation among security forces, improve communications, and address other regional issues, such as sharing electrical power and the use of Lake Victoria. Among the measures being taken to promote integration are freely exchangeable currencies (and ultimately the creation of a single currency) and the issuance of a common East African passport.

Although the EAC treaty does not earmark counterterrorism as an area of socioeconomic cooperation, regional measures to combat terrorism are being designed and undertaken under the aegis of cooperation on "political matters, and legal and judicial affairs." In its first development strategy (1997–2000), the EAC did not identify counterterrorism as one of the areas that it would act upon. It, however, identified "easing of border crossing" as one of the 12 "policy and program areas of action."[20] Nevertheless, in *The Second East African Community Development Strategy, 2001–2005*, the EAC identified "peace, security, and defence" as a program area of action under which, in combination with the actions taken under legal and judicial matters, counterterrorism measures have been designed and implemented in the region.

In the 2001–2005 development strategy, the EAC sought to harmonize all national laws and regulations in immigration and to take joint action in international agreements and protocols. Among the measures that the EAC committed itself to take are the promotion of peace and security—identified as being essential for the promotion of trade, investment, and other development efforts—and steps aimed at curbing criminal activities across borders and enhancing overall safety and security in the region.

Although its priority is economic cooperation, the EAC is aware, like other African regional organizations, that regional peace, security, and stability are factors that impinge on integration and must be addressed. Consequently, the three member states have signed a memorandum of understanding on cooperation in defense and have continuously put regional security as an agenda item for summit meetings. In this context, the EAC has established a Sectoral Committee on Cooperation in Defense as well as an Inter-State Security Committee. These committees have been meeting since 2003 to, inter alia, exchange information on implementation of the Nairobi Declaration on Small Arms and Light Weapons; draft modalities for a common refugee registration mechanism; and discuss joint exercises on peacekeeping operations, counterterrorism, and military level participation in disaster response.

On November 11, 2004, the EAC Sectoral Committee on Cooperation in Defense met in Mombasa, Kenya, to discuss a common strategy against terrorism as well as ways of developing an early warning mechanism. The committee also made a decision to develop and harmonize the EAC standard operating procedures for disaster management and to counter terrorism.[21] Additionally, the countries of the region have been integral in establishing the Eastern and Southern Africa Anti-Money Laundering Group, which cooperates with the Financial Action Task Force, and the Eastern Africa Police Chiefs Cooperation Organization (EAPCCO), which cooperates with Interpol.

Despite the economic benefits of integrating the East Africa region, Kenyan security analysts are concerned that "the ease of travel and the general liberalization of Customs and Immigration regulations" in the EAC would directly contribute to "the increase in cross border crimes in the region."[22] For instance, a criminal "can now commit a crime in, say, Kisumu and within a record time of sixty minutes, manage to cross the border to Uganda," where he will fall under a different criminal justice system, one that could complicate his extradition to Kenya. Likewise, a Kenyan criminal can "cross over to Tanzania, cause mayhem, run back to Kenya and get a Kenyan lawyer to argue successfully against extradition in court."

Nevertheless, during a high-level meeting of the East African Community Inter-State Security Committee at the EAC headquarters on November 5, 2004, the regional chiefs of police asserted their firm commitment to maintain peace and security in the East African region by ensuring that no criminal is allowed to hide in any place within the partner states. They said that criminals can now be easily apprehended because of the well-organized coordination of activities and operations among the police forces of the three partner states and because of the prevailing efficient and effective communication between the police forces.

Although this statement of assurance is laudable, it needs to be reflected in statutes and protocols that have yet to be drafted and adopted by the EAC. Despite the lack of regional statutes, the three countries have undertaken individual measures to counter terrorism, and it is hoped that these measures would soon be harmonized by the EAC Joint Committee set up to coordinate actions of the three countries against terrorism.

Actions of EAC Member States

Repeated terrorist attacks in East Africa have prompted the countries in the region to evaluate their counterterrorism measures, particularly those related to intelligence gathering, and their preparedness for dealing with the aftermath of terrorist acts. In addition to the EAC measures, the East African countries have also adopted counterterrorism programs and taken the following individual measures aimed at, among other things, transforming their security apparatus into modern units with unified prosecution, investigation, and intelligence structures.[23]

Antiterrorism Police Units

Efforts to coordinate law enforcement and other security service activities have been a positive development in EAC member states. Kenya formed an antiterrorist police unit[24] in February 2003 and has established a task force on money laundering and combating the financing of terrorism consisting of representatives from the ministries of finance, trade, and foreign affairs; the Central Bank; the police; the Criminal Investigation Department; and the National Security Intelligence Service. Other EAC countries also need to establish similar structures composed of various counterterrorism authorities drawn from security forces and the legislative, judicial, and financial authorities. As a step in the right direction, Tanzania has already formed a designated antiterrorist police unit, while the Ugandan government has established a joint antiterrorism task force comprised of the Department of Military Intelligence, the Police Criminal Investigation Department and Special Branch, the External Security Organization, and the Internal Security Organization.

Counterterrorism Legislation

All three EAC countries have taken steps to enact new counterterrorism legislation. Since 2001, the Kenyan government introduced in parliament a series of measures, including the 2003 Suppression of Terrorism Bill and the 2004 Proceeds of Crime and Money Laundering (Prevention) Bill. On the positive side, these bills endeavored to criminalize terrorist actions in Kenya, and the 2004 bill was designed to harmonize numerous existing laws that aim to check money laundering and related activities that might assist terrorist activities, including the Banking Act, Narcotic Drugs and Psychotropic Substances Control Act, Fugitive Offenders Pursuit Act, Extradition (Contiguous and Foreign Countries) Act, Extradition (Commonwealth Countries) Act, Capital Markets Authority Act, Insurance Act, Official Secrets Act, and Criminal Procedure Code and Evidence Act.

However, in the case of the 2003 Suppression of Terrorism Bill in particular, critics have vehemently opposed the government's initiatives. They charged that it would erode some of the rights and freedoms that Kenyans have gained since the introduction of multiparty democracy in the early 1990s and eventually forced the government to withdraw and redraft the proposed legislation for reintroduction in 2006. The critics—including legal watchdogs and civil society representatives—argued, for instance, against section 3(1) of the bill, which defines *terrorism* as "the use or threat of action designed to influence the Government or to intimidate the public or a section of the public; and made for the purpose of advancing a political, religious or ideological cause." This broad and vague definition, the critics argue, provides wide latitude for varied interpretations and potential abuse by the government against opposition parties, the free press, or civil society movements.

The bill was also opposed for stating in article 12(1) that a person will be suspected of being a terrorist merely by wearing clothing similar to that worn by known terrorists affiliated to organizations such as al Qaeda. Muslims in the country say this clause specifically targets them, as their religious and social practices include wearing garb similar to that worn by some traditional Middle Easterners. The Suppression of Terrorism Bill was also opposed for allegedly being strikingly similar to the USA PATRIOT Act and for the fact that it was being heavily supported by the U.S. Government, which some Kenyans resent for its handling of the war on terror.[25]

In Uganda, the Anti-Terrorism Act of 2002 was approved by the President on May 21, 2002, and came into force on June 7, 2002. This act aims "at suppressing acts of terrorism" and provides "for the punishment of persons who plan, instigate, support, finance, or execute acts of terrorism"; proscribes "terrorist organizations"; and provides "for the punishment of persons who are members of, or who profess in public to be members of, or who convene or associate with or facilitate the activities of terrorist organizations."[26] However, argue Solomy Bossa and Titus Mulindwa, "the definition of terrorism around which the legislation is constructed is so broad that it could be used to prosecute trade unionists involved in a strike or those engaged in civil disobedience. This is so because the definition does not specifically exclude legal strikes and protests that do not aim to seriously disrupt an essential service."[27] Furthermore, "the wide scope of the offence relating to these organizations damages freedom of expression and freedom of assembly—as it subjects political activities to criminal sanctions, even when there has been no criminal activity."

The fear that this law would be used to repress political dissent and limit freedom of expression, especially by the media, was highlighted in 2002 when Ugandan radio stations were threatened with prosecution under the act if they aired interviews with exiled opposition leader Colonel Kizza Besigye. After labeling Besigye a terrorist, the government warned that anyone who aided him would be guilty of an offense under the act.[28] This law also bears the potential for the government to abuse the provision on surveillance and does not provide safeguards to guarantee fair trials and to prevent extraditions to countries imposing the death penalty for "terrorist crimes."

In Tanzania, the Prevention of Terrorism Act was signed into law in December 2002. As in Kenya, the act has faced heavy criticism and opposition, particularly from the Muslim population that feels it is being specifically targeted. In a workshop on the Prevention of Terrorism Act organized by the Commission for Human Rights and Good Governance in Dar es Salaam in March 2005, the act was criticized for denying "individuals most rights, including the right to freedom of movement, privacy, and participation in political affairs."[29] The act was also criticized for borrowing "heavily from not only the USA PATRIOT Act, but also (from) the British Prevention of Terrorism (Temporary Provisions) Act of 1989 and the Suppression of Terrorism and Communism Act of Apartheid South Africa."

Therefore, there is a need to review the antiterrorism legislation of the East African countries to ensure that the security measures prescribed therein respect human rights and have adequate safeguards for their protection. As the cases of Kenya and Tanzania show, antiterrorism legislation that does not contain these guarantees is difficult to enact into law and to enforce once it has become law.

Border Controls and Immigration Procedures

Although there are adequate immigration provisions and procedures to deal with illegal persons, holders of forged documents, and the control of refugees, the countries of the region have been lax in implementing them. It has now been established that while some al Qaeda operatives entered the region legally, others passed through border and entry points without proper documents or scrutiny by entry point immigration personnel. Some of the terrorists were even able to acquire legal residences and travel documents that were reserved for citizens only. The laws in the three EAC countries require those seeking travel documents to produce identification cards and birth certificates, which can only be acquired through production of birth notifications or written reports from local administrators confirming citizenship. However, Fazul Abdullah Mohammed (also known as "Harun"), a Comoran citizen and one of the perpetrators of the August 1998 Embassy bombings, was able to acquire through fraudulent means Kenyan travel documents that he used to plan his terrorist activities. All of this points to the need for EAC countries individually and collectively to improve implementation of their existing procedures and laws. Since 2001, technical, material, and financial assistance from Western countries has been critical in starting the process to address these vulnerabilities. However, further action is obviously required.

Establishment of National Counterterrorism Centers

In Kenya, the government has established a National Counterterrorism Center (NCTC) that intends to collect, integrate, and disseminate timely and accurate intelligence on terrorism threats and vulnerabilities. The NCTC is mandated to work closely with the antiterrorism police unit. Furthermore, Kenya has drafted a national counterterrorism strategy and convened a National Security Advisory Committee. Although other countries in the region have yet to match Kenya's initiatives, it is hoped that they will in the short run benefit from them through the EAC framework. Once fully operational, the NCTC can liaise with the Algiers-based African Center for the Study and Research on Terrorism and other relevant organizations to conduct a feasibility study on further regional and international information sharing. Resulting databases would contain the names of individuals identified as associated with terrorism; analysis of previous acts of terrorism; assessments of the causes, characteristics of perpetrators, terrorist modus operandi, law enforcement responses, and related data; information on criminal groups, supply routes, financial support networks, and money laundering methods; and international connections. Once established, such a database should be made accessible to national police forces and other law enforcement agencies in the region, as well as other regional and international law enforcement agencies such as Interpol.

Regional Political and Diplomatic Action

EAC member states are also cooperating and exchanging information through meetings of national contact persons and offices and leaders. In January 2002, a regional summit of East African leaders occurred in Khartoum to endorse a resolution against international terrorism. However, because the countries differed over the definition of terrorism, the proposal that emerged did not include concrete policies. For instance, a draft proposal suggesting ministers of justice and heads of security meet within 2 months to begin work on a joint campaign against terrorism was dropped because leaders could not agree on the meaning of the concept.[30] Nevertheless, it is through such meetings that regional leaders have been given an opportunity to distance themselves and their countries from terrorism.

In September 2003, internal affairs ministers from the East Africa region met in the Seychelles and signed an agreement on a range of measures to combat transnational illegal activities. The agreement is intended to strengthen regional cooperation to fight cross-border organized crime, terrorism, and narcotics trade. In 2004, ministers representing the 10 member states of the Eastern Africa Police Chiefs Cooperation Organization signed three agreements designed to bolster cross-border work on the extradition of criminals, the fight against terrorism, and the struggle with the narcotics trade.[31] It was during the first EAPCCO meeting held in Kampala, Uganda, in 1998 that an institutionalized body was set up to establish a collective effort to curb the cross-border crime within the region.

In such instances, it is clear that the political leaders and diplomatic representatives of EAC countries are committed to participate in international counterterrorism efforts. However, further action is required to ensure that such commitments are translated into practice once the leaders return home from their various summits and conferences.

Accession to International Treaties

Of the various international instruments that exist to prevent and combat terrorism, ratification and implementation in the EAC area has met with mixed success. Kenya has ratified all 12 international counterterrorism conventions and protocols; Tanzania is a party to 7; and Uganda is a party to 10. Kenya acceded to the 1997 International Convention for the Suppression of Terrorism Bombings in November 2001, Tanzania in January 2003, and Uganda in

November 2003. Tanzania ratified the International Convention for the Suppression of the Financing of Terrorism in January 2003, Kenya in June 2003, and Uganda in November 2003. Kenya ratified the United Nations (UN) Convention Against Transnational Organized Crime in June 2004; Tanzania and Uganda have signed but not ratified it.[32] All three countries have ratified the Organization of African Unity (OAU) Convention on the Prevention and Combating of Terrorism. However, as described above, political commitments have not always led to full implementation.

International Assistance

Since 1998, counterterrorism in East Africa has been greatly boosted by the support and cooperation of the United States and other Western governments. Although Washington is concerned about attacks across Africa, it considers East Africa to be at particular risk. In June 2003, the Bush administration announced the $100 million East Africa Counterterrorism Initiative (EACTI). This initiative included military training for border and coastal security, programs to strengthen control of the movement of people and goods across borders, aviation security capacity building, assistance for regional efforts against terrorist financing, and police training.[33] EACTI also included an education program to counter extremist influence and an outreach program to Muslim populations of the region. In view of the role that negative perceptions of the West (in combination with other factors) have in fertilizing the ground for terrorist activities, these education programs can in the long term play an important role to counter radical extremism. Such programs, however, require a sustained commitment and effort. Following the conclusion of EACTI, Kenya and other East African countries have continued to benefit from military training and some investment in humanitarian activities by U.S. military forces assigned to the Combined Joint Task Force–Horn of Africa (CJTF–HOA).

Furthermore, the United States is working closely with East African governments through the U.S. Interagency Terrorist Finance Working Group to develop comprehensive anti–money laundering and counterterrorist financing regimes in their nations. In 2003, the State Department's Terrorist Interdiction Program established a computer system at selected airports and some border crossings in Kenya, Tanzania, Ethiopia, Djibouti, and Uganda to enable immigration and border control officials to identify suspects attempting to enter or leave the country. State Department officials involved in creating the sophisticated database program said it was developed after the 1998 Embassy bombings in response to Kenya's request for help in being able to quickly identify who is entering and leaving the country.

In addition, the United States is supporting police development programs for national police in Tanzania, Uganda, and Ethiopia. Although these programs are not specifically focused on counterterrorism, they "are introducing essential skills-based learning and problem-solving techniques to build the capacity of East African police forces to detect and investigate all manner of crime, including terrorist incidents."[34] Washington is "also funding forensic laboratory development programs in Tanzania and Uganda, designed to build the capacity to analyze evidence collected at crime scenes." The State Department's Antiterrorism Assistance Program provides a variety of courses to civilian law enforcement officials in East Africa as well as other parts of the world.

Regional and International Partnerships

The success of counterterrorism measures in East Africa also hinges on security cooperation between the members of the EAC and countries in the larger East Africa region and between the EAC and other regional and international organizations. The effectiveness of the EAC would, to a significant degree, depend on the relationship it builds with other similar organizations across Africa, including the Intergovernmental Authority on Development (IGAD), the Southern African Development Community, and the Common Market for Eastern and Southern Africa, as well as with the African Union. In this connection, given their overlapping membership, the EAC will have to work closely with IGAD to harmonize their counterterrorism strategies and plans. IGAD's efforts, as detailed elsewhere in this volume, contain measures to establish a regional approach to counterterrorism within a broader international strategy that looks at countering the financing of terrorism, enhancing the operational capacity to counter illegal cross-border movements, recording and sharing information, implementing measures to ensure the protection of human rights during counterterrorism operations, and incorporating education programs to enhance public support.

In the Declaration of the Second High-Level Inter-Governmental Meeting on the Prevention and Combating of Terrorism in Africa conducted in October 2004, the AU "underscore(d) the importance of regional cooperation in the prevention and combating of terrorism and particularly in the implementation of continental and international instruments."[35] Additionally, it stressed greater "intra and inter-regional cooperation, in facilitating exchange of information, mutual legal assistance, concluding extradition agreements and complementing the actions of Member States."

Since January 2005, the EAC has been recognized as a key partner in the promotion of AU objectives. Consequently, it is obligated to abide by Article 6 of the Protocol to the OAU Convention on the Prevention and Combating of Terrorism, adopted by the AU Assembly in July 2004. This article challenges Regional Economic Communities, through their mechanisms for conflict prevention, management, and resolution, to "play a complementary role in the implementation of this Protocol and the Convention." Among the activities they are called upon to engage in are having contact persons on terrorism at a regional level; liaising with the AU Commission in the development of counterterrorism measures; promoting cooperation at the regional level in the implementation of all aspects of the Protocol and the Convention on the Prevention and Combating of Terrorism; and harmonizing and coordinating national measures to prevent and combat terrorism in their respective regions.

Other activities include establishing modalities for sharing information on the activities of perpetrators of terrorist acts and on best practices for the prevention and combating of terrorism; assisting member states to implement regional, continental, and international instruments for preventing and combating terrorism; and reporting regularly to the commission on measures taken at the regional level to prevent and combat terrorist acts. The EAC will also need to play a key role in ensuring that its member states sign, ratify, or accede to both the OAU Convention and the Protocol on the Prevention and Combating of Terrorism in Africa. Following further coordination with the AU and IGAD, the EAC is potentially well positioned in the region to assist in implementing UN Security Council Resolution 1373 (2001), which calls on all national governments and subregional, regional, and international organizations to work closely together to combat "international terrorism and transnational organized crime, illicit drugs, money-laundering, illegal arms-trafficking, and illegal movement of nuclear, chemical, biological and other potentially deadly materials" that are a "serious challenge and threat to international security."

Lingering Terrorism Vulnerabilities

A major weakness of East African counterterrorism measures is that their short- and medium-term strategies are only aimed at "catching bad guys, providing training and, to a limited extent, building up counterterrorism infrastructure."[36] In order for such strategies to address the problem of terrorism in the region, they must also seek "to reduce poverty and social alienation." David Shinn warns that unless more resources are channeled "into improving the environment that encourages terrorism—namely poverty—it is difficult to see lasting progress against this enemy." Consequently, long-term strategies should aim at addressing the factors that create a conducive environment for terrorism, including poverty, intolerance, political alienation, and corruption. In the case of Kenya, investigations that followed the terrorist attacks revealed that all these factors played a part. For instance, al Qaeda operatives used corrupt government processes to enter the country and settle among a poor segment of the population that was alienated from the political system. The al Qaeda supporters established charitable organizations that were used as cover for laundering money, recruiting support, and planning and executing terrorist acts in Kenya and Tanzania. Although the three East African countries, particularly Kenya and Uganda, have little history of religious extremism and their diverse religious groups have peacefully coexisted for years, there is a fear that this situation might change if the material conditions of the population do not improve. Poverty is widely regarded as creating conditions that attract terror organizations to recruit impoverished youth populations.[37]

The three countries of the region have also been ranked high on Transparency International's corruption index. Besides instituting national measures such as enactment of anticorruption legislation and the setting up of anticorruption watchdog bodies, these countries have a long way to go in uprooting institutionalized corruption. But it is notable that concrete steps have been taken to deal with endemic corruption, including accession to international treaties. Kenya ratified the United Nations Convention Against Corruption in December 2003, and Uganda did in September 2004. Tanzania has yet to ratify this convention, which it signed in December 2003. The United States and other countries are also assisting in the long-term strategies by using foreign assistance funds and other developmental tools to help strengthen democratic institutions and support effective governance.[38]

Although the counterterrorism measures mentioned above, when fully implemented, will to a large extent prevent terrorist groups such as al Qaeda from recruiting followers and establishing bases in the region, the best prevention is a combination of improved economic and political conditions for the population, combined with the arrest of operators, planners, financiers, and supporters of terrorist organizations before they launch attacks on innocent civilians. However, there are serious concerns that the former prescription has generally been overlooked, while the other counterterrorism measures being implemented by the governments in East Africa could be counterproductive. First, as has already been noted, there is fear that the "governments have sought to exploit 'the war against terror' to pass draconian laws that limit freedom of the press and expression."[39] For instance, the Ugandan government is accused of introducing an antiterrorism bill that redefines "criticism of the government as a new form of 'terrorism.'" Furthermore, the government has also been accused of using the fight against terror to justify increases in "military and intelligence agency budgets, increasing the scope for 'classified expenditure' and its accompanying abuse." In 2004, the Mwai Kibaki administration was implicated in a scandal that involved a shadowy company, Anglo Leasing, being secretly awarded a lucrative government contract to build a modern forensic laboratory and supply new passports that would assist in the fight against terrorism.

The second concern is that the war on terrorism has been exploited by some countries to promote other interests. For instance, the Ugandan government is suspected of joining the U.S.-led global war on terror so that it can be seen to be on Washington's side and qualify for aid dollars that it needs to fight rebels opposed to the government of President Yoweri Museveni.[40] Critics have claimed that President Museveni joined the global war on terrorism, launched in the aftermath of September 11, 2001, to persuade the United States to add the Lord's Resistance Army (LRA) to its list of international terror groups. Thereafter, Museveni launched Operation *Iron Fist* in March 2002 to attack LRA bases in southern Sudan. The offensive not only failed but also emboldened the LRA to launch vicious attacks on civilians in northern Uganda in June 2002 and February 2004. In March 2004, General Charles Wald, who was at the time in charge of African operations in the U.S. Army, confirmed in an interview that the United States is directly involved in the fight against the LRA by giving Uganda "many things" that are "more than just moral support."[41]

Museveni drew the Americans into the war when he convinced them that "some of [LRA leader] Joseph Kony's commanders were trained by Osama bin Laden during the years he spent in Sudan."[42] Like Uganda, Ethiopia has been accused of using the war on terror to promote its own interests and benefit from assistance through EACTI and CJTF–HOA by feeding the United States with intelligence information that inflates the terrorist threat from Somalia.[43]

The third concern is that the long-term goal of supporting national security forces and strengthening regional alliances to fight terror may be undermined by continuing political instability, simmering border conflicts, and ethnic and religious tension in the region.[44] Although the war in southern Sudan ended with the signing of a comprehensive peace agreement in January 2005, the difficult task of postconflict peacebuilding and reconstruction has yet to start in earnest. In Somalia, despite the formation of a new government at peace talks in Kenya, it has yet to relocate to Mogadishu due to insecurity in the country. Additionally, the situation in the Democratic Republic of Congo has continued to deteriorate. There is, however, hope that the proposed expansion of EAC membership to

Rwanda and Burundi would bring with it peace and stability in the Great Lakes region of Central Africa.

Proposed EAC Counterterrorism Efforts

Despite its meager resources, the EAC has undertaken laudable steps to counter terrorism in East Africa. However, it still faces the challenges of harmonizing national strategies and plans and undertaking other counterterrorism measures. Priority actions that the EAC and its member states should consider include the following:

Draft a regional counterterrorism plan containing strategies and implementation measures highlighted in this paper. The EAC Secretariat should ensure that its implementation complies with and conforms to continental and international obligations such as those reflected in UN Security Council Resolution 1373, the OAU Convention on the Prevention and Combating of Terrorism, and the AU Declarations of the First and Second High-Level Inter-Governmental Meeting on the Prevention and Combating of Terrorism in Africa. Further coordination with IGAD and other regional communities is also required.

Implement existing political commitments at the operational level. Harmonized efforts with intelligence collection, information sharing, border control and immigration, and coordinated policing must move beyond rhetoric and be put into action. To meet this goal, the EAC must change the culture of the national security community in the region to focus on the protection of national and regional interests rather than the security of the states and their leaders. The intelligence community must also develop a network or a system of sharing information and analysis of regional trends that have an effect on the war on terror.

Conduct joint training programs for all agencies engaged in enforcing counterterrorism measures. In cooperation with the AU and IGAD, the EAC should spearhead a comprehensive assessment of the training and equipment of all agencies in the region engaged in countering terrorism. The EAC can also approach international organizations such as the UN and Interpol to provide assistance with capacity building, training, and resource mobilization.

Assess and harmonize instruments available to facilitate mutual legal assistance and extradition. This includes the adoption of procedures aimed at facilitating and speeding up investigations, the collection of evidence, and other measures that would enhance cooperation between law enforcement agencies.

Harmonize national legislation as it relates to terrorism. To this end, the EAC Secretariat could facilitate coordination of the technical and legal language to conform to and enhance regional integration efforts. This would include adoption of an agreed-upon definition of terrorism that does not conjure discrimination against people with different ethnic, racial, religious, and cultural backgrounds. Since "terrorism is a very complex phenomenon," it is crucial that it is properly defined and understood in order "to be able to work effectively against it."[45] As was pointed out in the case of Kenya, the definition of terrorism can very easily be interpreted to interfere with the traditions and way of life of a particular culture and religion. The EAC has the task of ensuring that the scope of the provisions of the antiterrorism legislation is clearly defined so that they do not target those who are not terrorists and do not belong to terrorist groups. Also, penalties for offenses should be harmonized, so terrorists will not try to take advantage, for example, of lighter penalties for money laundering in one country than in neighboring countries.

Ensure that member states have taken adequate measures to protect and promote human rights. As called for in article 3(1)(a) of the Protocol to the OAU Convention on the Prevention and Combating of Terrorism and set by the African Charter of Human and Peoples' Rights and the relevant UN Conventions, counterterrorism efforts must respect the law. However, this has not always been the case. For instance, Amnesty International has raised serious concerns about the way Kenya has carried out its measures to combat and prevent terrorism. In particular, Amnesty International has said that the rights of those suspected of involvement in terrorist activities have been flagrantly violated. The antiterrorism police unit is accused of unlawfully searching homes, arresting suspects without proper investigation, and detaining them in isolation. The suspects have also been subjected to torture and other cruel, inhumane, or degrading treatment or punishment and denied the rights to family visits and legal counsel.[46]

Amnesty International has warned that "measures to prevent 'terrorism' can only be effective if they also guarantee and protect human rights." The EAC should ensure that regional counterterrorism measures recognize that terrorism is a threat to the full enjoyment of civil liberties and human rights and that such measures must be designed in a manner that does not impermissibly limit human rights and fundamental freedoms. The EAC will also have the responsibility of ensuring that antiterrorism legislation would not be easily used to suppress or undermine democratic opposition, as in the case of Colonel Besigye in Uganda. It is important that measures put in place do not provide terrorists with opportunities to gain support for their cause, since terrorism thrives in environments in which human rights are violated.

Adopt public outreach programs. It remains essential for governments in East Africa to seize the current opportunity of public interest in terrorism and counterterrorism and sensitize the public through education, emphasizing the need to be vigilant in their daily routine and report suspicious people and activities to relevant authorities.

Coordinate the mobilization of resources and technical assistance. EAC member states need to build capacity to combat terrorism so as to minimize competition between themselves over foreign funds and to assist each other when necessary—for example, in responding to and treating mass casualties. Furthermore, the interest of the EAC members in fighting terrorism should not be based on the allure of the money that allies in the war are willing to give.

Continue implementing programs that have long-term goals of eliminating terrorism. The best approach for eliminating terrorist vulnerabilities and threats in the region is for the EAC to create conditions that would ensure development, good governance, democracy, peace, stability, security, and good secular education opportunities in all its member states.

Conclusion

East Africa, more than any other region on the continent, has been scarred and traumatized by terrorist attacks that could have been prevented had the countries in the region put in place measures that addressed their vulnerabilities. Since all of the terrorist activities in East Africa have international links, it is logical that measures for preventing and combating terrorism should have a regional approach and be tied to the broader continental and international counterterrorism strategies. The member states are aware of this and are working toward bringing their national counterterrorism measures under a regional umbrella. Consequently, the EAC is gradually acquiring the capability and operational capacity to implement a regional counterterrorism strategy and to ensure that the counterterrorism measures conform to international regimes and standards. The measures being undertaken through the EAC are mainly aimed at short- and medium-term goals, but, over time, the EAC would have to play a significant role in harmonizing and spearheading effective regional counterterrorism strategies that seek to eradicate poverty, rebuild local institutions, and address a host of regional issues such as border patrol, refugees, and immigration.

The EAC, in addition to the recommendations made above, can play a crucial role in ensuring that its member states adopt long-term strategies that would address the factors that help the development of domestic, transnational, and international terrorism. That said, further coordination with the African Union and IGAD is required in order to ensure that the EAC is not tasked with roles that are already assigned by its member states to other organizations. Once such coordination has been enhanced, the EAC is likely to have a substantial role remaining as efforts to prevent and combat terrorism are enormous, time-consuming tasks that require significant resources and a long-term commitment.[47] Ultimately, however, the main responsibilities of preventing and combating terrorism in East Africa lie with the individual states: engaging in good governance, eliminating corruption, and adopting sustainable development policies that eradicate poverty and generate gainful employment opportunities for their populations.

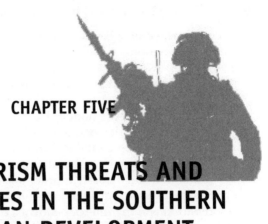

CHAPTER FIVE

TERRORISM THREATS AND RESPONSES IN THE SOUTHERN AFRICAN DEVELOPMENT COMMUNITY REGION

Julius E. Nyang'oro

The Southern African Development Community (SADC) is a regional organization consisting of 14 countries: Angola, Botswana, Democratic Republic of Congo (DRC), Lesotho, Madagascar, Malawi, Mauritius, Mozambique, Seychelles, South Africa, Swaziland, Tanzania, Zambia, and Zimbabwe. The declaration and treaty establishing the community were signed in Windhoek, Namibia, in August 1992. At the time of its formation, the SADC group consisted of 10 countries and, most significantly, excluded South Africa. The predecessor organization to SADC, the Southern African Development Coordination Conference (SADCC), had been established in July 1979 to harmonize economic development among countries in Southern Africa, promote regional integration, and, most importantly, lessen dependence on South Africa, which at the time was under apartheid rule.[1] Following the institution of a full democratic government in South Africa in 1994, that country became the eleventh member of the SADC group. Since then, the final three members—DRC, Mauritius, and Seychelles—have joined.

The transition from SADCC to SADC had one special element. While SADCC was specifically formed to counter the dominance of an apartheid-ruled South Africa in the region, with an explicitly political agenda of isolating and defeating the apartheid system, SADC's objectives now include promoting regional integration that would address emerging regional political, economic, and military challenges with post-apartheid South Africa a leading partner. Thus, the Common Agenda of SADC is geared to meet the following objectives for the region:

- development and economic growth
- alleviation of poverty
- enhancement of the standard and quality of life of the people of Southern Africa and support for the socially disadvantaged through regional integration
- evolution of common political values, systems, and institutions
- promotion and defense of peace and security, the promotion of self-sustaining development on the basis of collective self-reliance, and the interdependence of member states
- complementarity between national and regional strategies and programs and the promotion and maximum productive employment of the region's resources
- sustainable use of the natural resources and effective protection of the environment
- strengthening and consolidation of the longstanding historical, social, and cultural affinities and links among the people of the region.[2]

Thus, what emerges as a broad strategy for SADC is a comprehensive approach to development that does not delineate the imperatives of economic security from those of physical and other forms of security in the traditional sense.[3] It is therefore natural that as the world has become increasingly concerned with terrorism as a security threat, SADC would consider this to be a matter of interest.

This chapter evaluates SADC's efforts in the area of terrorism in light of global and regional security challenges emerging from the September 11 terrorist attacks in the United States and subsequent related incidents in other parts of the world, including Bali and Mombasa in 2002, Madrid in 2004, and London in 2005. It is also important to assess SADC's efforts because of the commitments that individual countries in the region have made through the Organization of African Unity (OAU) Convention on the Prevention and Combating of Terrorism (1999) and subsequent African Union (AU) documents, as well as United Nations (UN) Security Council Resolution 1373 (2001), which obligates all UN member states to take the necessary measures to fight international terrorism.

Besides the global nature of the terrorist menace, some SADC countries have also been directly affected by terrorist activities. The August 1998 bombings of the U.S. Embassy in Tanzania and the Planet Hollywood Café in Cape Town are cases in point. Further,

Khalfan Khamis Mohamed, the Tanzanian national who was implicated in the Dar es Salaam bombings, managed to travel through at least three countries in the region (Tanzania, Mozambique, and South Africa) before being caught; and Haroon Rashid Aswat, a Briton implicated in the London bombings of 2005, had operated in at least two countries in the SADC region (South Africa and Zambia). Given the transnational nature of the terrorist threat, SADC's efforts in the area of terrorism—specifically, whether SADC as a regional entity has a viable strategy to combat terrorism—need to be critically assessed.

Terrorism in the Southern African Context

Of all the subregions on the continent, Southern Africa has a very complex history with regard to terrorism. From its inception, SADCC was preoccupied with issues of security, particularly in response to the threat posed by South Africa vis-à-vis neighboring states during the apartheid years.[4] At the height of the antiapartheid struggle in the region, the South African government supported rebel movements for purposes of destabilizing states that supported liberation movements, particularly the African National Congress (ANC) and the Pan-Africanist Congress (PAC), in South Africa. The most prominent cases of South African support were for the *Resistencia Nacional de Mocambique* (RENAMO) in Mozambique and the United Movement for the Total Independence of Angola (UNITA) in Angola.

For its part, the South African government viewed the ANC and PAC as terrorist organizations bent on destroying the South African state. By contrast, SADCC viewed both RENAMO and UNITA as "reactionary" movements, carrying out terrorist activities under the sponsorship of the apartheid regime. South Africa justified its attacks on neighboring states and its sponsorship of these rebel movements on national security grounds and on the basis of a global war against communism in the context of the Cold War.

The collapse of the Soviet empire coincided with a rapidly changing political dynamic in Southern Africa. This included the recognition of Namibia as an independent country in 1990 under the leadership of the South West Africa Peoples' Organization (SWAPO), previously labeled a "terrorist movement" by South Africa. The altered dynamics also included the release of the ANC's Nelson Mandela from prison in February 1990. Thus, Southern Africa as a region has faced the age-old problem: "One person's terrorist is another person's freedom fighter." Further, the region also witnessed a transition in the political statutes of former rebel movements, many of which became part of the official political establishment by abandoning their campaigns of violence. The two most recent examples are RENAMO in Mozambique and UNITA in Angola.

A potential danger made apparent by the South African experience during the apartheid era is that the regime used laws labeled as "prevention of terrorism acts" to detain and imprison those who were opposed to its apartheid policies. This was a serious threat to democratic principles that, ironically, the regime claimed to uphold. Similar dangers are now arising in the context of the global war against terrorism. As has been reported in the case of Zimbabwe, the regime of Robert Mugabe is accused of developing counterterrorism laws to use as a pretext for quashing his domestic opposition.[5] Also, the region has seen examples of groups labeled as terrorists renouncing violence and becoming more respectable as they gain political power. The result of these dynamics is often an ambivalent posture by some countries—for instance, South Africa—toward a generalized global war against terror.[6]

Contemporary Terrorist Threats

While there is no universally agreed definition, terrorism can be broadly understood to be violence intended or calculated to provoke a state of terror in the general public, a group of persons, or particular persons for political purposes. By this measure, Southern Africa has definitely experienced the phenomenon in recent times.[7] One way to comprehend the threat of terrorism, both domestic and international, is to go beyond the Huntingtonian thesis of "clash of civilizations," which overemphasizes the cultural differences between the West and Islam and posits the difference between these two "civilizations" as the greatest political challenge of the modern era.[8] Instead, a contextualized analysis of terrorism—in historical, geographic, and regional terms—provides a better analytical basis upon which to address the threat.

In the Southern African context, the Institute for Security Studies based in South Africa has provided a useful approach to terrorism by categorizing the countries of the region into three groups in terms of threat perception: low, intermediate, and high.[9] According to this outline, *low* denotes countries that have had limited or no experience (Botswana and Lesotho); *intermediate* denotes countries that have experienced acts of terrorism around specific issues that have since been resolved (Angola, Namibia, Swaziland, South Africa, and Mozambique); *high* denotes those countries that have recently (since 1995) experienced or been directly influenced by acts of terrorism (Zimbabwe, the DRC, Tanzania, and Malawi).

Intermediate Threat Countries

The principal terrorist threat in these countries has been domestic, with significant reference to the unfinished business of liberation wars of the last half of the 20th century. For example, soon after Angola gained independence from Portugal in November 1975, UNITA leader Jonas Savimbi refused to recognize the legitimacy of the Movement for the Popular Liberation of Angola (MPLA) government. With help from apartheid South Africa, UNITA launched a war that did not end until the death of its leader in 2002. It would seem that the threat of terrorism from UNITA is now nonexistent, as remaining UNITA elements have been absorbed into the Angolan government. It is significant to note that although the Angolan war lasted almost three decades, UNITA could never control much territory beyond its Ovimbundu ethnic base. The Angolan case is a good illustration of ethnicity as a principal force in African domestic conflicts that in turn lead to complex political crises. Part of this complexity is the way in which the rebel movements are characterized. In reality, the ANC and UNITA, and even the Zimbabwe African National Union and Zimbabwe African Peoples' Union in Rhodesia, were really insurgency groups that sometimes may have used terrorist-type tactics to gain political control. As the world of international terrorism becomes more complex, we should not lose sight of the fact that there is a qualitative difference between insurgency and terrorist groups.[10]

In South Africa, the principal terrorist threat since the transition to democratic majority rule has come from two sources: right-wing extremism and the group People Against Gangsterism and Drugs (PAGAD). On the one hand, right-wing extremism has primarily been motivated by the changing nature of post-apartheid South African society in which minority groups no longer control the government and some individuals have disdain for the way the black majority is running the country. On the other hand, PAGAD started as a vigilante group primarily to protect the Muslim community in Cape Town from the menace of gangs and drugs. Initially, the group seemed to have a base of community support, as it was seen as an organization responding to the lack of institutional and security presence of the South African government in the years of transition toward democratic rule. However, as Anneli Botha tells us, "[T]he process of how an organization develops from a pressure group, which functions within the boundaries of legitimate dissent, into an organization that commits acts associated with terrorism, is illustrated in the development of PAGAD's selecting of targets."[11]

Thus, up to May 1998, PAGAD's targets of attacks were largely suspected drug dealers, gangsters, and illegal alcohol establishments in Muslim communities in the Western Cape. However, in June 1998, Muslim-owned businesses became targets, apparently because people saw PAGAD's increasingly indiscriminate attacks on individuals as bad for business and spoke against PAGAD's tactics. In July 1998, academics and clerics who spoke against PAGAD's tactics also became targets. PAGAD further expanded its attacks to include restaurants, police stations, and other law enforcement agencies. The weapons used for attacks also became more sophisticated, including the use of cellular phones as remote-controlled detonators for explosive devices. Although PAGAD denied responsibility for the attacks on the Planet Hollywood restaurant at the popular tourist destination of the Cape Town waterfront, it was the strongest suspect. The speculation at the time was that Planet Hollywood became a target because it symbolized the decadence of the West and undermined societal moral values. This attitude linked PAGAD to a larger global campaign led by al Qaeda. Nonetheless, PAGAD maintained its innocence in this case. Naturally, the South African government has reacted very strongly against PAGAD. The arrest of the group's leaders prompted the demise of its activities.[12]

The South African government's harsh reaction was partly dictated by the fact that foreign tourism would suffer if the country was perceived to be unsafe. As an example of the impact of terrorism on tourism, it is instructional to note that Kenya lost more than half of its receipts from tourism following the 2002 al Qaeda attacks near Mombasa and the subsequent issuance of a U.S. State Department travel advisory.

High Threat Countries

High threat countries can be divided into two categories. The first—including Zimbabwe and the DRC—consists of countries whose political stability is at serious risk. There, the threat of terrorism is associated not with groups whose interest is to maximize violence and create disorder but rather with the failure of the state to establish a legitimate governing environment, a case of "failing" or "failed" states.[13] In the case of Zimbabwe, some observers have accused the government of Robert Mugabe of conducting de facto terrorism against its own citizens, as witnessed by the brutality against opposition party members and the more recent leveling of shanties and stalls in some of the townships. This, in effect, is the use of terrorist tactics by the state. However, the word *terrorism* is commonly associated with nongovernment actors, while violence by governments against civilians is usually classified as civil rights or human rights violations.

The political situation in the Democratic Republic of Congo since the 1997 overthrow of President Mobutu Sese Seko has been one of crisis of governance. The central government has hardly functioned and its reach and effectiveness are under serious challenge, a situation that was also true during much of Mobutu's regime. To date, rebel groups have operated freely in much of the country, largely supported by neighboring governments (particularly Rwanda and Uganda). In fact, the DRC may not technically qualify as a state since it hardly meets the traditional criteria of one, such as having an accepted legitimate government and control of its territory.[14] In the DRC's case, therefore, the traditional concepts of terrorism are problematic, given the ubiquitous nature of violence and the goals of some rebel movements, which are not to kill people and cause destabilization but rather to ultimately take over the government themselves.

The second category in the high threat countries includes Tanzania and Malawi. Their case actually poses an interesting paradox. Historically, these two countries have been among the most stable in the region. Until the mid-1990s, Malawi's political stability had been premised on the authoritarian rule of the late Kamuzu Banda and the Malawi Congress Party (MCP). The successor regime of Bakili Muluzi had to deal with the pent-up frustrations of three decades of tyrannical rule. Muslims, who form perhaps as much as 20 percent of the population, felt especially aggrieved. The post–September 11 environment has made for a more tense relationship between the government and Muslims in Malawi, although much of the tension arose because of the Malawi government's cooperation with the United States in arresting and deporting five suspected al Qaeda members in June 2003. Given the fact that Muluzi himself was Muslim, many Malawians would have thought him to be less enthusiastic in cooperating with Americans on this issue. However, Malawi has historically been perceived as pro-West in its foreign policy—thus, the natural inclination of the Muluzi government to go along with the American demand. There is little evidence that terrorism—whether domestic or with international connections—is considered a major problem in Malawi. However, the growing numbers of refugees and asylum seekers from numerous African countries are seen as a potential political threat.[15] In addition, the new government in Malawi under President Bingu wa Mutharika is committed to following its predecessor in keeping a closer eye on potential al Qaeda influence in the country.

Of all the countries in the SADC region, Tanzania is the only country that has faced a major and catastrophic experience with transnational terrorism. On August 7, 1998, terrorists associated with al Qaeda simultaneously blew up American Embassies in Nairobi, Kenya, and Dar es Salaam, Tanzania. Although it has now been authoritatively determined that the explosions were part of al Qaeda's international terrorism, it is also true that some of the participants in the planning and execution of the plot were Tanzanians, including Khalfan Khamis Mohamed, who was the local

connection to the bombing. However, he seems to have been motivated by the wider al Qaeda agenda of anti-Americanism rather
than opposition to the Tanzanian government. That distinction is
important to make because it influences the way the local population may perceive terrorists and the threat of terrorism. Although
the majority of the victims of the bombing in Dar es Salaam were
Tanzanians, most citizens still may not consider the terrorist threat
as a central concern to their lives. Rather, they see it as a clash between al Qaeda and the United States in which Tanzania just happened to be one venue for an attack. In spite of the attack, Tanzania
continues to be a favorite tourist destination and has not suffered
the same loss of revenue as Kenya.

Counterterrorism Measures in the SADC Region

In the post–September 11 environment, SADC joined the rest of
the world in publicly condemning international terrorism. However, there is little evidence that SADC as a group has taken substantial initiatives to deal with this threat. There are no specific
SADC protocols dealing with terrorism as such, and much of the
counterterrorism activity in the region is conducted within and by
individual countries.[16] In a broader sense, this is a statement about,
or an indication of, the general weakness of SADC as an organization and the lack of strong leadership at the SADC Secretariat. Much
SADC business is conducted at its annual gatherings of heads of
state, without mandating further actions by the group's secretariat
between these meetings. Terrorism as an issue is not an exception
to this reality, thus making initiatives by individual countries, as
opposed to SADC as an organization, to be the most important
measure of counterterrorism activities in the region.

Perhaps one of the best ways to determine the efficacy and success of counterterrorism activity in the region is to measure them
against specific United Nations conventions and protocols dealing
with international terrorism. The 12 relevant conventions are:

- Convention on Offences and Certain Other Acts Commit-
  ted Aboard Aircraft, Tokyo, 1963
- Convention for the Suppression of Unlawful Seizure of Air-
  craft, The Hague, 1970
- Convention for the Suppression of Unlawful Acts Against
  the Safety of Civil Aviation, Montreal, 1971
- Convention on the Prevention and Punishment of Crimes
  Against Internationally Protected Persons, Including Dip-
  lomatic Agents, New York, 1973
- International Convention Against the Taking of Hostages,
  New York, 1979

- Convention on the Physical Protection of Nuclear Material, Vienna, 1980
- Protocol for the Suppression of Unlawful Acts of Violence at Airports Serving International Aviation (Supplementary to the 1971 Montreal Convention), Montreal, 1988
- Convention for the Suppression of Unlawful Acts Against the Safety of Maritime Navigation, Rome, 1988
- Protocol for the Suppression of Unlawful Acts Against the Safety of Fixed Platforms Located on the Continental Shelf, Rome, 1988
- Convention on the Marking of Plastic Explosives for the Purpose of Detection, Montreal, 1991
- International Convention for the Suppression of Terrorist Bombings, New York, 1997
- International Convention for the Suppression of the Financing of Terrorism, New York, 1999.

In line with much of the world, the SADC region has become more active in adopting the UN conventions against terrorism in the wake of the September 11 attacks and the issuance of UN Security Council Resolution 1373. As Kenny Kapinga has noted:

> The aftermath of 9/11 had a remarkable impact on the decision of countries to commit to international and regional counter-terrorism conventions. Of the UN Conventions, 64% of the countries in the SADC Sub-region are now parties, in contrast to 36% before 9/11. In addition to becoming parties to international instruments, countries are also required to implement national legal instruments, a step that requires specific attention and assistance.[17]

The 64 percent adoption rate for UN conventions dealing with terrorism does not indicate in any meaningful way whether the respective national governments are working hard, if at all, to implement these conventions in their own countries. All it says is that these countries have adopted a stand that is politically expedient so that they do not look to be out of step with the rest of the international community in terms of counterterrorism measures. It may be argued that the nonaggressive approach to terrorism by SADC countries is based on member countries viewing it as a low risk, a view supported by outside observations as well:

> For most observers Southern Africa is so insignificant on the global stage that it is easy to ignore and overlook

it. In a Study by the World Markets Research Centre, a global terrorism index that ranked 186 countries revealed that countries in Southern Africa are likely to remain relatively free of terrorism. South Africa, at 74 on the index, was given a medium-to-low-risk ranking as a result of the activities of People Against Gangsterism and Drugs (PAGAD) and of right-wing extremism. Of the other countries in the region, Zimbabwe was placed at 113 and Botswana even lower, at 174.[18]

In cases where Southern African governments have been proactive in enacting counterterrorist legislation, the primary motivation appears to have been a concern about internal governance issues. In this regard, the primary concern of SADC member countries has been

TABLE 5–1
Compliance with United Nations Resolution 1373: Status of National Legislation

Country	Dedicated Counter-terrorism Legislation	Dedicated Legislation Related to the Financing of Terrorism	Dedicated Extradition Legislation	Dedicated Mutual Legal Assistance Legislation
Angola	No specific legislation, but has ratified the Organization of African Unity (OAU) Terrorism Convention	No specific legislation	Insufficient extradition legislation	None
Botswana	Draft legislation only	None	Sufficient	Sufficient
Democratic Republic of Congo	None	No specific legislation	None	None
Lesotho	None	None	Legislation appears sufficient but not specific	Legislation appears sufficient but not specific
Malawi	None	None	Legislation appears sufficient but not specific	Legislation appears sufficient but not specific
Mauritius	Has specific counter-terrorism legislation	Sufficient	Sufficient	Sufficient

Source: Kenny Kapinga et al., "Towards a SADC Counter-Terrorism Strategy," in *Terrorism in the SADC Region*, ed. Anneli Botha (Pretoria: Institute for Security Studies, March 2005), 89.

the proliferation of cross-border criminal activities, particularly in the area of illegal drugs in the region. Although criminality and terrorism have sometimes been conflated, their causes and consequences are significantly different, and they require different approaches. For common crimes, adequate legislation is already on the books in every SADC country.

Nonetheless, UN Security Council Resolution 1373 places specific obligations on all UN member states to report on individual initiatives taken to combat terrorism. This has forced countries in the region to show evidence of compliance with the resolution (see table 5–1).

Article 2 of the OAU Convention on the Prevention and Combating of Terrorism obliges member countries to adopt all relevant United Nations conventions on terrorism and to translate them into domestic legislation. Except for Zambia and Zimbabwe, all SADC

TABLE 5–1 *(Continued)*
Compliance with United Nations Resolution 1373:
Status of National Legislation

Country	Dedicated Counter-terrorism Legislation	Dedicated Legislation Related to the Financing of Terrorism	Dedicated Extradition Legislation	Dedicated Mutual Legal Assistance Legislation
Mozambique	No specific domestic legislation, but has ratified the OAU Terrorism Convention	None	Insufficient	None
Namibia	None; draft legislation in progress	None	Insufficient	None
Seychelles	None	None	Insufficient	Sufficient
South Africa	Domestic counter-terrorism legislation; draft legislation	Sufficient	Sufficient	Sufficient
Swaziland	None	None	Sufficient	Sufficient
Tanzania	Has specific counter-terrorism legislation	None	Sufficient	Sufficient
Zambia	None	None	Sufficient	Sufficient
Zimbabwe	Domestic counter-terrorism legislation	None	Sufficient	Sufficient

countries are signatory to the convention, with Angola, Lesotho, Malawi, Mauritius, Mozambique, Seychelles, South Africa, and Tanzania having ratified the treaty. But as has been the case with UN Security Council Resolution 1373, the implementation of the provisions of the OAU Convention still has a long way to go. Simply signing or ratifying treaties does not mean that governments in Southern Africa have made the necessary investments in state capacity to ensure their implementation.

To some extent, the less than enthusiastic response by governments to the threat of terrorism is predictable. Even though some of the countries have experienced terrorism directly, the majority of the governments view their territories as transit points used by terrorists whose interests and targets are beyond their direct concerns. These governments also view their countries as victims that are caught in the global crossfire between al Qaeda and the United States, thus requiring no special effort in the partnership against global terrorism. Naturally, this is not a wise position to take, as evidence increasingly shows that some local elements, particularly in South Africa, are buying into the "radicalization" of Islam.[19]

Southern Africa: A Balance Sheet

Countries in the SADC region generally do not view terrorism with the same urgency as the United States or other countries that are at the forefront of the battle with al Qaeda, such as Pakistan. Rather, SADC countries have viewed contemporary issues of terrorism as remote from their daily concerns of security. The slowness of SADC and its member states to react to current threats of terrorism is partly the result of a regional political environment that emphasizes new forms of governance in a post-apartheid world. The threat of terrorism, while publicly acknowledged by the political leadership, has not been taken as seriously as more local concerns about democratization, unemployment, health issues, and so forth.

In those cases where incidents of domestic terrorism have occurred in the past, such as in South Africa, these threats have been viewed as associated with the problems of political transition (right-wing extremism and PAGAD), as opposed to acts of groups that have threatened the stability of the political system and general security. Similarly, for those countries that have been touched by transnational terrorism, such as Tanzania, the reaction by both the government and the population at large has been to concentrate on only the external nature of the problem. However, the perception that terrorism is largely an external problem might quickly change if tourism and foreign investment flows to the subregion are affected by terrorism.

Because of a general perception of the low threat of terrorism in the region, SADC has been absent from the formulation of a regional strategy to combat terrorism, despite many public condemnations of it. However, there is a more serious issue concerning SADC as an institution. Its secretariat lacks both the personnel and financial resources that would be required to coordinate any counterterrorism measures that may be needed to align SADC strategy with its commitments to the AU and UN. Part of the issue here may be that countries in the region are not sufficiently convinced that terrorism should be high on the agenda vis-à-vis other concerns, such as economic development.

Countries in the region could therefore use some incentives to be part of a larger global effort by receiving more support to build their domestic competencies in law enforcement. They also need to be made more aware that some of their countries have been used in the past as transit points in the movement of individuals who are associated with global networks of terrorism. The key would be to convince and encourage countries in the region, and SADC as a regional organization, to see the big picture that economic development, foreign investment, and domestic spending requirements could be seriously affected if terrorists attack their territory or use their territory to attack others.

Ironically, as Michael Rifer points out, SADC as both a region and a regional organization actually already has much of the institutional framework that could be used to create an antiterrorism architecture.[20] SADC has an overall regional security structure in the form of the organization on policy, defense, and security cooperation; the organization also has adopted protocols on transnational threats on small arms and drug trafficking and on mutual legal assistance. If these elements are combined with the efforts of other multinational groups in the subregion outside SADC, such as the Interpol-supported group Southern African Regional Police Chiefs Cooperation Organization or the East and Southern Africa Anti-Money Laundering Group, the results in terms of the war against terror would be quite effective. As the old saying goes, the wheel is already there; SADC countries do not have to invent it.

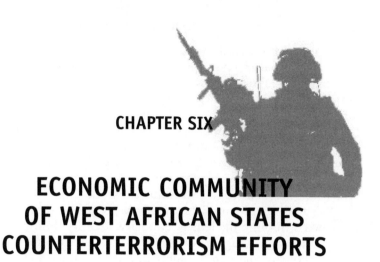

CHAPTER SIX

ECONOMIC COMMUNITY OF WEST AFRICAN STATES COUNTERTERRORISM EFFORTS

Eboe Hutchful

With several of the world's poorest countries, a number of failing states, a history of violent conflict, and the presence of rebel groups, West Africa is often seen as a region potentially vulnerable to terrorism. The subregion covered by the Economic Community of West African States (ECOWAS)—including Benin, Burkina Faso, Cape Verde, Côte d'Ivoire, The Gambia, Ghana, Guinea, Guinea-Bissau, Liberia, Mali, Niger, Nigeria, Senegal, Sierra Leone, and Togo—has several distinctive political and geographical features that make it conducive to movement by terrorist groups. These features include vast stretches of desert in the Sahel region, long and virtually unpatrolled borders in several of the landlocked states, and Africa's only free movement protocol. All of these factors are compounded by open and pervasive corruption by border officials.[1]

While ECOWAS is a leader in several aspects of conflict management, it lags behind other African subregions (such as the Inter-Governmental Authority on Development [IGAD] in the Horn of Africa) in counterterrorism initiatives.[2] ECOWAS is at the forefront of global efforts to establish subregional mechanisms for defense and security collaboration, peace support operations, conflict mediation, the development of a framework for controlling small arms proliferation, and implementation of an effective conflict early warning system. However, its role in counterterrorism specifically is a limited one.

Much of this situation can be understood in terms of differences in the histories, experiences, and locations of the various African

113

subregions with regard to international terrorism. The reasons include attitudinal and perceptual factors as well as institutional and resource gaps. First, terrorism appears to be relatively low on the scale of priorities of ECOWAS, which currently has no institutional structures or resources devoted specifically to fighting terrorism. Second, ECOWAS organizational systems are characterized by significant gaps in human and material resources. Further, existing resources have been severely strained by the organization's attempts to grapple with ongoing conflicts in Liberia and Côte d'Ivoire, as well as the crises in Togo and Guinea-Bissau.

Third, although conflicts are pervasive in the subregion, they are viewed through the lens of ethnicity, identity politics, poverty, governance, and struggles over natural resources, rather than terrorism.[3] Fourth, many in the subregion tend to regard ECOWAS as distant from the main theaters of terrorism and counterterrorism operations, even though concerns have been expressed about al Qaeda connections and pro-Taliban sentiments in Nigeria,[4] and the infiltration of the Algerian-based Salafist Group for Preaching and Combat.[5] Hence, transforming both attitudes and institutional capabilities will be the critical challenge for counterterrorism in the subregion.

The ECOWAS Counterterrorism Role

As a subregional organization, ECOWAS does not have its own working definition of terrorism. Rather, it applies the comprehensive definition adopted by the African Union (AU)—namely, the 1999 Organization of African Unity (OAU) Convention and Plan of Action on the Prevention and Combating of Terrorism—and follows the requirements of United Nations (UN) Security Council Resolution 1373.

In addition, ECOWAS and its member states abide by the AU Plan of Action that was adopted to provide details of how African governments should go about implementing their regional and global obligations for improved counterterrorism cooperation and coordination. The plan enjoins African member states to take a number of specific measures in the areas of legislation and judiciary, police and border controls, suppression of terrorist financing, and exchange of information. It also provided for the establishment of an African Center for the Study and Research on Terrorism in Algiers.

While it is accepted that the primary responsibility for counterterrorism initiatives and enforcement belongs at the national level, the AU clearly regards regional collaboration (and international support) as an indispensable cornerstone of its own counterterrorism strategy. Hence, Article 6 of the Protocol to the OAU Convention, as adopted in Addis Ababa on July 8, 2004, specified the role of subregional organizations. This included the following:

- establish contact points on terrorism at the regional level
- liaise with the AU Peace and Security Commission in developing measures for the prevention and combating of terrorism
- promote cooperation at the regional level, in the implementation of all aspects of this protocol and the convention, in accordance with article 4 of the convention
- harmonize and coordinate national measures to prevent and combat terrorism in their respective regions
- establish modalities for sharing information on the activities of the perpetrators of terrorist acts and on the best practices for the prevention and combating of terrorism
- assist member states to implement regional, continental, and international instruments for the prevention and combating of terrorism
- report regularly to the commission on measures taken at the regional level to prevent and combat terrorist acts.

That said, the coordinating role in counterterrorism contemplated by the AU Plan of Action was already anticipated, and specifically provided for, in an ECOWAS protocol relating to the formation of the ECOWAS Conflict Mechanism adopted in December 1999. This mechanism sought to "strengthen cooperation in the areas of conflict prevention, early-warning, peace-keeping operations, the control of cross-border crime, *international terrorism* [emphasis added] and proliferation of small arms and anti-personnel mines."[6] However, while words such as *conflict, crises*, and *natural disasters* recur in the 1999 protocol, there is no further reference to *terrorism* in the text. Further, while the mechanism spells out detailed provisions and frameworks for each of these issue areas, there are no such provisions on counterterrorism, suggesting that, among the hierarchy of ills afflicting the subregion, terrorism is far down the ladder.

This omission is remedied to an extent in the subsequent ECOWAS Protocol on Democracy and Good Governance, in which ECOWAS directs its member states to "strengthen their national agencies responsible for preventing and combating terrorism"[7] and instructs the office of the Deputy Executive Secretary for Political Affairs, Defense, and Security (DES/PADS) in the ECOWAS Secretariat to "initiate joint activities for the national agencies of member states in charge of preventing and combating terrorism."[8]

ECOWAS has proposed several additional initiatives to enhance subregional capability to deal with terrorism and other cross-border threats.

Among them:

- a suggestion that each of its constituent states establish a specific integrated counterterrorism task force at the national level
- a decision by the Conference of Heads of State and Government of ECOWAS on December 12, 1999, to establish an Intergovernmental Action Group Against Money Laundering (*Groupe Inter-gouvernemental d'Action contre le Blanchiment en Afrique*, or GIABA) to provide a common framework for combating money laundering and the financing of terrorist activities and to promote cooperation between member states with different legal and financial systems
- a decision to draft a protocol on the establishment of an ECOWAS Criminal Intelligence Bureau, first discussed by ECOWAS ministers of justice, internal security, and social affairs in Dakar in 2001. This bureau was to collate intelligence from member states on criminal activities, monitor the movement of criminals, and generally facilitate collaboration in the control of cross-border crime and terrorists.[9]
- imposition of a moratorium on small arms to prevent and control the proliferation of small arms in the subregion
- support from ECOWAS and its member states toward the establishment of the AU African Center for the Study and Research on Terrorism, including the designation of a subregional focal point for information sharing and cooperation activities
- convening of the first-ever ECOWAS regional conference of security and intelligence chiefs (sponsored by Nigeria) during 2004. At this level, currently two mechanisms facilitate rapid exchange of information among ECOWAS states on potential terrorist activity: the International Criminal Police Organization (Interpol), based in Abidjan and covering 26 West and Central African countries, and the West African Police Chiefs Committee (WAPCCO). In its annual regional meeting in Accra, Ghana, in July 2005, Interpol reiterated the need to intensify the fight against terrorism and to strengthen regional collaboration (including with WAPCCO) toward this end.
- participation by ECOWAS officials in foreign training and cooperation efforts, including seminars hosted by the U.S. Africa Center for Strategic Studies regarding counterterrorism efforts of the African Union and subregional organizations, and the particular role of the U.S.-led Trans-Sahara Counterterrorism Initiative.

Evaluating ECOWAS Effectiveness

The measures adopted by ECOWAS are striking in that few of them relate specifically to terrorism. In particular, there has been little systematic effort to fulfill the AU mandate for subregional organizations. To date, ECOWAS lacks even a rudimentary structure or agenda for prosecuting terrorism. There has also been little effort to actually enforce ECOWAS recommendations, and general exhortations have not always been backed up with specific policies, guidelines, or resources.

Action on the proposal to establish GIABA has been uneven. While the mainly Francophone member states of the West African Economic and Monetary Union (WAEMU)[10] have established their own legislative framework and are already implementing GIABA objectives through the Central Bank of West African States,[11] many of the Anglophone and Lusophone members of ECOWAS have yet to take the required actions. Similarly, the ECOWAS Criminal Intelligence Bureau (proposed in Dakar 2001) apparently has still not materialized,[12] and implementation of the Moratorium on Small Arms has been limited by capacity and resource constraints.[13]

Even the successes are sometimes double edged. Although all ECOWAS countries now issue machine-readable passports, the utility of this measure is defeated by the corruption that still attends to the procurement of passports, as well as the continuing porosity of borders and the fact that much cross-border movement still dispenses with formal documents.

To be sure, the fault does not lie exclusively with ECOWAS. Member states generally have been slow and incomplete in responding to requests from the ECOWAS Secretariat for information on actions relating to the implementation of the OAU Convention. Similarly, while almost all ECOWAS member states have signed, and most have ratified,[14] the relevant UN counterterrorism conventions, actual implementation remains spotty. For instance, few ECOWAS countries have taken action toward putting in place specific counterterrorist legislation. At least two ECOWAS states—The Gambia and Côte d'Ivoire—have passed or drafted such legislation. In The Gambia, the Anti-Terrorism Act of 2000 and the Money Laundering Act of 2003 both provide for measures to combat terrorism and related matters. The legislation on counterterrorism proposed by the government of Côte d'Ivoire defines for the first time specific terrorist offenses and lays down relevant sanctions.

At the same time, a new mechanism for combating cross-border crime and terrorism in all its forms is evolving to replace the defunct Agreement on Non-Aggression and Assistance in Matters of Defense. Some states (such as Senegal and Niger) have responded by tweaking existing penal codes (or adopting new ones) to better respond to counterterrorism exigencies. Other states (such as Benin and Burkina Faso) have argued against the need for such legislation, insisting that they already have legal instruments on their statute books adequate for countering terrorism.

For that matter, only a few states in the subregion (such as Sierra Leone and Cape Verde) appear to have established an integrated counterterrorism task force (and therein, the dominant approach has been to create counterterrorism units within existing security forces). Even in those countries that claim to have established them (such as Ghana), such centers do not seem to be very active, or at least they seem to have assumed a very low profile. Lack of a proper reporting system within ECOWAS and the absence of independent research make it difficult to determine the scope and overall effectiveness of the counterterrorism measures undertaken by individual ECOWAS countries. What is clear is that the diversity of these measures, and their lack of consistency, indicate an absence of regional coordination.

It is not entirely surprising that these national efforts have tended to be driven more by bilateral relations with Western donors than by ECOWAS directives. Practically every state in West Africa enjoys a bilateral counterterrorism program with the United States, the United Kingdom, France, or Germany, often as part of a broader security assistance regime. Unlike ECOWAS initiatives, these programs are actually backed by resources (such as training programs and provision of equipment). While some donors have also tried to channel assistance through ECOWAS (although by no means do all countries offering security assistance to ECOWAS prioritize "counterterrorism"), many of these programs are occurring by accident or design[15] outside the ECOWAS framework, are selective in the countries that they target, and are not always transparent.

While these programs have undoubtedly helped to compensate for ECOWAS inaction and lack of leadership, a legitimate concern is whether they may be competing with, or supplanting, efforts focused on the subregion and may even help to explain the low level of responsiveness to ECOWAS initiatives. A broader concern is the potential to stimulate the militarization of the Africa region (a process already under way in the Horn, at least),[16] and for counterterrorism to become entangled in broader strategic objectives (such as protection of U.S. access to West African oil reserves). On the other hand, to the extent that paying lip service to the global war against terrorism or entering into an antiterrorist alliance with a major power has come to be regarded as a convenient and painless way of currying political favor, there is clearly an element of political opportunism among African leaders. Enhanced responsiveness to

ECOWAS initiatives requires cultivating greater local ownership of counterterrorism policy and methodology, with the assistance of multilateral and bilateral partners.

Legal, Political, and Administrative Constraints

One of the most important challenges confronting ECOWAS in the harmonization and coordination of its counterterrorism efforts, and indeed in its integration efforts in general, relates to the contrasting legal and administrative traditions inherited from the varied Anglophone, Francophone, and Lusophone colonial backgrounds of its member states. A result of this heritage is the existence of multiple (and often competing) subregional organizations, in some cases with cross-cutting memberships, driven by divergent legal and policy frameworks and moving at different rates on collective decisions. The most important example of this is, of course, the existence of WAEMU and ECOWAS and their contrasting performance on the GIABA and on a wider range of integration issues.

There are also institutional and infrastructural constraints to consider. The most important of these relates to the lack of capacity within the ECOWAS Secretariat itself, in terms of both human and financial resources required to engage member states in the implementation of the OAU Convention.[17] In theory, enforcement and coordination of counterterrorism actions in ECOWAS are undertaken by the DES/PADS in the ECOWAS Secretariat. In reality, ECOWAS still does not have a counterterrorism office or center and has only a single dedicated officer to deal with counterterrorism cooperation issues. In addition, ECOWAS does not yet have a subregional strategy, plan, road map, or—as far as one can tell—a specific budget for counterterrorism activities.

At the national level as well, most ECOWAS states lack the infrastructure and equipment required for a credible counterterrorism campaign. Most are characterized by a number of shortcomings:

- poor border controls and the lack of even a rudimentary ability to mount the necessary surveillance over their national territories
- limited intelligence and information gathering, storage, and retrieval capability
- a lack of essential coordination and communication across government agencies (including the security bureaucracy, which is often rife with rivalries)
- the absence of appropriately trained and equipped emergency and civil protection teams (police, fire, medics, humanitarian relief agencies, etc.)
- weak financial interdiction tools

- justice systems that often are overstressed to the breaking point.

As counterterrorism experience in other countries has indicated, collaboration between the state and the private sector is essential for successful prevention and prosecution of terrorism, and in most African countries such collaboration is virtually nonexistent.

However, there are also wider political constraints that make ECOWAS governments reluctant to press harder on the issue of terrorism. In the multiethnic, multicultural, and multireligious societies found in West Africa, there is a danger that counterterrorism may be perceived as a form of racial, ethnic, or religious profiling. Indeed, this has already emerged in those states (such as Kenya, Nigeria, and South Africa) where there has been a robust response to terrorism.[18] Many Africans are uncomfortable with the thrust of the present discourse on terrorism, which they see as designed to achieve the security interests of rich and powerful countries in the West. This skepticism is deepened by what is widely perceived as fabricated rationales for the U.S. invasion of Iraq. Four "ideological" perceptions in particular deter wider public endorsement of counterterrorism efforts in ECOWAS and its member states. These are that:

- counterterrorism is engineered by the United States and its Western allies and is of concern primarily to those states
- counterterrorism is "anti-Islamic"
- current counterterrorism strategy is designed to deal with the symptoms rather than the root causes of terrorism, which are perceived to lie in poverty, marginalization, and alienation
- indiscriminate application of the "terrorist" label may hinder authentic struggles for national liberation and global justice, implying that terrorist acts are in some sense legitimate in the context of such struggles.[19]

Overall, the skeptical view was expressed at a counterterrorism workshop hosted by the U.S. Government in Mali in 2003,[20] when some participants asserted:

> Why is there a need to prioritize the global war on terrorism in Africa, particularly when juxtaposed against the immediate challenges posed by civil strife, poverty, and disease, which claim thousands of lives each day? In many Africans' views, African states must prioritize their meager resources and devote more attention to the

essential challenges of combating poverty, disease, and civil wars. They alluded that while the global war on terrorism is an overarching priority for the United and Great Britain, the immediacy of the problem for Africa is debatable.

Such skepticism of the counterterrorism agenda is fairly wide-spread among ECOWAS, national officials, and the citizenry of West Africa, and continues to undermine political support for robust policy.

There are also specific political concerns that are more local in origin. In societies with recent histories of authoritarian governance, a tradition of impunity among security forces, and weak legal structures, counterterrorism may pose a direct threat to human rights. Current fears of the possible emergence of a tiered justice system within Western societies in the context of the struggle against terrorism (with one set of laws for alleged terrorists and another for everyone else)[21] resonate more sharply among states with much weaker legal and judicial traditions.[22] Stringent counterterrorism measures and muscular reassertion of a national security ideology may undermine ongoing security sector reforms and further weaken accountability among security agencies.[23] In many cases, counterterrorism has allowed African states to intensify their already familiar repertoire of repression and deflect pressures for democratization and accountability.[24]

Enhancing ECOWAS Capacity

In light of both the successes and shortcomings of ECOWAS efforts to date, a number of steps are required to transform this situation and to put in place the underpinnings of a comprehensive ECOWAS counterterrorism strategy.

Strengthen ECOWAS Internal Capabilities

The starting point of a comprehensive ECOWAS counterterrorism strategy has to be the strengthening of the organization's own capability to execute the roles identified for subregional organizations in the AU Plan of Action. This can be done by establishing a properly staffed counterterrorism center in the ECOWAS Secretariat[25] to undertake research, monitor national policies, provide strategic and capacity-building advice to ECOWAS member states, and co-ordinate the design of a subregional road map. Such a center will also liaise with national counterintelligence centers and the African Center for the Study and Research on Terrorism in Algiers, as well as identify and coordinate access to external resources.[26]

It is important to ensure that this counterterrorism center does not become an island within ECOWAS, with few overarching links with other ECOWAS departments. Rather, it requires internal coordination, bringing together the different departments to discuss common strategies for combating terrorism in the financial, legal, political, social, and humanitarian domains, thus building overall capacity across the board with the secretariat and elsewhere. Important organs such as the Defense and Security Commission and the ECOWAS Parliament should have their roles clearly identified as well.

Linking the above with broader institutional reform within ECOWAS is imperative. Both the Office of the Executive Secretary and that of the DES/PADS, the office under which a counterterrorism center would likely fall, suffer from capacity challenges and constitute major bottlenecks in the policy and administrative structure of ECOWAS. In addition to problems of staffing levels and quality, top officers are often away from head offices on one crisis-management assignment after another. As a consequence, major decisions as well as implementation are held up.

Further, capacity constraints within the ECOWAS Secretariat need to be addressed by calling on the wide range of multilateral (especially UN) and bilateral assistance that has become increasingly available.[27] It can also be alleviated through collaboration with nongovernmental organizations, think tanks, and research centers.[28]

Develop a Road Map for ECOWAS

There is a need for an ECOWAS road map as the basis for a coherent subregional counterterrorism strategy. The IGAD road map can serve as a model.[29] ECOWAS already has many of the elements for such a strategy in place in its various conventions on extradition,[30] small arms, money laundering, and cross-border crime. Furthermore, ECOWAS (relative to IGAD) has the distinct advantage of already having a comprehensive conflict prevention and management system in place. A road map would pull all these together and establish time lines for implementing specific measures.

Elements of such a road map would include conducting a survey of terrorist threats and challenges, as well as counterterrorism capabilities, in the subregion. Critically, this will need to be followed by a road map that confronts the following issues.

Enhance and Coordinate Judicial Measures and Capabilities

To accomplish this task, it is critical to ensure that all ECOWAS states sign, ratify, and implement all UN, AU, and ECOWAS conventions and protocols on terrorism and related matters. Once this is accomplished, it will be possible to design or adapt model counterterrorism legislation for adoption by ECOWAS member states, taking advantage of existing drafts provided by institutions such as the African Center for the Study and Research on Terrorism, the UN Office on Drugs and Crime, and the Commonwealth Secretariat, as a means of harmonizing national legislation on all aspects of terrorism and related matters (including money laundering, organized crime and corruption, and drugs and arms trafficking) and bringing them in line with the relevant international and continental instruments.

Further, ECOWAS can facilitate access to technical assistance and capacity building of the judiciary in member states, including training of members of the judiciary and law enforcement communities in best practices in investigation and prosecution techniques relative to terrorism cases. Finally, ECOWAS can work to establish a regional judicial forum for information and the exchange of best practices between member states in relation to judicial responses to the threat of terrorism.

Enhance National and Subregional Coordination

Improved bilateral and multilateral cooperation in the ECOWAS subregion will require the establishment of national counterterrorism bureaus in each member state to coordinate all terrorism-related activities. This will entail the creation of focal points on terrorism in every ministry and governmental body. Then it will be possible to bring together the different ministries (interior, finance, security, defense and external relations, and so forth) in workshops, seminars, and other forums and through joint national and regional training programs to ensure interoperability.

ECOWAS can also encourage member states to cultivate and pursue bilateral initiatives to enhance their national counterterrorism efforts; promote collaboration with regional partners such as Interpol and WAPCCO; and encourage regional collaboration to reexamine the issue of border controls in the context of the free movement protocol. The latter may include the establishment of an ECOWAS commission to work on reconciling and monitoring the free movement protocol in light of the need for increased border vigilance to deter cross-border movement of terrorist elements. While machine-readable passports have been introduced at major entry points such as airports, anyone who has crossed ECOWAS borders recently can verify that border controls remain extremely problematic, with large numbers of undocumented crossings and pervasive and open extortion by police, immigration, and customs officials. Indifferent controls have contributed to cross-border crime,[31] but the potential problems they pose for effective counterterrorism have yet to be acknowledged within ECOWAS itself.[32]

Finally, ECOWAS should build further capacity for its efforts to settle the proliferation of conflicts in the region that provide receptive soil for both domestic and (potentially) international terrorism.

Promote Best Practices, Training, and Capacity Building

The ECOWAS Secretariat and the proposed counterterrorism center should act as clearinghouses for information sharing on international best practices in preventing and combating terrorism (including maintaining and sharing a list of terrorist organizations) and sourcing and coordinating external training and capacity building opportunities. One valuable initiative would be the convening of an annual meeting of high-level ECOWAS national experts from the security, financial, and diplomatic communities to share lessons learned and provide an update on terrorist modus operandi in the region.

Promote Education and Sensitization

Attempts should be made to raise the profile of counterterrorism on the ECOWAS list of priorities through education and other forms of sensitization—for instance, by integrating counterterrorism into the curricula of national military and security training institutions, regional centers like the Kofi Annan International Peacekeeping Training Center, and multidisciplinary, multiagency courses such as Ghana's new Security Sector Governance and Management Course.[33]

Public and media education (targeting in particular the youth of ECOWAS member states) is also important to teach about the dangers of terrorism and change the perception that counterterrorism is foisted on African states by the United States and the West. This can be done most successfully by stressing the negative impact of terrorism on the global economy and the variety of ways in which terrorism hurts the development process and poverty alleviation (through the diversion of aid, impact on tourism, lower commodity prices, etc.);[34] the reality that terrorist targets are often indiscriminate and unpredictable and cost the lives of too many Africans each year; and the fact that countries that are not themselves targets of terrorism are nevertheless potential actors in the drama of terrorism, through their role (often unintended) as conduits for financing, havens for fugitives, and launching pads for attacks.

Finally, overall credibility of, and support for, counterterrorism in the ECOWAS subregion may be enhanced by undertaking the following initiatives. First, it is critical to make a clearer and less ambiguous link between the incidence of terrorism and issues of development, democracy, and the rule of law. There is the perception that counterterrorism is pushing issues of development and poverty—and hence what many regard as the structural causes of violence—off the global agenda,[35] and at the same time undermining the rule of law. For example, while the United States insists that one of the qualifications for inclusion in counterterrorism initiatives is democratic governance, this does not always appear to be the case in practice, and there is a widespread perception both in Africa and elsewhere that counterterrorism has bolstered authoritarian regimes.

Second, it is important to link counterterrorism and security sector reform efforts in Africa. Many of the security agencies at the forefront of counterterrorism strategies in Africa are not only ineffective in operational terms, but also often lack public legitimacy and respect for human rights. Greater operational capability must therefore be linked with improved security sector governance and respect for the rule of law.

Third, there is a need to link counterterrorism and capacity building for national crisis and disaster management. Both draw critically on capable first responder and civil protection units and high levels of interagency coordination. It is obvious that most ECOWAS countries are extremely weak in such respects. Developing counterterrorism capability thus has real potential payoffs for national disaster management and vice versa. These links need to be stressed, insofar as countries lack the political will and tend to balk at the cost of counterterrorism measures but may be open to making the appropriate investments once they become aware of their multidimensional roles.

Conclusion

Recent terrorist attacks, including those in the United Kingdom and Egypt, have signaled once again that terrorist actions cannot be expected to subside in the foreseeable future, and at the same time underscored the massive challenges involved in countering this threat, even among states much better endowed than ECOWAS. As a subregional organization, ECOWAS remains bound by decisions on counterterrorism taken at the levels of the United Nations and the African Union. However, as this chapter has indicated, dedicated counterterrorism efforts within ECOWAS have been hindered by both objective factors, particularly a lack of capacity, and subjective considerations, such as perceived biases in existing counterterrorism strategies.

While none of these factors entirely excuse the level of inaction (and complacency) that has come to characterize the subregional posture on terrorism, it is obvious that many of the issues transcend ECOWAS and need to be addressed within a wider framework. They include, in particular, the need for:

- assurances that counterterrorism measures will not or do not infringe on fundamental human rights or shift the focus from issues of development

- a universally agreed definition of what constitutes terrorism as the basis for a comprehensive antiterrorism convention
- accompanying guidelines within ECOWAS as to what can be accepted as legitimate counterterrorism action (preferably within the context of UN Security Council Resolution 1373 and the AU Plan of Action)[36]
- capacity building for states that lack the resources to respond adequately to UN and AU decisions.

Fortunately, these issues are already on the international agenda. They formed the core of the remit of the UN Secretary-General's "High-Level Panel on Threats, Challenges, and Change" and resulted in comprehensive (and often innovative) recommendations.[37] Particularly noteworthy were the deliberate efforts of the High-Level Panel to craft a "new security consensus" designed to reconcile and synthesize the concerns of those who see the issue in terms of security service responses to terrorism on the one hand and those who tend to prioritize development and poverty alleviation on the other.[38]

Responding to the recommendations of the panel, the UN Secretary-General has defined five elements of a "principled, comprehensive strategy" for counterterrorism, laying particular stress on the need to "develop state capacity to prevent terrorism" and to "defend human rights in the struggle against terrorism."[39] What remains to be determined, however, is the response of the Security Council itself to these far-reaching proposals. Otherwise, barring significant terror attacks in an ECOWAS member state, it is likely that future counterterrorism efforts in West Africa will be determined at the global, UN level and at the level of national, bilateral cooperation, rather than significantly involving ECOWAS.

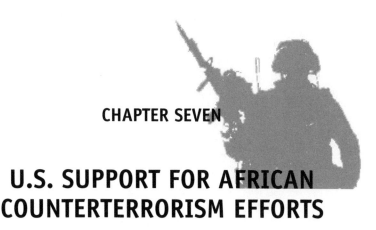

CHAPTER SEVEN

U.S. SUPPORT FOR AFRICAN COUNTERTERRORISM EFFORTS

Andre Le Sage

The idea and practice of regional cooperation are not new to Africa. Indeed, the benefits of collaboration have been clear since the early days of independence, leading to the creation of the Organization of African Unity (OAU) in 1963. Since then, numerous regional and subregional forums for multilateral cooperation on matters ranging from security to trade to development have sprung up across the continent. In 1999, the OAU itself was transformed by its member states into the African Union (AU) in order to enhance their cooperation activities and accelerate efforts to build peace and prosperity.

In these forums, African governments have particularly recognized the importance of security cooperation. This is largely premised on the transnational nature of many of the challenges facing the continent, including organized crime, disease, massive population movements, and, increasingly, terrorism. Just as critically, individual countries have come to appreciate the potential that unified action brings for addressing complex issues, such as improved border security and intelligence sharing, where limited resources can be combined and thereby amplified.

African Union Counterterrorism Efforts

The African Union recognizes that terrorism, regardless of its geographical location, is a threat to African and international security. The AU maintains that primary responsibility in this effort lies with its member states, with subregional and international organizations assisting in these endeavors. The AU also stresses that counterterrorism measures should not infringe on human and civil rights or undermine international law and must not be confused with legitimate political opposition.

The AU concluded several agreements related to terrorism over the past two decades, including a 1992 OAU resolution against extremism and the 1999 OAU Convention on the Prevention and Combating of Terrorism. Based on the convention, AU member states committed to outlaw "terrorist acts" according to the following definition:

> (a) any act which is a violation of the criminal laws of a State Party and which may endanger the life, physical integrity or freedom of, or cause serious injury or death to, any person, any number or group of persons or causes or may cause damage to public or private property, natural resources, environmental or cultural heritage and is calculated or intended to:
>
> (i) intimidate, put in fear, force, coerce, or induce any government, body, institution, the general public or any segment thereof, to do or abstain from doing any act, or to adopt or abandon a particular standpoint, or to act according to certain principles; or
>
> (ii) disrupt any public service, the delivery of any essential service to the public or to create a public emergency; or
>
> (iii) create general insurrection in a State.
>
> (b) any promotion, sponsoring, contribution to, command, aid, incitement, encouragement, attempt, threat, conspiracy, organizing, or procurement of any person, with the intent to commit any act referred to in paragraph (a) (i) to (iii).[1]

After the attacks in Kenya and Tanzania in 1998, as well as the events of September 11, the continent took stock of its approach to terrorism to date and realized that the 1999 convention needed a mechanism to support its implementation. This resulted in 2004 in a Protocol to the OAU Convention and, most practically, the AU Plan of Action (POA) for the Prevention and Combating of Terrorism.

The POA details specific strategies for implementing international counterterrorism instruments—particularly the 13 conventions and protocols registered with the United Nations (UN) to criminalize various terrorist acts—as well as the means through which AU member states can enhance their bilateral and multilateral cooperation. In particular, the POA also calls for member states to undertake the following:

- enhance police and border control capacities
- enact necessary legislative and judicial reforms
- suppress the financing of terrorism
- increase exchanges of information and intelligence
- build further cooperation at the subregional, continental, and international levels
- charge the AU's Peace and Security Commission and other organs to monitor and support these actions.[2]

To date, the AU and its member states have taken three main steps to implement the POA, including the creation of a group of experts to design a road map for execution, the creation of projects to construct a comprehensive African counterterrorism model law and a common African arrest warrant, and the establishment of the AU's African Center for the Study and Research on Terrorism (ACSRT), based in Algiers.[3]

The AU charged ACSRT with several key functions, including sensitization of member states to the threat of terrorism in Africa; provision of technical assistance to develop national and subregional counterterrorism strategies; creation of coordination procedures for member states to access expert guidance; construction of a database with information and shared intelligence related to terrorism; harmonization and standardization of national legislation against terrorism in accordance with African and international conventions, resolutions, and judicial instruments; and dissemination of research and information on policy issues.

Subregional Counterterrorism Efforts

Article 16 of the 2004 Protocol to the OAU Convention specifically endorses the supportive role to be played by African subregional organizations, some of which the AU officially recognizes as Regional Economic Communities. On paper, their objectives and strategies largely duplicate what the AU has already set out to accomplish in the POA. However, by virtue of greater proximity to their member states and possibly due to greater political buy-in by key governments, the subregional organizations have a strong role to play. Key among these organizations are the following.

Inter-Governmental Authority on Development (IGAD). IGAD member states have committed to establishing a subregional approach to counterterrorism that fits within the AU and UN frameworks. In this vein, IGAD has developed a Draft Implementation Plan to Counter Terrorism, which has yet to be adopted. However, measures within that plan are already at various stages of implementation, including initiatives to counter the financing of terrorism, enhance operational capacities to counter illegal cross-border movements, increase the sharing of information and intelligence on common security concerns, implement measures ensuring the protection of human rights during counterterrorism operations, and incorporate education and other social service programs to enhance public support. In addition, IGAD's support of and, at times, leading role in international efforts to build peace agreements in Somalia and Sudan are considered by the organization as substantial counterterrorism contributions. Finally, in 2006, the IGAD Capacity-building Program Against Terrorism was initiated to provide training and research with support from the Institute for Security Studies in South Africa and funding from European donors.

East African Community (EAC). Comprised of Kenya, Tanzania, and Uganda, the EAC was inaugurated in January 2001 to promote cooperation in the areas of transport and communication, trade and industry, security, immigration, and foreign investment. Although the EAC's founding treaty does not specify counterterrorism as an area of cooperation, the organization's activities include efforts aimed at curbing cross-border criminal activities. In addition, the three member states have signed a memorandum of understanding on cooperation in defense, which has led to further action to combat the proliferation of small arms and light weapons; to draft modalities for refugee registration; and to conduct joint military training exercises for peacekeeping, counterterrorism, and disaster response.

Economic Community of West African States (ECOWAS). ECOWAS and its member states have also taken important measures toward cooperation on international security and terrorism. Given the formation of the ECOWAS Monitoring Group to intervene as a peacekeeping force in Liberia, Sierra Leone, and Guinea-Bissau, the organization's member states are already experienced in multilateral security cooperation. In addition, ECOWAS has enacted a number of general measures that relate to counterterrorism, including a 1992 convention on extradition, a 1999 peace and security protocol, a 2001 protocol to combat corruption, and a 2003 accord for police cooperation. Currently, an accord specifically designed to combat terrorism is under consideration by ECOWAS.

Southern African Development Community (SADC). Although SADC and its member states regularly condemn terrorism and certain attacks that take place around the world, there are no protocols adopted that deal specifically with terrorism. Rather, the organization's member states confront their terrorist threats and vulnerabilities through wide-ranging commitments to enhance security and development. These have resulted in various initiatives and protocols with regard to democratization, harmonization of legal regimes, and efforts to combat weapons proliferation and crime. If the organization sought to pursue more specific counterterrorism planning, SADC could do so within the terms of the Protocol for Policy, Defense, and Security Cooperation.[4] As a first step in this direction, in late 2006, SADC did announce the intention of creating an antiterrorist unit in conjunction with the International Criminal Police Organization (Interpol). The office, to be based in Harare, Zimbabwe, is intended to focus on police cooperation and information sharing.[5]

In addition to these four largest African subregional organizations, similar roles are played in other parts of the continent by the Arab Maghreb Union, the Economic Community of Central African States, the Economic and Monetary Community of Central African States, and the Common Market for Eastern and Southern Africa. However, the specific counterterrorism role that these organizations play has yet to be fully elaborated.

Police and Financial Cooperation

Two additional sets of initiatives related to counterterrorism have evolved at the African subregional level in cooperation with international organizations. They have been endorsed by the AU and relevant subregional organizations, and their level of practical success is far greater than the political processes at those larger and political institutions. First, Interpol and its Africa Sub-Directorate have promoted, facilitated, and supported efforts by African national police agencies to improve their coordination. This has led to the establishment of four subregional cooperation efforts, including the East African Police Chiefs Committee, Southern African Regional Police Chiefs Committee, *Comité des Chefs de Police de l'Afrique de l'Ouest*, and *Comité des Chefs de Police de l'Afrique Centrale*. In conjunction with Interpol, they share information and provide training and investigational support.[6] Given the presence of national Interpol bureaus in many countries, these mechanisms are particularly important in such regions as North Africa, where no functional subregional political organization exists to invest in counterterrorism efforts and provide assistance to member states.

Second, the Financial Action Task Force—an intergovernmental body charged with developing standards and measures to combat money laundering and terrorist financing—has three local affiliate organizations in Africa. They include:

- Eastern and Southern African Anti-Money Laundering

Group (ESAAMLG), comprised of 14 countries from Eastern and Southern Africa and Indian Ocean states

- Intergovernmental Action Group Against Money Laundering (GIABA), comprised of West African member states of ECOWAS
- Middle East and North Africa Financial Action Task Force (MENAFATF), comprised of 14 countries, including Algeria, Egypt, Morocco, and Tunisia, on the African continent.

The program of work for these organizations includes reviewing the legal and regulatory frameworks of their members, assessing their strengths and weaknesses, and working to consolidate a comprehensive regional regime compatible with global standards. They also conduct an ongoing program of mutual evaluation and capacity building assistance to ensure consistent implementation and forward movement.

Assessing Regional and Subregional Efforts

Despite these efforts, experience has shown that African regional security cooperation has faced numerous challenges, and translating commitments into effective practice has proven difficult. This is demonstrated by the fact that only 36 of the 53 AU member states have ratified the 1999 OAU Convention, and only 21 of these have established national counterterrorism focal points.[7] Furthermore, ACSRT encountered significant difficulties in funding and staffing due to the delayed arrival of AU funding until mid-2006. Until then, it was forced to rely on direct support from the Algerian government.

There are at least five key areas for a framework for implementing regional and subregional counterterrorism commitments, including clarification of the roles and responsibilities of the AU and subregional organizations; building AU and subregional organizational capacity; the importance of identifying counterterrorism focal points for member states and subregional organizations; building political will by member states' leaders; and ensuring broad knowledge of AU and subregional counterterrorism efforts within African governments and among their citizens.

Clarification of Roles and Responsibilities. The roles and responsibilities of the AU and subregional organizations in combating terrorism are very similar. The primary functions of these organizations are the coordination and harmonization of the counterterrorism efforts of their member states and the development and implementation of a coordinated strategy for the entire organization. The only real difference in mandates is geographical: while the AU is responsible at the continental level, the others assume these tasks at the subregional level. At best, the subregional organizations are more able to tailor capabilities to meet their specific, local terrorist threats and vulnerabilities and may have additional political interest on the part of their member states' leaders. However, the AU should assist the subregional organizations in formulating strategies to meet their specific needs while fitting into the AU's continental strategy and should coordinate implementation of these measures.

Building Organizational Capacities. Both the AU and subregional organizations face a serious lack of human, financial, and logistical resources. In addition, while most subregional organizations understand that successful economic integration and development—usually their primary institutional purpose—are impossible without security, not all have recognized the critical threats posed by terrorism. Without these critical capacities and sufficient education and training for the organizations' staff, counterterrorism practices cannot keep pace with commitments.

Counterterrorism Focal Points. Designation of counterterrorism focal points by each member state and subregional organization is an essential and immediate need in establishing and implementing coordinated strategies. Focal points are needed to serve as authoritative points of contact to provide and disseminate information between the national, subregional, and regional levels. It is likely that a single individual is not sufficient to act as a reliable focal point that builds sustained capacity in a country or organization. Rather, the focal point in each instance should be a well-staffed office led by a high-ranking official with the necessary institutional and personal qualifications.

Building Political Will. Lack of national level political support among African states is a serious challenge to the formulation and implementation of successful counterterrorism strategies. The deficit of political will quickly translates into human resource and funding shortages and severely constrains implementation of AU and subregional counterterrorism commitments. In response, many African countries and organizations with support from international donors have tried to establish well-resourced and well-staffed counterterrorism units that function relatively independently of the wider government bureaucracy. However, such units do not have the capacity to cover the whole of Africa on their own, and they do not serve the needs of coordination if they are not fully integrated into national bureaucracies and supported by their governments.

Increasing Public Information. While it is important to generate political will at the national and multilateral levels, this is not possible without the support of all elements of a country's government bureaucracy and individual citizens. If decisions and commitments made at the AU or a subregional organization are not widely disseminated, no country's security personnel, border patrols, customs officials, or other civil servants will know their responsibilities. Further, the level of information provided to the general public is insufficient and serves to cut off counterterrorism efforts from wider understanding and support.

National Efforts and U.S. Counterterrorism Support

Despite the wide range of African regional and subregional counterterrorism efforts described above, it is clear that they only operate in support of practical national implementation. In short, most counterterrorism responsibilities lie at the national level. The terrorist threat is unique in every country in Africa, and, as a result, no single template for the necessary counterterrorism response exists. However, over the past 30 years, governments throughout the world have developed a range of instruments to confront substate extremist threats. Many countries have built up considerable counterterrorism experience through an assortment of legislative, financial, security, and coordinating mechanisms.

Taken together, these strategic initiatives constitute the tools of counterterrorism. The basic aims are, first, to create an environment that is hostile to the penetration and recruitment of terrorist operatives; second, to develop the capacities of government's legal and security services in order to identify and preempt any attacks that are planned; and third, to create the necessary crisis response capacities to manage the humanitarian impact and civil disruption that would follow an attack.

National Level Efforts

Some of the best examples of African counterterrorism efforts at the national level include the following:

Creation of National Coordination Bodies. Many African countries have created national bodies to oversee the counterterrorism response, coordinate the collection and sharing of intelligence and other information, and give higher profile and priority to counterterrorism within their national bureaucracies. In East Africa alone, this includes the creation of the National Counter-Terrorism Center in Kenya, the Joint Anti-Terrorism Task Force in Uganda, the formation of the National Intelligence and Security Service in Ethiopia, and a similar effort under way in Tanzania.

Creation of Specially Trained and Equipped Forces. Groups such as Kenya's Anti-Terrorism Police Unit and other countries' dedicated counterterrorism military forces have been trained and equipped through the Trans-Sahara Counterterrorism Partnership (TSCTP), East African Counterterrorism Initiative (EACTI), and the Combined Joint Task Force–Horn of Africa (CJTF–HOA) to conduct both intelligence collection and rapid response actions in cases of terrorism.

Creation of Targeted Counterterrorism Legislation. Many countries have amended their national penal codes or drafted new legislation to outlaw terrorism. Those that have succeeded include Uganda, South Africa, Ethiopia, Algeria, Tunisia, and Morocco. Similar efforts are also under way with the preparation of draft legislation—although it is often highly controversial—in Tanzania, Nigeria, Kenya, Zimbabwe, and Senegal.

Creation of Financial Intelligence Units. Other countries have also enhanced their capacity to monitor national financial transactions and investigate suspect cases in order to prevent terrorists from laundering and transferring funds. This includes South Africa's Financial Intelligence Center, a draft Anti-Money Laundering Bill in Tanzania, and the efforts of subregional groups such as ESAAMLG, GIABA, and MENAFATF.

U.S. Support for National Efforts

The United States has recognized that combating terrorism will not be accomplished effectively by any single government working alone. Rather, it requires cooperation from like-minded countries around the world. The United States continues to invest in building strong partnerships to confront shared security threats as well as to help build the capacity of its allies to take independent action at their national, subregional, and regional levels.

U.S. counterterrorism programs endeavor to ensure that local and foreign security services, diplomatic efforts, and humanitarian and development capacities are effectively employed in unison to combat both terrorist actors and the political, social, and economic conditions that enable them to operate and build support. The military assistance component of U.S. counterterrorism efforts is usually the most visible, particularly in media and scholarly assessments. U.S. Special Operations Forces have been engaged in training their counterparts in several African countries in appropriate military tactics and strategies to address the small, mobile networks of militants. Key aspects of the training include basic marksmanship, planning, communications, land navigation, patrolling, and medical care.

Nonmilitary factors are equally important to the success of African efforts to combat terrorism. Addressing the prevalence of local political conflicts, organized criminal activities, marginalized populations, poverty, and the need for greater socioeconomic development, as well as governance concerns over democratization, the rule of law, and corruption, are all critical to ensure that terrorist organizations cannot exploit the weaknesses of African states in order to recruit followers, find sanctuary, strengthen their movements, and eventually launch attacks within the region or abroad.

Finally, U.S. Government efforts are designed to help strengthen regional counterterrorism information sharing and coordinated action and to institutionalize the willingness of African governments to address this shared security threat at the levels of bilateral, subregional, and regional cooperation among security forces, promote democratic governance, and ultimately improve U.S. bilateral relationships with each of these states.

Some of the most important and widespread programs to support and develop national capacities across the continent are described here.

Broad, Multisector Initiatives in High-Risk Areas. Counterterrorism requires small, highly trained, and highly mobile forces to respond to terrorist threats in arid, maritime, and urban areas. More African forces need to be trained and deployed for border surveillance and control and to support initiatives of nonmilitary agencies. They use an array of human and technical intelligence assets to identify terrorists, penetrate terrorist cells, and preempt planned attacks. All of this must be accomplished with constitutional and other legal guarantees in mind to allow opposition groups to express themselves openly within the confines of the legal political system, thus diminishing the need to resort to violence.

- Combined Joint Task Force–Horn of Africa: security assistance, capacity building, and cooperation with host governments and international organizations to enhance long-term stability; enhanced liaison relationships in intelligence, law enforcement, and military; analysis and investigation of al Qaeda's operational and support network in the region; civil affairs projects to combat ideological support for terrorism
- East Africa Counterterrorism Initiative: capacity building programs for border, coastal, and aviation security, counterterrorism financing, and police training; education programs and outreach to marginalized communities
- Trans-Sahara Counterterrorism Partnership: builds indigenous capacity and facilitates cooperation among

governments in the region that are willing partners. Activities include training and equipment, security conferences, intelligence capabilities enhancement, intelligence sharing and fusion center, and border security assistance. Some funds are dedicated to promoting democracy and economic growth.

- Gulf of Guinea Initiative: training in security, maritime operations, search and rescue, and antiterrorism force protection operations; community relations projects, technical assistance, and HIV prevention programs.

Investment in Law Enforcement, Legislative, and Judicial Capabilities. At its root, terrorism is a violation of national and international law, and whenever possible, the role of police in bringing terrorist leaders and operatives to justice has been prioritized as the most transparent and legitimate means of addressing the threat. Efforts are required to ensure that the planning, incitement, and conduct of terrorism are illegal, allow for extradition and other forms of international cooperation, and equip the criminal justice system to combat terrorism within the bounds of the rule of law.

- Anti-Terrorism Assistance Program: provides training to foreign partners in law enforcement, protection of national leadership, border control, critical infrastructure protection, crisis management, and other technical aspects of combating terrorism
- FBI Legal Attaché Program: special agents stationed at U.S. missions overseas work with foreign law enforcement to combat common crime and terrorism
- International Criminal Investigative Training Assistance Program: assists foreign governments in developing the capacity to provide professional law enforcement services based on democratic principles and respect for human rights
- Mutual Legal Assistance Treaties and Mutual Legal Assistance Agreements: set out the protocols for the investigation of terrorists by U.S. law enforcement in sovereign nations, protect U.S. agents working in those nations, and speed response time to a terrorist-related event
- Resident Legal Adviser: provides technical expertise and training to partner governments on combating corruption, money laundering, and other financial crimes
- International Civilian Police Program: recruits police officers from the United States to participate in international civilian police activities and local police development programs in foreign countries

- International Law Enforcement Academy, Botswana: strengthens regional partnerships, provides training and technical assistance for foreign law enforcement personnel, and fosters cooperation by foreign law enforcement authorities with U.S. law enforcement entities engaged in criminal investigations.

Improved Financial Monitoring and Regulation. These efforts are aimed at freezing and otherwise disrupting the monetary flows terrorist groups rely on to sustain and augment their activities.

- Financial Systems Assessment Team: examines existing laws, regulations, customs and border patrol effectiveness, and financial investigative capabilities; offers technical assistance and training based on team recommendations
- Financial Crimes Enforcement Network: supports law enforcement efforts on countering terrorism financing and money laundering
- Support for development of Financial Intelligence Units: technical assistance and diplomatic engagement to help countries create a national agency to combat financial crimes and terrorist financing.

Enhanced Border, Port, and Customs Controls. These are programs to improve security standards at land and maritime points of entry and decrease the ease of movement of terrorists, weapons, money, and goods used to support terrorism.

- Container Security Initiative: identifies high-risk containers and prescreens containers prior to their shipment to the United States
- International Port Security Program: facilitates bilateral and multilateral discussions to exchange information and share best practices that support implementation of international maritime security standards
- Foreign Port Security Assessment: assesses effectiveness of antiterrorism measures maintained in foreign ports in regions engaged in trade or tourism with the United States; assists foreign officials with corrective actions
- U.S. Coast Guard International Training Program: deploys teams worldwide each fiscal year to train partners on Coast Guard missions, including maritime security–related topics
- Safe Skies for Africa: offers technical advice on aviation security and facilitation of improvements made by partner countries

- Export Control and Border Security Assistance Program: helps to establish the practical basis for cooperation among states in the region as well as encourage cooperation with the United States and other Proliferation Security Initiative participants to prevent shipments of weapons of mass destruction, their delivery systems, and related material
- Terrorist Interdiction Program: enhances border security by providing foreign governments with a computerized database that allows border control officials to identify and detain or track individuals of interest.

Good Governance and Development Strategies. These are intended to diminish underlying conditions (for example, grievances, frustration, and sources of tension, including poverty and weak government institutions) and deny sanctuary and access to recruits by adapting development programs to high-risk areas and populations that provide tangible benefits. Such efforts should also ensure that an emergency management system is in place in the case of a terrorist attack or other national disaster.

- Support for International Organizations: contributions to the United Nations Development Program; World Bank; African Development Fund; Global Fund to Fight AIDS, Tuberculosis, and Malaria; and other international efforts
- Middle East Partnership Initiative: supports economic, political, and educational reform in the Middle East and North Africa and increased opportunity for all people in the region, especially women and children
- President's Emergency Plan for AIDS Relief: provides health services and drug treatment for people with HIV/AIDS, supports children orphaned by AIDS, and supports HIV prevention programs
- Human Rights and Democracy Fund: administers programs designed to strengthen democracy, promote human rights, and build civil society in countries that are strategically critical to the United States
- Women's Justice and Empowerment in Africa Initiative: administers programs to combat sexual violence and abuse against women, as well as to empower them in society
- Anti-Human Trafficking Initiative: funds programs that increase criminal prosecutions of traffickers and programs for rescuing, rehabilitating, and reintegrating trafficking victims
- English Language Programs: offer training, materials, and personnel (including regional English language officers, English

Access Microscholarships, and academic specialists) to build English language skills in a partner country

- African Education Initiative: increases access to quality basic education in Africa through scholarships, textbooks, and teacher training programs
- Middle East Free Trade Initiative: supports accession to World Trade Organization as part of the mission to help Middle East and North African countries achieve economic growth and increased trade and investment with the United States
- African Growth and Opportunity Act: provides beneficiary countries with the most liberal access to the U.S. market available to any country or region not having a free trade agreement with the United States; reinforces African reform efforts, provides improved access to U.S. credit and technical expertise, and establishes a high-level dialogue on trade and investment in the form of a U.S.–Sub-Saharan Africa Trade and Economic Forum.

Capacity Building for African Military and Civilian Organizations. These are broad efforts to build professional capacity among African military commanders and civilian defense leaders and provide them with exposure to critical thinking on contemporary global security challenges.

- Africa Center for Strategic Studies: conducts academic programs to counter ideological support for terrorism, foster regional cooperation on security issues, promote democracy, and assist African nations in improving their security and strengthening their defense establishments by promoting good governance, security sector professionalism, and democratic civil-military relations
- Near East–South Asia Center for Strategic Studies: conducts academic programs to counter ideological support for terrorism, foster regional cooperation on security issues, promote democracy, and assist North African nations in improving their security and strengthening their defense establishments by promoting good governance, security sector professionalism, and democratic civil-military relations
- Center for Civil-Military Relations: trains foreign civilian and military participants through resident and nonresident courses at the Naval Postgraduate School; programs assist foreign nations in resolving civil-military issues resulting from defense transformation, stability and support operations, combating terrorism, and other security challenges

- Counterterrorism Fellowship Program: offers education and training to build counterterrorism capabilities in the militaries and civilian agencies of partner nations
- National Guard State Partnership Program: pairs state National Guard units with foreign militaries to build partnerships, conduct training, and enhance familiarity. Program is overseen by combatant commander in coordination with the U.S. chief of mission.
- Joint Combined Exchange and Training: provides U.S. Special Operations Forces opportunities to maintain their skills and to train foreign militaries and other groups to combat terrorism overseas
- Golden Spear: ongoing multilateral working group of East African countries and U.S. Central Command to discuss and collaborate on strategic issues with particular reference to natural and manmade disaster response preparedness.

Conflict Resolution Processes. These measures are aimed at mitigating sectarian divisions and promoting peaceful interethnic or religious coexistence and tolerance in order to stem violence and prevent refuge and use by terrorist groups.

- Peace and Reconciliation Programs: promote reintegration of ex-combatants, political party training, election assistance, governance programs, textbooks, health services, civil society strengthening, anticorruption, agricultural production, education, and anti–gender-based-violence programs
- Global Peace Operations Initiative: aims to train and equip 75,000 military troops, a majority of them African, for peacekeeping operations by 2010; will also promote the development of an international transportation and logistics support system for peacekeepers, and is encouraging an information exchange to improve international coordination of peace operations training and exercises in Africa
- Humanitarian Mine Action: protects victims of conflict and creates conditions for the return of refugees and displaced persons to their homes; restores access to land and infrastructure; promotes conflict resolution and peacebuilding efforts; develops host nation capacity to effectively manage and execute mine action.

Public Information Campaigns. These are used to explain U.S. foreign policy, delegitimize terrorist actions, foster free and independent media, and promote cultural, educational, and professional ties between the United States and partner countries.

- Voice of America, al-Hurra TV, Radio Sawa: broadcasts news and information in countries that lack strong, independent media
- American Corners: partners U.S. missions and host institutions to provide access to current and reliable information about the United States via book collections, Internet access, and local programming available to the general public
- Increased public diplomacy: encourages participation by senior U.S. Government and Arabic-speaking officials, especially diplomats, in outreach activities with regional media, universities, secondary schools, and mosques
- International Information Programs: sponsor media programs, publications, and special events to encourage international support for the war on terrorism, understanding of U.S. foreign policy, and good governance in partner countries
- Professional and Educational Exchange Programs: bring current or potential leaders in government, politics, media, education, and other fields to meet and confer with their professional counterparts and experience the United States firsthand.

Coordinating Modalities. These are partnership forums to ensure that separate security and counterterrorism efforts do not duplicate one another and work in tandem under the auspices of a single, well-planned, and coherent framework.

- Africa Clearinghouse Initiative: multinational forum for officials from the North Atlantic Treaty Organization (NATO), United Nations, the European Union, and African governments to share information about security issues, security assistance programs, and counterterrorism activities
- Mediterranean Dialogue: ongoing cooperation between NATO countries and North African countries; combats terrorism through information sharing and maritime cooperation
- G–8 Counterterrorism Action Group: meets to facilitate cooperation on counterterrorism policy, including international assistance to partner countries
- Proliferation Security Initiative: collaborates on implementation of effective measures, either alone or in concert with other states, for interdicting the transfer or transport of weapons of mass destruction, their delivery systems, and related materials to and from states and nonstate actors of proliferation concern. Participants conduct exercises together, share information, and have meetings of operational experts.

U.S. Support for African Counterterrorism Capacities

Finally, it is useful to consider the big picture of U.S. assistance to Africa from the fiscal years 2004 to 2007. Figures presented here are drawn from Congressional Budget Justifications and are rounded. Overall, Africa receives approximately $51 million annually from the International Military Education and Training (IMET) and Foreign Military Financing (FMF) accounts. For the International Narcotics Control and Law Enforcment and Non-proliferation, Anti-terrorism, De-mining, and Related Programs accounts, the annual combined total ranges from $33 million to $62 million. Annual Economic Support Funds (ESF) spending in Africa is between $200 million and $300 million. Finally, the total for "softer" accounts is between $2.7 billion and $3.5 billion per year.[8] This summary excludes efforts of the Millennium Challenge Account, which estimates committing more than $2 billion to Africa by 2007. It also excludes Egypt— the second largest recipient of U.S. assistance worldwide—whose annual sum for ESF, FMF, and IMET has averaged above $3 billion.

Conclusion

The investment made in counterterrorism efforts by both African governments and organizations and their foreign partners obviously has been substantial. The impact of individual programs, however, remains difficult to gauge, and all require program-by-program and country-by-country evaluation. Nonetheless, 5 years after the September 11 attacks in the United States, it is possible to assess the remaining terrorist threats and vulnerabilities to terrorist operations that exist in Africa and to identify further actions required to address these dynamics.

Limited and Specific Terrorist Threats

As detailed in chapter 1, the threat from transnational terrorists such as al Qaeda and its associated movements, and from domestic terrorist groups operating in Africa, is limited and specific. The number of hardened extremists and their core operatives and supporters is finite and generally restricted to key areas of Somalia and East Africa, the Trans-Sahara area, and Southern Africa. In many ways, however, the limited nature of the threat makes it harder to combat effectively: operatives are fewer in number, without significant bases, and easily disperse within innocent civilian populations in dense urban areas and arid lands.

While current African and U.S. counterterrorism efforts appear to have disrupted terrorists' abilities to launch further catastrophic attacks in Africa since 2002, there has been no absence of terrorist activity in the region. However, U.S. counterterrorism efforts have not resulted in the seizure of key al Qaeda operatives based in the

Horn of Africa and East Africa, prevented the expansion of territorial control and influence by al Qaeda–associated movements in Africa (including militants associated with al Ittihad al Islami, the Salafist Group for Preaching and Combat [*Groupe Salafiste pour la Predication et le Combat*, or GSPC], and the Salafiya Jihadiya networks in North Africa), or decreased ideological support for extremism on the continent. In addition, efforts to build the counterterrorism capacities of African governments through partnership and training have had limited success.

In Africa, foreign terrorists remain successful at integrating into local contexts. They often enter African countries on credible pretexts and establish family, business, and criminal ties to garner local protection. Foreign operational organizers and planners can discreetly cultivate local support, either through the persuasive power of money and ideology, or by trying to appropriate local conflicts and grievances as synonymous with their own agenda. At the same time, in an effort to secure foreign support against their local enemies and link up with a wider, global jihad, a growing number of local militant groups appear to be seeking out affiliation with terrorists such as al Qaeda.

Even if these threats are limited in number, the opportunities for their success are significant. Vulnerabilities to terrorism are rife across the continent. Porous borders, corrupt officials, available weapons, numerous soft Western targets, and the large number of disenfranchised, often politically marginalized people—all of these provide opportunities for foreign terrorist operatives to gain operational access to Africa and to initiate a process of radicalization and recruitment locally. Terrorists have also proven successful at coopting a variety of "extremist force multipliers" in Africa, including local shari'a courts, the staff of some Islamic charities, radical preachers from the continent or from abroad, criminal networks used for smuggling, and even some legal businesses.

Responding to African Terrorism Vulnerabilities

The overall U.S. Government response to terrorist vulnerabilities in Africa appears to address the key variables that enable terrorists to penetrate and operate in a given country. This includes programs to identify terrorist leaders and foot soldiers, efforts to reduce terrorists' freedom of movement and access to physical safe havens, support for regulatory and monitoring mechanisms to prevent the financing of terrorism, and programs to reduce ideological support for terrorism and extremism. However, even if U.S. Government programs are targeted to the correct vulnerabilities, the question that must be answered concerns the extent to which these programs are having the necessary impact. Given the persistence of the vulnerabilities identified above, the answer must unfortunately be that the majority are not yet having the required impact to safeguard African and American interests. While some efforts such as the Terrorist Interdiction Program are already paying off, most cannot fairly be evaluated for several—and in some cases many—more years to come.

Given the persistence, if not expansion, of terrorist activities across Africa since the September 11 terrorist attacks, current responses clearly are at best containing—but not eliminating—the threats posed by violent extremists, both foreign and local. Further, medium- and long-term responses have not yet ameliorated the socio-economic conditions and public opposition to foreign and national political policies that have fed a rising tide of radicalization toward conservative, if not militant, political Islam. Despite increased foreign aid investments in some parts of Africa, it is necessary to question what signs exist of tangible impacts of international and national development aid investments made after September 11. Further work is also required to build public support against terrorism to isolate extremists and militants from broader society so that investigations and terrorist targeting can be carried out expeditiously and effectively.

Limitations of Security Training. A key component of U.S. counterterrorism efforts in Africa has been to provide targeted training to African militaries and, to a lesser extent, African police forces in two subregions facing the most substantial vulnerabilities. This includes the partner countries that comprise the Trans-Sahara area in northwest Africa that benefit from TSCTP and those in the Horn and East Africa that benefit from CJTF–HOA and EACTI. As detailed above, these efforts have multiple goals. Most obviously, they aim to increase host nations' military professionalism and access to interoperable equipment in order to enhance their direct action capacity against terrorists.

Small, mobile military and paramilitary police forces are useful in direct action efforts once terrorist targets are identified and provide U.S. forces access and partners in African countries for joint operations. However, terrorists in Africa are hard targets—either operating in distant rural areas or hidden within dense urban areas. While a well-trained security service is needed to take action against these groups, the prerequisite for them to act effectively is intelligence. Further, small and mobile forces will not single-handedly be able to collect sufficient intelligence, consistently monitor vast border areas, or patrol ungoverned spaces. In addition, there is a danger that deploying specialized counterterrorism military forces outside capital cities may increase antagonisms between African governments, rebel movements, and marginalized tribes, who fear that the security forces will act abusively.

This necessarily leads to questions about the breakdown of U.S. resource commitments to combat terrorism in Africa. There is a need to redirect funding from IMET and FMF efforts toward additional programs to promote economic development, access to essential social services, and stronger nonmilitary capacities within African governments' legal, financial, and other sectors. The TSCTP effort is a frequently cited example, given the media spotlight that has focused on training given by U.S. Special Operations Forces to North and West African militaries.

However, if one focuses on TSCTP, the usage of funds does not seem too far out of balance. TSCTP is a $500 million allocation of funds for 10 countries over 5 years. The resulting annual TSCTP investment per African country averages out to $10 million per year, which is then roughly split between hard security efforts and softer nonmilitary, diplomatic, and development efforts. In short, rather than needing to transfer funds from military training to other efforts, there is more likely a need to increase the overall level of commitment in a way that simultaneously balances the distribution of resources between military, intelligence, diplomatic, and developmental initiatives. Further, efforts are required to ensure that African public perceptions and concerns about the balance in U.S. counterterrorism support are taken into account.

Further Capacity Building Required. To address the limitations of a military-focused counterterrorism response, additional security training efforts are required for police forces, intelligence services, border and customs control officers, port authorities, and other parts of African government bureaucracies. These must complement the creation of specialized counterterrorism forces by creating a broad capacity across the spectrum of African government services to monitor their areas of expertise and gather and disseminate information on active and evolving threats to allow for a coordinated counterterrorism response.

It is a major strength that the U.S. Government has such a wide range of programs designed to provide exactly this sort of assistance in improving the nonmilitary aspects of African "homeland security" and building antiterrorism capacities. However, there are a number of requirements for this assistance to become more effective than it has been in Africa thus far. First and foremost, such programs should not be implemented in an ad hoc manner across the continent. Rather, every African country—starting particularly with those countries facing significant and moderate vulnerabilities—should receive every form of assistance. It makes little sense to help an African country improve its legal framework to combat terrorism if that country lacks the necessary police and judicial capacities to implement the framework. Similarly, it makes little sense to build an effective financial monitoring and regulation capacity if terrorists can continue to access funds through criminal endeavors or the transport of funds via couriers past weak border, customs, and ports controls.

Finally, unless such capacity building efforts are expanded over time to cover the entire continent, there is a danger that efforts to close down terrorists' potential for operations in one country simply push that problem to other countries. The nature of capacity building assistance to combat terrorism in Africa must be both sustained and broadened. Providing one-off courses to mid-level officials who regularly rotate through different assignments, both terrorism-related and not, is insufficient. The base of counterterrorism professional knowledge must be substantial and widespread enough to create sustainable government capacities that can perform over time, even in the face of many countries' problems with corruption and limited political will and managerial oversight.

Combating Ideological Support for Extremism. A common conclusion of the country studies and subregional summaries of terrorist vulnerabilities in Africa is that ideological support for terrorism may be limited to a handful of militants in each country but that ideological support for extremism may be growing on the continent. This is the case despite the gradual democratization and development of the continent since the early 1990s. First, repressive and unrepresentative governance, combined with popular anger toward a government's inability to effect positive change, may preclude options for nonviolent political reform and lead to militancy. Second, high rates of poverty, unemployment, and other factors leading to marginalization of entire social groups are persistent grievances. Third, Africans—both Muslim and non-Muslim— are often widely opposed to U.S. foreign policies in the Middle East, as well as the conduct of the war on terrorism and the war in Iraq. In this context, Southern Africa has become a hub for foreign fundamentalist groups, including Jama'at al Tabliq and a number of Islamic charities associated with terrorism in other countries. All of these factors combine to make extremist and terrorist indoctrination, recruitment, and training highly possible.

These problems persist despite U.S. investments in good governance, democratization and conflict resolution, economic development, and strategic communications, as outlined above. First, combating ideological support for terrorism and extremism is a declared priority, but no obvious strategy is currently in place or being effectively implemented for either Africa as a whole or on a consistent country-by-country basis. In fact, U.S. efforts to promote democracy and respect for human rights in Africa are often perceived as casualties in the American effort to strengthen African government partners and build cooperation against terrorism. Second, there is no obvious remedy for the fact that strategic communications and public diplomacy have not succeeded in countering people's genuine opposition to specific U.S. foreign policies—the outcomes of which are regularly broadcast across the world's media.

Third, although the U.S. Government commits hundreds of millions of dollars each year to humanitarian and development initiatives across Africa, their aggregate success over the past four decades has yet to lift the continent out of poverty and recurring catastrophe. This begs a question—the answer to which is outside the scope of this chapter—of what the U.S. Government is doing differently in providing aid to Africa today that is more likely to yield success, "win hearts and minds," and prevent terrorists from exploiting African grievances.

A fourth concern about combating ideological support for terrorism relates to ongoing African conflict and civil tensions. Terrorists, particularly al Qaeda and affiliated movements, often gain access and build support in the African context by coopting local grievances. This is particularly the case in the Trans-Sahara and the Horn of Africa areas, where militant Islamist movements have made common cause with tribal or clan groups that are engaged in conflicts against national political structures. In particular, the GSPC can only function in northern Mali with the cooperation of elements of the Tuareg tribe, while militants in Somalia who associated with the Supreme Council of Islamic Courts and al Ittihad al Islami rely heavily on support from southern Somali clans that are opposed to the Transitional Federal Government.

Coordinating African Counterterrorism. Given the complexity of terrorist threats and vulnerabilities in Africa and the multifaceted counterterrorism response that is under way, a coordinated response strategy involving the available diplomatic, intelligence, military, and development tools is imperative. As mentioned above, the U.S. Government first needs to ensure that all such tools are made available in every African country, particularly those facing significant and moderate levels of vulnerability. Second, even where all of these approaches are being implemented simultaneously, intra- and interagency coordination will be a key to success, especially at the field level.

First, broad multi-sector counterterrorism efforts such as EACTI and TSCTP must go beyond coordinating funding appeals to congressional appropriators to become interagency operational partnerships. While headquarters-level coordination efforts such as the Regional Action Plan and National Implementation Plan processes are often useful in the planning stages, further efforts are likely required to ensure coordinated action on the ground in Africa. Efforts through the State Department's Office for the Coordinator for Counterterrorism known as Regional Security Initiatives (RSIs) to promote field-level coordination of diplomatic, developmental, military, and intelligence efforts are already geared toward this end and require serious engagement by all parties. Thus far, however, on the African continent, only the Horn and East Africa area have benefited from RSI efforts in a meeting that took place in May 2006. Further, such meetings held at the behest of officials in Washington, DC, need to develop into lasting interagency partnerships within Africa. In addition to applying this model to the planning and implementation of EACTI, CJTF–HOA, and TSCTP, a similar initiative for Southern Africa would help U.S. priorities fall into line with the distribution of terrorist threats and vulnerabilities across the continent.

Second, U.S. counterterrorism efforts in Africa too often appear to fall at one of two extremes. On the one hand, aggressive counterterrorism efforts in a small number of countries focus on achieving short-term success through direct action against terrorists, wherein intelligence support is critical to track and remove high-value terrorist targets. On the other hand, in the remainder of African countries, long-term transformative efforts are under way in the expectation that limited investments in capacity building, diplomacy, and development assistance will create effective partnerships and undermine public support for terrorism and extremism.

In order to find the best middle ground, U.S. counterterrorism efforts in Africa require further information support to design effective strategies to build counterterrorism coalitions that include partners outside of African governments, including opposition politicians, leaders of traditional and reformist Islamic movements, the business community, and civil society at large. In part, this should come from increased country and area expertise on the part of U.S. Government officials working in Africa. Further support for U.S. intelligence efforts may also be required in order to collect and analyze information related to the wider dynamics and complexities of African politics and societies. This would require focusing not only on the intelligence required to capture high-value terrorist targets, but also on issues and trends related to ideological support for extremism.

There is no single key to success in combating terrorism in Africa. However, a number of critical elements can be identified. First,

African governments—despite their commitments to counterterrorism as evidenced by international treaty obligations, regional strategies, and national policy statements—must develop the political will to provide the human and material resources required to implement their commitments. Second, Western governments working in partnership with African countries need to expand and broaden their counterterrorism assistance efforts to build the capacities listed above across the board, not on a case-by-case basis. Without such increased investments, it appears a question of when, not if, another terrorist atrocity will occur on the African continent.

APPENDIXES

APPENDIX ONE

Organization of African Unity Convention on the Prevention and Combating of Terrorism (1999)

The Member States of the Organization of African Unity:

Considering the purposes and principles enshrined in the Charter of the Organization of African Unity, in particular its clauses relating to the security, stability, development of friendly relations and cooperation among its Member States;

Recalling the provisions of the Declaration on the Code of Conduct for Inter-African Relations, adopted by the Thirtieth Ordinary Session of the Assembly of Heads of State and Government of the Organization of African Unity, held in Tunis, Tunisia, from 13 to 15 June 1994;

Aware of the need to promote human and moral values based on tolerance and rejection of all forms of terrorism irrespective of their motivations;

Believing in the principles of international law, the provisions of the Charters of the Organization of African Unity and of the United Nations and the latter's relevant resolutions on measures aimed at combating international terrorism and, in particular, resolution 49/60 of the General Assembly of 9 December 1994, together with the annexed Declaration on Measures to Eliminate International Terrorism as well as resolution 51/210 of the General Assembly of 17 December 1996 and the Declaration to Supplement the 1994 Declaration on Measures to Eliminate International Terrorism, annexed thereto;

Deeply concerned over the scope and seriousness of the phenomenon of terrorism and the dangers it poses to the stability and security of States;

Desirous of strengthening cooperation among Member States in order to forestall and combat terrorism;

Reaffirming the legitimate right of peoples for self-determination and independence pursuant to the principles of international law and the provisions of the Charters of the Organization of African United Nations as well as the African Charter on Human and People's Rights;

Concerned that the lives of innocent women and children are most adversely affected by terrorism;

Convinced that terrorism constitutes a serious violation of human rights and, in particular, the rights to physical integrity, life, freedom and security, and impedes socio-economic development through destabilization of States;

Convinced further that terrorism cannot be justified under any circumstances and, consequently, should be combated in all its forms and manifestations, including those in which States are involved directly or indirectly, without regard to its origin, causes and objectives;

Aware of the growing links between terrorism and organized crime, including the illicit traffic of arms, drugs and money laundering;

Determined to eliminate terrorism in all its forms and manifestations;

HAVE AGREED AS FOLLOWS:

Part 1
Scope of Application

Article 1
For the purposes of this Convention:
1. "Convention" means the OAU Convention on the Prevention and Combating of Terrorism.

2. "State Party"means any Member State of the Organization of African Unity which has ratified or acceded to this Convention and has deposited its instrument of ratification or accession with the Secretary General of the Organization of African Unity.

3. "Terrorist act"means:

   (a) any act which is a violation of the criminal laws of a State Party and which may endanger the life, physical integrity or freedom of, or cause serious injury or death to, any person, any number or group of persons or causes or may cause damage to public or private property, natural resources, environmental or cultural heritage and is calculated or intended to:

(i) intimidate, put in fear, force, coerce or induce any government, body, institution, the general public or any segment thereof, to do or abstain from doing any act, or to adopt or abandon a particular standpoint, or to act according to certain principles; or

(ii) disrupt any public service, the delivery of any essential service to the public or to create a public emergency; or

(iii) create general insurrection in a State;

(b) any promotion, sponsoring, contribution to, command, aid, incitement, encouragement, attempt, threat, conspiracy, organizing, or procurement of any person, with the intent to commit any act referred to in paragraph (a) (i) to (iii).

Article 2
States Parties undertake to:

(a) review their national laws and establish criminal offences for terrorist acts as defined in this Convention and make such acts punishable by appropriate penalties that take into account the grave nature of such offences;

(b) consider, as a matter of priority, the signing or ratification of, or accession to, the international instruments listed in the Annexure, which they have not yet signed, ratified or acceded to; and

(c) implement the actions, including enactment of legislation and the establishment as criminal offences of certain acts as required in terms of the international instruments referred to in paragraph (b) and that States have ratified and acceded to and make such acts punishable by appropriate penalties which take into account the grave nature of those offences;

(d) notify the Secretary General of the OAU of all the legislative measures it has taken and the penalties imposed on terrorist acts within one year of its ratification of, or accession to, the Convention.

Article 3
1. Notwithstanding the provisions of Article 1, the struggle waged by

peoples in accordance with the principles of international law for their liberation or self-determination, including armed struggle against colonialism, occupation, aggression and domination by foreign forces shall not be considered as terrorist acts.

2. Political, philosophical, ideological, racial, ethnic, religious or other motives shall not be a justifiable defence against a terrorist act.

Part II
Areas of Cooperation

Article 4
1. States Parties undertake to refrain from any acts aimed at organizing, supporting, financing, committing or inciting to commit terrorist acts, or providing havens for terrorists, directly or indirectly, including the provision of weapons and their stockpiling in their countries and the issuing of visas and travel documents.

2. States Parties shall adopt any legitimate measures aimed at preventing and combating terrorist acts in accordance with the provisions of this Convention and their respective national legislation, in particular, they shall do the following:

(a) prevent their territories from being used as a base for the planning, organization or execution of terrorists acts or for the participation or collaboration in these acts in any form whatsoever;

(b) develop and strengthen methods of monitoring and detecting plans or activities aimed at the illegal cross-border transportation, importation, export, stockpiling and use of arms, ammunition and explosives and other materials and means of committing terrorist acts;

(c) develop and strengthen methods of controlling and monitoring land, sea and air borders and customs and immigration checkpoints in order to pre-empt any infiltration by individuals or groups involved in the planning, organization and execution of terrorist acts;

(d) strengthen the protection and security of persons, diplomatic and consular missions, premises of regional and international organizations accredited to a State Party, in accordance with the relevant conventions and rules of international law;

(e) promote the exchange of information and expertise on terrorist acts and establish data bases for the collection and analysis of information and data on terrorist elements, groups, movements and organizations;

(f) take all necessary measures to prevent the establishment of terrorist support networks in any form whatsoever;

(g) ascertain, when granting asylum, that the asylum seeker is not involved in any terrorist act;

(h) arrest the perpetrators of terrorist acts and try them in accordance with national legislation, or extradite them in accordance with the provisions of this Convention or extradition treaties concluded between the requesting State and the requested State and, in the absence of a treaty, consider facilitating the extradition of persons suspected of having committed terrorist acts; and

(i) establish effective co-operation between relevant domestic security officials and services and the citizens of the States Parties in a bid to enhance public awareness of the scourge of terrorist acts and the need to combat such acts, by providing guarantees and incentives that will encourage the population to give information on terrorist acts or other acts which may help to uncover such acts and arrest their perpetrators.

Article 5

States Parties shall co-operate among themselves in preventing and combating terrorist acts in conformity with national legislation and procedures of each State in the following areas:

1. States Parties undertake to strengthen the exchange of information among them regarding:

(a) acts and crimes committed by terrorist groups, their leaders and elements, their headquarters and training camps, their means and sources of funding and acquisition of arms, the types of arms, ammunition and explosives used, and other means in their possession;

(b) the communication and propaganda methods and techniques used by the terrorist groups, the behaviour of these groups, the movement of the leaders and elements, as well as their travel documents.

2. States Parties undertake to exchange any information that leads to:

(a) the arrest of any person charged with a terrorist act against the interests of a State Party or against its nationals, or attempted to commit such an act or participated in it as an accomplice or an instigator;

(b) the seizure and confiscation of any type of arms, ammunition, explosives, devices or funds or other instrumentalities of crime used to commit a terrorist act or intended for that purpose.

3. State Parties undertake to respect the confidentiality of the information exchanged among them and not to provide such information to another State that is not party to this Convention, or to a third State Party, without the prior consent of the State from where such information originated.

4. States Parties undertake to promote co-operation among themselves and to help each other with regard to procedures relating to the investigation and arrest of persons suspected of, charged with or convicted of terrorist acts, in conformity with the national law of each State.

5. States Parties shall co-operate among themselves in conducting and exchanging studies and researches on how to combat terrorist acts and to exchange expertise relating to control of terrorist acts.

6. State Parties shall co-operate among themselves, where possible, in providing any available technical assistance in drawing up programmes or organizing, where necessary and for the benefit of their personnel, joint training courses involving one or several States Parties in the area of control of terrorist acts, in order to improve their scientific, technical and operational capacities to prevent and combat such acts.

Part III
State Jurisdiction

Article 6
1. Each State Party has jurisdiction over terrorist acts as defined in Article 1 when:

(a) the act is committed in the territory of that State and the perpetrator of the act is arrested in its territory or outside it if this is punishable by its national law;

(b) the act is committed on board a vessel or a ship flying the flag of that State or an aircraft which is registered under the laws of that State at the time the offence is committed; or

(c) the act is committed by a national or a group or nationals of that State.

2. A State Party may also establish its jurisdiction over any such offence when:

(a) the act is committed against a national of that State; or

(b) the act is committed against a State or government facility of that State abroad, including an embassy or other diplomatic or consular premises, and any other property, of that State; or

(c) the act is committed by a stateless person who has his or her habitual residence in the territory of that State; or

(d) the act is committed on board an aircraft which is operated by any carrier of that State; and

(e) the act is committed against the security of the State Party.

3. Upon ratifying or acceding to this Convention, each State Party shall notify the Secretary General of the Organization of African Unity of the jurisdiction it has established in accordance with paragraph 2 under its national law. Should any change take place, the State Party concerned shall immediately notify the Secretary General.

4. Each State Party shall likewise take such measures as may be necessary to establish its jurisdiction over the acts set forth in Article 1 in cases where the alleged offender is present in its territory and it does not extradite that person to any of the States Parties which have established their jurisdiction in accordance with paragraphs 1 or 2.

Article 7
1. Upon receiving information that a person who has committed or who is alleged to have committed any terrorist act as defined in Article 1 may be present in its territory, the State Party concerned shall take such measures as may be necessary under its national law to investigate the facts contained in the information.

2. Upon being satisfied that the circumstances so warrant, the State Party in whose territory the offender or alleged offender is present shall take the appropriate measures under its national law so as to ensure that person's presence for the purpose of prosecution.

3. Any person against whom the measures referred to in paragraph 2 are being taken shall be entitled to:

(a) communicate without delay with the nearest appropriate representative of the State of which that person is a national or which is otherwise entitled to protect that person's rights or, if that person is a stateless person, the State in whose territory that person habitually resides;

(b) be visited by a representative of that State;

(c) be assisted by a lawyer of his or her choice;

(d) be informed of his or her rights under sub-paragraphs (a), (b) and (c).

4. The rights referred to in paragraph 3 shall be exercised in conformity with the national law of the State in whose territory the offender or alleged offender is present, subject to the provision that the said laws must enable full effect to be given to the purposes for which the rights accorded under paragraph 3 are intended.

Part IV
Extradition

Article 8
1. Subject to the provision of paragraphs 2 and 3 of this Article, the States Parties shall undertake to extradite any person charged with or convicted of any terrorist act carried out on the territory of another State Party and whose extradition is requested by one of the States Parties in conformity with the rules and conditions provided for in this Convention or under extradition agreements between the States Parties and within the limits of their national laws.

2. Any State Party may, at the time of the deposit of its instrument of ratification or accession, transmit to the Secretary General of the OAU the grounds on which extradition may not be granted and shall at the same time indicate the legal basis in its national legislation or international conventions to which it is a party which excludes such extradition. The Secretary General shall forward these grounds to the State Parties.

3. Extradition shall not be granted if final judgement has been passed by a component authority of the requested State upon the person in

respect of the terrorist act or acts for which extradition is requested. Extradition may also be refused if the competent authority of the requested State has decided either not to institute or terminate proceedings in respect of the same act or acts.

4. A State Party in whose territory an alleged offender is present shall be obliged, whether or not the offence was committed in its territory, to submit the case without undue delay to its component authorities for the purpose of prosecution if it does not extradite that person.

Article 9
Each State Party undertakes to include as an extraditable offence any terrorist act as defined in Article 1, in any extradition treaty existing between any of the State Parties before or after the entry into force of this Convention.

Article 10
Exchange of extradition requests between the States Parties to this Convention shall be effected directly either through diplomatic channels or other appropriate organs in the concerned States.

Article 11
Extradition requests shall be in writing, and shall be accompanied in particular by the following:

(a) an original or authenticated copy of the sentence, warrant of arrest or any order or other judicial decision made, in accordance with the procedures laid down in the laws of the requesting State;

(b) a statement describing the offences for which extradition is being requested, indicating the date and place of its commission, the offence committed, any convictions made and a copy of the provisions of the applicable law; and

(c) as comprehensive a description as possible of the wanted person together with any other information which may assist in establishing the person's identity and nationality.

Article 12
In urgent cases, the competent authority of the State making the extradition may, in writing, request that the State seized of the extradition request arrest the person in question provisionally. Such provisional arrest shall be for a reasonable period in accordance with the national law of the requested State.

Article 13

1. Where a State Party receives several extradition requests from different States Parties in respect of the same suspect and for the same or different terrorist acts, it shall decide on these requests having regard to all the prevailing circumstances, particularly the possibility of subsequent extradition, the respective dates of receipt of the requests, and the degree of seriousness of the crime.

2. Upon agreeing to extradite, States Parties shall seize and transmit all funds and related materials purportedly used in the commission of the terrorist act to the requesting State as well as relevant incriminating evidence.

3. Such funds, incriminating evidence and related materials, upon confirmation of their use in the terrorist act by the requested State, shall be transmitted to the requesting State even if, for reasons of death or escape of the accused, the extradition in question cannot take place.

4. The provisions in paragraphs 1, 2 and 3 of this Article shall not affect the rights of any of the States Parties or bona fide third parties regarding the materials or revenues mentioned above.

Part V
Extra-territorial Investigations (Commission Rogatoire)
and Mutual Legal Assistance

Article 14

1. Any State Party may, while recognizing the sovereign rights of States Parties in matters of criminal investigation, request any other State Party to carry out, with its assistance and cooperation, on the latter's territory, criminal investigations related to any judicial proceedings concerning alleged terrorist acts and, in particular:

(a) the examination of witnesses and transcripts of statements made as evidence;

(b) the opening of judicial information;

(c) the initiation of investigation processes;

(d) the collection of documents and recordings or, in their absence, authenticated copies thereof;

(e) conducting inspections and tracing of assets for evidentiary purposes;

(f) executing searches and seizures; and

(g) service of judicial documents.

Article 15
A commission rogatoire may be refused:

(a) where each of the States Parties has to execute a commission rogatoire relating to the same terrorist acts;

(b) if that request may affect efforts to expose crimes, impede investigations or the indictment of the accused in the country requesting the commission rogatoire; or

(c) if the execution of the request would affect the sovereignty of the requested State, its security or public order.

Article 16
The extra-territorial investigation (commission rogatoire) shall be executed in compliance with the provisions of national laws of the requested State. The request for an extra-territorial investigation (commission rogatoire) relating to a terrorist act shall not be rejected on the grounds of the principle of confidentiality of bank operations or financial institutions, where applicable.

Article 17
The States Parties shall extend to each other the best possible mutual police and judicial assistance for any investigation, criminal prosecution or extradition proceedings relating to the terrorist acts as set forth in this Convention.

Article 18
The States Parties undertake to develop, if necessary, especially by concluding bilateral and multilateral agreements and arrangements, mutual legal assistance procedures aimed at facilitating and speeding up investigations and collecting evidence, as well as cooperation between law enforcement agencies in order to detect and prevent terrorist acts.

Part VI
Final Provisions

Article 19
1. This Convention shall be open to signature, ratification or accession by the Member States of the Organization of African Unity.

2. The instruments of ratification or accession to the present Convention shall be deposited with the Secretary General of the Organization of African Unity.

3. The Secretary General of the Organization of African Unity shall inform Member States of the Organization of the deposit of each instrument of ratification or accession.

4. No State Party may enter a reservation which is incompatible with the object and purposes of this Convention.

5. No State Party may withdraw from this Convention except on the basis of a written request addressed to the Secretary General of the Organization of African Unity. The withdrawal shall take effect six months after the date of receipt of the written request by the Secretary General of the Organization of African Unity.

Article 20
1. This Convention shall enter into force thirty days after the deposit of the fifteenth instrument of ratification with the Secretary General of the Organization of African Unity.

2. For each of the States that shall ratify or accede to this Convention shall enter into force thirty days after the date of the deposit by that State Party of its instrument of ratification or accession.

Article 21
1. Special protocols or agreements may, if necessary, supplement the provisions of this Convention.

2. This Convention may be amended if a State Party makes a written request to that effect to the Secretary General of the Organization of African Unity. The Assembly of Heads of State and Government may only consider the proposed amendment after all the States Parties have been duly informed of it at least three months in advance.

3. The amendment shall be approved by a simple majority of the State Parties. It shall come into force for each State which has accepted it in accordance with its constitutional procedures three months after the Secretary General has received notice of the acceptance.

Article 22
1. Nothing in this Convention shall be interpreted as derogating from the general principles of international law, in particular the principles

of international humanitarian law, as well as the African Charter on Human and Peoples' Rights.

2. Any dispute that may arise between the States Parties regarding the interpretation or application of this Convention shall be amicably settled by direct agreement between them. Failing such settlement, any one of the State Parties may refer the dispute to the International Court of Justice in conformity with the Statute of the Court or by arbitration by other States Parties to this Convention.

Article 23
The original of this Convention, of which the Arabic, English, French and Portuguese texts are equally authentic, shall be deposited with the Secretary General of the Organization of African Unity.

Annex: List of International Instruments

(a) Tokyo Convention on Offences and Certain Other Acts Committed on Board Aircraft of 1963;

(b) Montreal Convention for the Suppression of Unlawful Acts against the Safety of Civil Aviation of 1971 and the Protocol thereto of 1984;

(c) New York Convention on the Prevention and Punishment of Crimes against Internationally Protected Persons, including Diplomatic Agents of 1973;

(d) International Convention against the Taking of Hostages of 1979;

(e) Convention on the Physical Protection of Nuclear Material of 1979;

(f) United Nations Convention on the Law of the Sea of 1982;

(g) Protocol for the Suppression of Unlawful Acts of Violence at Airports Serving International Civil Aviation, supplementary to the Convention for the Suppression of Unlawful Acts against the Safety of Civil Aviation of 1988;

(h) Protocol for the Suppression of Unlawful Acts against the Safety of Fixed Platforms located on the Continental Shelf of 1988;

(i) Convention for the Suppression of Unlawful Acts against Maritime Navigation of 1988;

(j) Convention on the Marking of Plastic Explosives of 1991;

(k) International Convention for the Suppression of Terrorist Explosive Bombs of 1997;

(l) Convention on the Prohibition of the Use, Stockpiling, Production and Transfer of Anti-Personnel Mines and on their Destruction of 1997.

APPENDIX TWO

Plan of Action of the African Union
for the Prevention and Combating of Terrorism

Algiers, Algeria
11–14 September 2002

I. Preamble

1. Member States of the African Union have long espoused the need to counter terrorism at both the individual and collective levels. This concern led to the adoption of the Convention on the Prevention and Combating of Terrorism by the 35th Assembly of Heads of State and Government of the Organization of African Unity in Algiers in July 1999.

2. In the Dakar Declaration against Terrorism, adopted by the African Summit of October 2001, Member States reaffirmed their unequivocal rejection of terrorism. The Declaration recognized the destructive effects of terrorism, and the obstacle it poses to development and stability on the African Continent.

3. Eradicating terrorism requires a firm commitment by Member States to pursue common objectives. These include: exchange of information among Member States on the activities and movements of terrorist groups in Africa; mutual legal assistance; exchange of research and expertise; and the mobilization of technical assistance and cooperation, both within Africa and internationally, to upgrade the scientific, technical and operational capacity of Member States.

4. Joint action must be taken at the inter-governmental level. This includes: coordinating border surveillance to stem illegal cross-border movement of goods and persons; developing and strengthening border control-points; and combating the illicit import, export and

stockpiling of arms, ammunition and explosives. These actions would assist in curbing terrorist networks' access to Africa. Informal and illegal channels for the transfer of funds and goods used to finance and support terrorism must be closed.

5. The concerted response reflected in this Plan of Action is situated in the context of the provisions contained in the Constitutive Act establishing the African Union, particularly the principles enunciated in Article 4, and in the operationalization of the New Partnership for Africa's Development (NEPAD) and the Conference on Security, Stability, Development and Co-operation in Africa (CSSDCA).

6. Severe conditions of poverty and deprivation experienced by large sections of the African population provide a fertile breeding ground for terrorist extremism. Few African governments are in a position, on their own, to marshal the requisite resources to combat this threat. Pooling resources, therefore, is essential to ensure the effectiveness of counter-terrorism measures.

7. Terrorism is a violent form of transnational crime that exploits the limits of the territorial jurisdiction of States, differences in governance systems and judicial procedures, porous borders, and the existence of informal and illegal trade and financing networks.

8. The implementation of the Algiers Convention is urgent, given Africa's vital role in the global struggle against terrorism, and its international legal obligations in terms of the United Nations Security Council Resolution 1373.

9. This Plan of Action is intended to give concrete expression to these commitments and obligations, to enhance and promote African countries' access to appropriate counter-terrorism resources through a range of measures establishing a counter-terrorism co-operation framework in Africa. To this end, Member States of the African Union hereby agree to take the measures detailed hereunder, in the spirit of the Constitutive Act of the African Union, particularly Articles 9(e) and 23(2) thereof, on monitoring implementation of the policies and decisions of the Union.

II. General Provisions

10. Member States undertake to:

>   a. sign, ratify and fully implement the Algiers Convention on the Prevention and Combating of Terrorism and, where necessary,

seek the assistance of other Member States or the international community to amend national legislation so as to align such legislation with the provisions of this Convention;

b. sign, ratify and fully implement all relevant international instruments concerning terrorism and, where necessary, seek assistance for amendments to national legislation so as to comply with the provisions of these instruments;

c. encourage interaction amongst various institutional players engaged in counter-terrorism and terrorism prevention activities, namely: legislative authorities; security forces; judicial authorities; financial authorities; investigative authorities, police, border surveillance and customs authorities; the military; civil protection services etc.;

d. take into consideration the intimate relationship between terrorism and related scourges such as drug trafficking, illicit proliferation and trafficking of small arms and light weapons, corruption and money laundering—all of which are variants of transnational organized crime; and

e. promote policies aimed at addressing the root causes of terrorism, in particular poverty, deprivation and marginalization. To this end, steps should be taken for the speedy establishment of the World Solidarity Fund referred to in UN General Assembly Resolution 55/210 adopted on 20 December 2001, and the decisions of the World Summit on Sustainable Development held in Johannesburg from 26 August to 4 September 2002.

III. Specific Provisions

A. Police and Border Control

11. Member States undertake to:

a. enhance border control and surveillance, as well as the necessary means to prevent the forgery and falsification of travel and identity documents;

b. ensure that identity documents contain advanced security features that protect them against forgery;

c. issue machine-readable travel documents that contain security features which protect them against forgery;

d. keep a Passport Stoplist containing information of individuals whose applications would require special attention or who may not be issued with travel documents;

e. check applications against the Passport Stoplist and the population register before the document is issued;

f. develop and upgrade the regulations governing border control and security procedures including land, sea and air exit and entry points so as to curb infiltration and promote co-operation among police agencies having due regard for relevant provisions of relevant regional and continental agreements on the free movement of persons and goods;

g. computerize all points of entry in order to monitor the arrival and departure of all individuals;

h. inspect all passports for authenticity, acceptability and prior endorsement;

i. provide regular training to immigration officials with regard to the profiling of travelers and the verification of the authenticity of documents;

n. ensure that an asylum seeker is not involved, directly or indirectly, in terrorism related activities prior to granting asylum to the concerned person; and

o. expedite the finalization and adoption of the draft Convention on Extradition and the draft Convention on Mutual Legal Assistance.

B. Legislative and Judicial Measures

12. Member States undertake to:

a. amend, where necessary, national laws relating to bail and other criminal procedural issues so as to give effect to the requirements of expeditious investigation and prosecution of those involved directly or indirectly in the crime of terrorism. These measures should include issues such as the protection of witnesses, access to dockets and information, and special arrangements on detention and access to hearings;

b. harmonize the standards and procedures regarding proof for terrorism-related crimes;

c. promote specialized training and reinforce the capacities of the judiciary;

d. harmonize legal frameworks pertaining to the prevention and combating of terrorism;

e. improve knowledge of the legal institutions of Member States, such as the judiciary and the different levels of jurisdiction, and facilitate access to these institutions within the framework of official proceedings initiated by Member States;

f. conclude extradition and mutual legal assistance agreements, where necessary, and adopt the legislation that would enable Member States to cooperate effectively;

g. identify, if need be, the national authorities for processing extradition and mutual legal assistance requests and, where necessary, establish mechanisms to ensure coordination between competent national authorities in this regard;

h. review existing extradition and mutual legal assistance legislation, and adapt such legislation with a view to ensuring effective and expeditious handling of extradition and mutual legal assistance requests;

i. simplify and streamline extradition and mutual legal assistance procedures, including the provision of sufficient information to the concerned States, to enable extradition and mutual legal assistance, as well as explore new arrangements for the transfer of criminal proceedings;

j. give effect to the principle of systematic extradition to the State where the terrorist act has been perpetrated and ensure, in conformity with international law, that claims of political motivation are not recognized as grounds for refusing requests for the extradition of persons directly or indirectly involved in the commission of terrorist acts. If a Member State does not extradite an alleged terrorist, it should take measures to prosecute the person so accused;

k. make provision in the national laws of Member States, for the establishment of jurisdiction over persons accused of terrorist acts, in conformity with relevant international obligations;

l. for purposes of criminal responsibility, place the mastermind, the apologist, the accomplice, the instigator and the sponsor of a terrorist act on the same pedestal as the perpetrator of such an act;

m. describe, in national legislation, a terrorist act as a particularly serious crime, and establish levels of punishment proportionate to the gravity of such acts; and

n. take adequate measures to prevent and outlaw the printing, publication and dissemination, by one or several persons residing on the territory of any Member State, of news items and press releases initiated by apologists of terrorist acts which are prejudicial to the interest and security of any other Member State.

C. Suppressing the Financing of Terrorism

13. Member States undertake to:

a. operationalize the International Convention for the Suppression of the Financing of Terrorism (1999), which criminalizes the act of financing terrorism and makes it mandatory to take all measures to detect, identify and freeze or seize any funds used or allocated for the purpose of committing terrorist acts;

b. carry out a stringent control of funds belonging to individuals, enterprises or organizations suspected of financing terrorist groups. Make it mandatory for financial institutions and other business entities to alert competent authorities in the event of movements of capital suspected of being linked to terrorism;

c. introduce legislation to criminalize the financing of terrorism and money laundering;

d. ensure that financial institutions in Africa take reasonable measures to obtain information about the true identity of the person or institution on whose behalf an account is opened or being operated;

e. put an end to the keeping of anonymous accounts or accounts in obviously fictitious names. Financial institutions should be required to identify such accounts, on the basis of official or reliable identifying documents, and record the identity of their clients, either occasional or casual, when establishing business relations or conducting fiduciary transactions, renting safe deposit boxes or performing large cash transactions;

f. regulate the public collection of funds and ensure that the proceeds are not used to finance terrorism;

g. confiscate movable and immovable assets intended for the financing of terrorist acts, and which may give shelter to terrorist groups and elements, and access to their support networks;

h. establish financial intelligence units in Member States in accordance with the recommendations of international financial institutions and, where necessary, seek bilateral, regional or international assistance;

i. train personnel in charge of preventing and combating money laundering, with international technical assistance where necessary; and

j. cooperate with International Financial Institutions for the development of a global, comprehensive, Anti-Money Laundering and Combating the Financing of Terrorism (AML/CFT) methodology and assessment process.

D. Exchange of Information

14. Member States undertake to:

a. enhance exchange of information and intelligence on:

i. the activities and criminal acts of terrorist groups as well as their regroupement and training camps; their means and sources of finance; the weapons, types of arms, ammunitions and explosives used, and other attack, massacre and destruction devices; and

ii. the communication and propaganda devices used by terrorist groups, their methods of work and means of travel as well as travel documents used, and steps that should be taken to counter the falsification and forgery of identity and travel documents.

b. enhance intelligence exchange, training and capacity-building (with the assistance of INTERPOL), including basic and improved specialized training for staff in charge of combating terrorism;

c. identify individuals, groups and entities engaged in terrorist activities, including those who encourage and support such individuals, groups or entities financially or by other means, and take action under appropriate national laws against such individuals, groups and entities;

d. share lessons learnt and experience gained on counterterrorist tactics;

e. establish a common Terrorism Activity Reporting (TAR) schedule as data collection instrument on names of identified organizations, persons, places and resources by Member States. The TAR should then provide the source information to the content of an AU database that shall provide timely exchange of information, experience and lessons learnt on counter terrorism tactics over a secured electronic network;

f. facilitate exchange of experience and lessons learnt on counter-terrorism tactics, including evaluation of emergency communication and response systems;

g. establish or develop anti-terrorist units and provide them with access to specific equipment and the requisite training to enhance the efficiency of their counter-terrorism units, particularly in matters of intervention, protection and detection;

h. establish a register within the Departments, responsible for processing travel documents, to ensure that such documents are only issued to those persons entitled thereto; and

i. encourage access to specialized training and capacity-building in counter-terrorism operations relying on the resources available in Africa and internationally.

E. Coordination at Regional, Continental, and International Levels

15. Member States undertake to:

a. establish contact points at regional level to follow-up and liaise on matters relating to implementation of the Plan of Action; and

b. prepare model legislation and guidelines to assist Member States to adapt their legislation to the provisions of the relevant African Union and international instruments.

F. Role of the Peace and Security Council (PSC)

16. Under Article 7 of the Protocol relating to the Establishment of the Peace and Security Council of the African Union, the Peace and

Security Council is charged to, among other things, ensure the implementation of the Convention on the Prevention and Combating of Terrorism and other relevant international, continental and regional conventions and instruments, and harmonize and coordinate efforts at regional and continental levels to combat international terrorism.* It is understood that pending the entry into force of the Peace and Security Council, the Central Organ shall assume responsibilities for all matters relating to terrorism. The Peace and Security Council shall:

a. prepare, publicize and regularly review a list of persons, groups and entities involved in terrorist acts. The list shall be drawn up on the basis of precise information or material proof from Member States and other sources that indicate that a decision has been taken by a competent authority in respect of the persons, groups and entities concerned. To this end, the Council shall make appropriate contacts with Member States as well as non-Member States on all matters relating to terrorism and the activities of terrorist groups;

b. request all Member States, on an annual basis, to report on the steps taken to prevent and combat terrorism and, where appropriate, on the implementation of the Algiers Convention;

c. present an annual report to the Assembly of the Union on the situation in the continent as far as terrorism is concerned; and

d. monitor and make recommendations on the implementation of this Plan of Action.

G. Role of the Commission

17. The Commissioner in charge of Peace and Security shall be entrusted with the task of following-up on terrorist related matters, as provided for under the Statutes of the Commission of the African Union.

18. The Commissioner, who will be assisted by professional staff, shall, inter alia:

---

* The delegation of Nigeria submitted a Terrorism Activity Reporting Format to the Commission during the meeting for the consideration by member states in the future.

a. examine the reports submitted by Member States in relation to paragraph 16.b. of the Plan of Action;

b. review and make recommendations to update the Plan of Action;

c. provide advice on matters pertaining to counter-terrorism action including preparation of model legislation and guidelines to assist Member States; and

d. follow-up with Member States and any other States on decisions taken by the Peace and Security Council and other organs of the Union on terrorism and activities of terrorist groups.

H. African Center for the Study and Research on Terrorism

19. Member States undertake to establish an African Center for Study and Research on Terrorism in Algiers, Algeria.

20. The African Center for the Study and Research on Terrorism shall serve to centralize information, studies and analyses on terrorism and terrorist groups and develop training programs by organizing, with the assistance of international partners, training schedules, meetings, and symposia.

21. Member States request the Commission to submit proposals on the modalities for the establishment of the Center, including the financial aspects.

APPENDIX THREE

Protocol to the Organization of African Unity Convention on the Prevention and Combating of Terrorism (2004)

We, the Heads of State and Government of the Member States of the African Union;

Gravely concerned at the increasing incidence of terrorist acts worldwide, including in Africa, and the growing risks of linkages between terrorism and mercenarism, weapons of mass destruction, drug trafficking, corruption, transnational organized crimes, money laundering, and the illicit proliferation of small arms;

Determined to combat terrorism in all its forms and manifestations and any support thereto in Africa;

Aware of the capabilities of the perpetrators of terrorist acts to use sophisticated technology and communication systems for organizing and carrying out their terrorist acts;

Bearing in Mind that the root causes of terrorism are complex and need to be addressed in a comprehensive manner;

Convinced that acts of terrorism cannot be justified under any circumstances;

Determined to ensure Africa's active participation, cooperation and coordination with the international community in its determined efforts to combat and eradicate terrorism;

Guided by the principles and regulations enshrined in international conventions and the relevant decisions of the United Nations (UN) to prevent and combat terrorism, including resolution 1373 adopted by the Security Council on 28 September 2001, and the relevant General Assembly resolutions;

Reaffirming our commitment to the OAU Convention for the Elimination of Mercenarism in Africa, adopted in Libreville, Gabon, in July 1977;

Reaffirming our commitment to the Code of Conduct for Inter-African Relations adopted by the Thirtieth Ordinary Session of the Assembly of Heads of State and Government of the Organization of African Unity (OAU) held in Tunis, Tunisia, from 13 to 15 June 1994;

Reaffirming our commitment to the OAU Convention on the Prevention and Combating of Terrorism adopted by the 35th OAU Summit in Algiers, Algeria, in July 1999;

Recalling the Dakar Declaration against terrorism adopted by the African Summit meeting, held in Dakar, Senegal, in October 2001;

Further Recalling the Plan of Action for the Prevention and Combating of Terrorism adopted by the Intergovernmental High Level meeting of Member States of the African Union, held in Algiers, Algeria, in September 2002;

Considering the Constitutive Act of the African Union, as well as the Protocol Relating to the Establishment of the Peace and Security Council of the African Union adopted by the Inaugural Summit of the Union in Durban, South Africa, in July 2002;

Reiterating our conviction that terrorism constitutes a serious violation of human rights and a threat to peace, security, development, and democracy;

Stressing the imperative for all Member States of the African Union to take all necessary measures to protect their populations from acts of terrorism and to implement all relevant continental and international humanitarian and human rights instruments; and

Desirous of ensuring the effective implementation of the OAU Convention on the Prevention and Combating of Terrorism.

Hereby agree as follows:

Article 1
Definitions

1. "Assembly" means the Assembly of Heads of State and Government of the African Union;

2. "Chairperson" means the Chairperson of the African Union;

3. "Commission" means the Commission of the African Union;

4. "Commissioner" means the Commissioner in charge of peace and security issues at the Commission of the African Union;

5. "Convention" means the OAU Convention on the Prevention and Combating of Terrorism adopted by the 35th OAU Summit in Algiers in July 1999;

6. "Member State" means any Member State of the African Union;

7. "Peace and Security Council (PSC)" means the Peace and Security Council of the African Union;

8. "Plan of Action" means the African Union Plan of Action on the Prevention and Combating of Terrorism in Africa;

9. "Protocol" means this Protocol to the Convention;

10. "Regional Mechanisms" means the African Regional Mechanisms for conflict prevention, management and resolution as established by the Regional Economic Communities;

11. "State Party" means any Member State of the African Union which has ratified or acceded to this Protocol;

12. "Terrorist Act" means any act as defined in Articles 1 and 3 of the Convention;

13. "Union" means the African Union;

14. "Weapons of Mass Destruction (WMD)" means biological, chemical and nuclear devices and explosives and their means of delivery.

Article 2
Purpose

1. This Protocol is adopted pursuant to Article 21 of the Convention as a supplement to the Convention.

2. Its main purpose is to enhance the effective implementation of the Convention and to give effect to Article 3(d) of the Protocol. Relating to the Establishment of the Peace and Security Council of the African Union, on the need to coordinate and harmonize continental efforts in the prevention and combating of terrorism in all its aspects, as well as the implementation of other relevant international instruments.

Article 3
Commitments by States Parties

1. States Parties commit themselves to implement fully the provisions of the Convention. They also undertake, among other things, to:

    a. take all necessary measures to protect the fundamental human rights of their populations against all acts of terrorism;

    b. prevent the entry into, and the training of terrorist groups on their territories;

    c. identify, detect, confiscate and freeze or seize any funds and any other assets used or allocated for the purpose of committing a terrorist act, and to establish a mechanism to use such funds to compensate victims of terrorist acts or their families;

    d. establish national contact points in order to facilitate the timely exchange and sharing of information on terrorist groups and activities at the regional, continental and international levels, including the cooperation of States for suppressing the financing of terrorism;

    e. take appropriate actions against the perpetrators of mercenarism as defined in the OAU Convention for the Elimination of Mercenarism in Africa, adopted in Libreville, in 1977, and other relevant applicable international instruments;

    f. strengthen national and regional measures in conformity with relevant continental and international Conventions and Treaties, to prevent the perpetrators of terrorist acts from acquiring weapons of mass destruction;

    g. cooperate with the international community in the implementation of continental and international instruments related to weapons of mass destruction;

    h. submit reports to the PSC on an annual basis, or at such regular intervals as shall be determined by the PSC, on measures taken to prevent and combat terrorism as provided for in the Convention, the AU Plan of Action and in this Protocol;

i. report to the PSC all terrorist activities in their countries as soon as they occur;

j. become parties to all continental and international instruments on the prevention and combating of terrorism; and

k. outlaw torture and other degrading and inhumane treatment, including discriminatory and racist treatment of terrorist suspects, which are inconsistent with international law.

2. States Parties shall implement the provisions of paragraph 1 above on the basis of all relevant African and international Conventions and Treaties, in conformity with Article 22 of the Convention.

Article 4
Mechanism for Implementation

The Peace and Security Council (PSC) shall be responsible for harmonizing and coordinating continental efforts in the prevention and combating of terrorism. In pursuing this endeavor, the PSC shall:

a. establish operating procedures for information gathering, processing and dissemination;

b. establish mechanisms to facilitate the exchange of information among States Parties on patterns and trends in terrorist acts and the activities of terrorist groups and on successful practices on combating terrorism;

c. present an annual report to the Assembly of the Union on the situation of terrorism on the Continent;

d. monitor, evaluate and make recommendations on the implementation of the Plan of Action and programmes adopted by the African Union;

e. examine all reports submitted by States Parties on the implementation of the provisions of this Protocol; and

f. establish an information network with national, regional and international focal points on terrorism.

Article 5
The Role of the Commission

1. Under the leadership of the Chairperson of the Commission, and in conformity with Article 10 paragraph 4 of the Protocol Relating to the Establishment of the Peace and Security Council, the Commissioner in charge of Peace and Security shall be entrusted with the task of following-up on matters relating to the prevention and combating of terrorism.

2. The Commissioner shall be assisted by the Unit established within the Peace and Security Department of the Commission and the African Centre for the Study and Research on Terrorism, and shall, among other things:

a. provide technical assistance on legal and law enforcement matters, including on matters relating to combating the financing of terrorism, the preparation of model laws and guidelines to help Member States to formulate legislation and related measures for the prevention and combating of terrorism;

b. follow-up with Member States and with regional mechanisms on the implementation of decisions taken by the PSC and other Organs of the Union on terrorism related matters;

c. review and make recommendations on up-dating the programmes of the Union for the prevention and combating of terrorism and the activities of the African Centre for the Study and Research on Terrorism;

d. develop and maintain a database on a range of issues relating to terrorism including experts and technical assistance available;

e. maintain contacts with regional and international organizations and other entities dealing with issues of terrorism; and

f. provide advice and recommendations to Member States on a needs basis, on how to secure technical and financial assistance in the implementation of continental and international measures against terrorism.

Article 6
The Role of Regional Mechanisms

Regional mechanisms shall play a complementary role in the

implementation of this Protocol and the Convention. They shall among other activities undertake the following:

a. establish contact points on terrorism at the regional level;

b. liaise with the Commission in developing measures for the prevention and combating of terrorism;

c. promote cooperation at the regional level, in the implementation of all aspects of this Protocol and the Convention, in accordance with Article 4 of the Convention;

d. harmonize and coordinate national measures to prevent and combat terrorism in their respective Regions;

e. establish modalities for sharing information on the activities of the perpetrators of terrorist acts and on the best practices for the prevention and combating of terrorism;

f. assist Member States to implement regional, continental and international instruments for the prevention and combating of terrorism; and

g. report regularly to the Commission on measures taken at the regional level to prevent and combat terrorist acts.

Article 7
Settlement of Disputes

1. Any dispute or differences between States Parties arising from interpretation or application of the provisions of this Protocol shall be resolved amicably through direct consultations between the States Parties concerned.

2. In the event of failure to settle the dispute under sub paragraph 1 above, either State Party may refer the dispute to the Assembly through the Chairperson, pending the entry into force of the Court of Justice of the African Union, which shall have jurisdiction over such disputes.

3. In the case where either or both States Parties are not Members of the Court of Justice of the African Union, either or both State Parties may refer the dispute to the International Court of Justice for a settlement in conformity with its Statutes.

Article 8
Extradition

1. The Convention shall constitute an adequate legal basis for extradition for States Parties that do not have extradition arrangements.

2. Should any dispute arise between States Parties on the interpretation or applicability of any existing bilateral extradition agreement or arrangement, the provisions of the Convention shall prevail with respect to extradition.

Article 9
Signature, Ratification, and Accession

1. The present Protocol shall be open for signature, ratification or accession by the Member States of the Union in accordance with their respective constitutional procedures.

2. The ratification of or accession to this Protocol shall require the prior ratification of or accession to the Convention by Member States concerned.

Article 10
Entry Into Force

This Protocol shall enter into force thirty days after the deposit of the fifteenth (15th) instrument of ratification or accession.

Article 11
Amendments

1. Any State Party may propose amendment(s) to this Protocol by submitting a written request to the Commission, which shall circulate the said proposed amendments to all States Parties thereof.

2. The amendment(s) shall be approved by a simple majority of States Parties.

3. The amendment(s) approved shall enter into force for each State Party which has accepted it, in accordance with its constitutional procedures, three months after the Chairperson of the Commission has received notice of the acceptance.

Article 12
Depository Authority

This Protocol and all instruments of ratification or accession shall be deposited with the Chairperson of the Commission, who shall transmit certified true copies to all Member States and notify them of the dates of deposit of instruments of ratification by Member States and shall register it with the United Nations and any other Organization as may be decided by the Union.

Adopted by the Third Ordinary Session of the Assembly of the African Union

Addis Ababa, 8 July 2004

APPENDIX FOUR

Modalities for the Functioning of the African Centre for the Study and Research on Terrorism (2005)

I. Establishment

1. The African Centre for the Study and Research on Terrorism (herein after referred to as the Centre) is established as constituted under Section H, Paragraphs 19 to 21 of the AU Plan of Action on the Prevention and Combating of Terrorism and pursuant to the relevant decisions adopted by the policy Organs of the Union including in particular, Assembly/AU/Dec.15 (II); EX.CL/Dec.13 (II); EX/CL/Dec.82 (IV); and EX.CL/Dec.126 (V).

2. The Centre is established as a structure of the Commission, in conformity with the Protocol to the OAU Convention on the Prevention and Combating of Terrorism, which confer on the Peace and Security Council of the African Union, the responsibility for implementing regional, continental and international counter-terrorism instruments as well as harmonize and coordinate continental efforts in the prevention and combating of terrorism.

II. Headquarters

The Headquarters of the Centre shall be in Algiers, Algeria. The African Union shall enter into a Host Agreement with the host country based on the practice and principles of the African Union and the international rules governing such agreements.

III. Operational Status

1. The Centre shall:

   a. be a structure of the Commission of the African Union, to strengthen the capacity of the Union to deal with issues relating to

184

the prevention and combating of Terrorism. It shall function as a research centre of excellence in matters concerning the prevention and combating of terrorism in Africa;

b. serve the interest of the African Union, in providing expertise in matters relating to the prevention and combating of terrorism in Africa;

c. be guided by the objectives and principles enshrined in the Constitutive Act of the African Union, the Protocol Relating to the Establishment of the Peace and Security Council of the African Union, the OAU Convention on the Prevention and Combating of Terrorism and its Protocol thereto, and the Plan of Action adopted in September 2002, and other relevant instruments and decisions of the Union, as well as the Charter of the United Nations, and other relevant international legal instruments that African countries have acceded to;

d. function in coordination with National Focal Points designated by Member States;

e. develop its curriculum, programme of activities and budget for each year, in consultation with the National Focal points.

IV. Purpose
The purpose of the Centre is to contribute to and strengthen the capacity of the African Union in the prevention and combating of terrorism in Africa, with the ultimate objective of eliminating the threat posed by terrorism to peace, security, stability and development in Africa. To this end, the Centre shall serve to collect and centralize information, studies and analyses on terrorism and terrorist groups and develop training programs by organizing, with the assistance of international partners, training schedules, meetings and symposia.

V. Functions
1. Pursuant to the purpose stated in Section IV above, the functions of the Centre shall be to:

a. assist Member States of the African Union in developing strategies for the prevention and combating of terrorism;

b. establish operating procedures for information gathering, processing and dissemination;

c. provide technical and expert advice on the implementation of the African Union counter-terrorism regimes, in particular, the 1999 OAU Convention and its Protocol thereto, the Plan of Action on the Prevention and Combating of Terrorism, as well as on the updating and strengthening of policies and programmes of the Union relating to counter-terrorism;

d. develop and maintain a database on a range of issues relating to the prevention and combating of terrorism, particularly on terrorist groups and their activities in Africa, as well as on experts and technical assistance available. Such a database as well as analyses shall be accessible by all Member States of the Union;

e. promote the coordination and standardization of efforts aimed at enhancing the capacity of Member States to prevent and combat terrorism;

f. initiate and disseminate research studies and policy analyses periodically to sensitize Member States, based on the current trends, and/or on the demand of Member State(s). The Centre shall publish, periodically its research and analyses, in an "African Journal for the Prevention and Combating of Terrorism";

g. develop cooperation and assistance programmes with similar and/or interested institutions at the national, regional, continental and international levels, in the areas of research, information gathering and analyses on issues relating to the prevention and combating of terrorism;

h. undertake research and converging studies on other global security problems with links to terrorism, which pose a threat to peace and security in Africa;

i. develop capacity for early warning to encourage early response, integrating the concept of Preventive Management of Crisis;
j. provide technical and expert advice on how best Africa can contribute in a more meaningful way to the international campaign against terrorism, particularly the implementation of relevant international instruments by Member States of the African Union;

k. undertake studies and make recommendations on strengthening and standardization of legal norms and cooperation in matters of information-sharing among Member States, mutual assistance, extradition, police and border control (including land, maritime and air) in Africa;

l. conduct studies and analyses on the best strategies and methods for suppressing the financing of terrorism;

m. organize workshops, seminars, symposia and training programs for enhancing the capacity of Member States and Regional Mechanisms in the prevention and combating of terrorism in Africa;

n. submit annual reports on its activities to the Chairperson of the Commission, for consideration by the policy Organs of the Union. The annual report shall include a financial statement on the activities undertaken in the previous year and the budget of activities envisaged for the next fiscal year.

2. The Centre may also carry out such duties as may be assigned to it by the Commission of the African Union or the Peace and Security Council, on matters relating to the prevention and combating of terrorism in Africa.

VI. Conduct of Business
1. Given the sensitive nature of the issues the Centre will be dealing with, and in order to safeguard its credibility, the Centre shall:

a. maintain a degree of confidentiality and tight security procedures in the collection and dissemination of information and data on terrorism;

b. ensure that the information it publishes or disseminates is reliable and verifiable;

c. be guided by the academic and ethical code of conduct for research and analysis;

d. organize regularly, symposia, at the level of all Member States to raise awareness, address the prevailing challenges, and to promote efforts aimed at preventing and combating terrorism in Africa.

VII. Composition and Structure
1. The Centre shall be headed by a Director. The Director shall report to the Chairperson of the Commission through the Commissioner for Peace and Security. The Commission shall work out a detailed

Organigram and structure of the Centre for consideration and approval by the relevant policy Organs of the Union.

2. The Centre shall be equipped with a Library, technical/electronic equipment (hardware and software);

3. The Centre shall comprise of international and local staff. The recruitment of Staff of the Centre shall be governed by the rules and regulations of the Union.

4. The Director shall be assisted by an Advisory Board, appointed by the Chairperson of the Commission for one year renewable term. The composition of the Board shall include one (1) representative from each of the five regions and one (1) representative from each of the RECs, drawn from the Focal Points of the Centre, in consultation with Member States and the RECs as well as representatives from the Commission. The Board shall serve as a mechanism of the Commission for the periodic review and/or evaluation of the curriculum, programmes, budget and finance, and other operational and administrative aspects of the Centre for the purpose of ensuring the efficient performance of the Centre, in line with the rules and regulations of the Union. It shall, among others, perform the following functions:

> a. Review and assess the curriculum and programmes of the Centre to ensure that they are focused and practicable within a given timeframe, consistent with the mandate and functions of the Centre as contained in this Modalities, and up-to-date with prevailing trends on terrorism as well as meet the needs of Member States of the Union;

> b. Review the structure and budget of the Centre vis-à-vis its activities and needs with the view to making recommendations to the policy Organs of the Union;

> c. Make recommendations to the Chairperson of the Commission on how to achieve the maximum performance of the Centre.

VIII. Funding
1. Without Prejudice to the autonomy and status of the Centre as a structure of the Commission,

> a. It shall be funded from the regular budget and Extra-budgetary sources of funding to be mobilized by the Commission;

> b. It shall prepare and submit its annual budget to the AU Commission for consideration and approval by the relevant policy Or-

gans of the Union.

IX. Conditions of Service

The conditions of work and terms of Service, including remuneration of Staff of the Centre shall be based on the AU Staff Rules and Regulations.

APPENDIX FIVE

List of Acronyms

ACSRT	African Center for the Study and Research on Terrorism
ACSS	Africa Center for Strategic Studies
ADF	Allied Democratic Forces
AIAI	al Ittihad al Islami
ANC	African National Congress
AU	African Union
CJTF–HOA	Combined Joint Task Force–Horn of Africa
DHDS	Djamaat Houmet Dawa Salafiya
DRC	Democratic Republic of Congo
EAC	East African Community
EACTI	East African Counterterrorism Initiative
EAPCCO	East African Police Chiefs Cooperation Organization
ECOWAS	Economic Community of West African States
EIG	Egyptian Islamic Group
EIJ	Egyptian Islamic Jihad
EIJM	Eritrean Islamic Jihad Movement
ESAAMLG	Eastern and Southern African Anti-Money Laundering Group
ESF	Economic Support Funds
FDLR	Democratic Liberation Forces of Rwanda
FMF	Foreign Military Financing
FTO	Foreign Terrorist Organization
GIA	Armed Islamic Group
GIABA	Intergovernmental Action Group Against Money Laundering
GICM	Moroccan Islamic Combatant Group
GMPJ	Mauritanian Group for Preaching and Jihad
GSPC	Salafist Group for Preaching and Combat
HAMAS	Harakat al-Muqawama al-Islamiyya

IGAD	Inter-Governmental Authority on Development
IMET	International Military Education and Training
Interpol	International Criminal Police Organization
JIR	Jama'at Ibadu Rahmane
LIFG	Libyan Islamic Fighting Group
LRA	Lord's Resistance Army
MENAFATF	Middle East and North Africa Financial Action Task Force
MWM	Moustarchidine wal Moustarchidates
NATO	North Atlantic Treaty Organization
NCTC	National Counterterrorism Center
OAU	Organization of African Unity
PAGAD	People Against Gangsterism and Drugs
POA	Plan of Action
PSC	Peace and Security Council
REC	Regional Economic Community
RSI	Regional Security Initiative
RUF	Revolutionary United Front
SADC	Southern African Development Community
SCIC	Supreme Council of Islamic Courts
S/CT	State Department Office for the Coordinator for Counterterrorism
SJ	Salafiya Jihadiya
SWAPO	South West Africa People's Organization
TCG	Tunisian Combatant Group
TEL	Terrorist Exclusion List
TFG	Transitional Federal Government
TIP	Terrorist Interdiction Program
UN	United Nations

NOTES

Chapter One: Terrorism Threats and Vulnerabilities in Africa

1   *The UN Human Development Report 2005* is available at <http://hdr.undp.org/reports/global/2005/>, and the *2006 UNAIDS Report* is available at <http://data.unaids.org/pub/GlobalReport/2006/>.

2   Transparency International's 2005 Corruption Perception Index is available at <www.transparency.org/policy_research/surveys_indices/gcb/2005>.

3   Martha Crenshaw, "The Causes of Terrorism," in *The New Global Terrorism: Characteristics, Causes, Controls*, ed. Charles Kegley (New York: Prentice Hall, 2002).

4   United Nations, Report of the Secretary-General's High-Level Panel on Threats, Challenges, and Change, *A More Secure World: Our Shared Responsibility*, 2004, available at <www.un.org/secureworld/>.

5   For further details, see, in this book, appendix one, "Organization of African Unity Convention on the Prevention and Combating of Terrorism (1999)," and chapter two, "The African Union Role in Global Counterterrorism," by Ibrahim J. Wani.

6   United States Department of State, Office of the Coordinator for Counterterrorism, *Country Reports on Terrorism 2005*, April 2006, available at <http://www.state.gov/documents/organization/65462.pdf>.

7   United States Department of State, Office of the Coordinator for Counterterrorism, "Fact Sheet: Terrorist Exclusion List," December 29, 2004, available at <www.state.gov/s/ct/rls/fs/2004/32678.htm>.

8   United States Department of the Treasury, Office of Foreign Assets Control, "Terrorism: What You Need to Know About U.S. Sanctions (Executive Order 13224)," available at <www.treas.gov/offices/enforcement/ofac/programsterror/terror.shtml>.

9   Project for the Research of Islamist Movements, "Africa: The Gold Mine of Al-Qaeda and Global Jihad?" *Islam in Africa Newsletter* 4, no. 2 (June 2006); "Terrorism: The New Scramble for Africa," *Mail and Guardian* (South Africa), August 30, 2006.

10   *Jane's Terrorism and Security Monitor*, "East Africa: Bin Laden's New Front,"August 3, 2006. See also BBC News, "Bin Laden Call Falls on Deaf Ears,"April 24, 2006.

11   CNN, "Islamic Militia to Open 'Holy War' Camps in Somalia," September 19, 2006.

12   See Jeffrey Tayler, "Worse Than Iraq?" *The Atlantic Monthly* 297, no. 3 (April 2006).

13   See Theresa Whelan, "Africa's Ungoverned Space: A New Threat Paradigm," briefing at the "Rethinking the Future Nature of Competitions

and Conflict" Seminar, December 19, 2005. It is also important to note that many African leaders reject the term *ungoverned* and prefer usage of *undergoverned* or a phrase that denotes a government's weakness in controlling an area rather than its complete incapacity to do so.

14 Patricia Weiss Fagen with Micah N. Bump, "Remittances in Conflict and Crises: How Remittances Sustain Livelihoods in War, Crises, and Transitions to Peace," International Peace Academy, February 2006. Also see Mark Basile, "Going to the Source: Why al Qaeda's Financial Network Is Likely to Withstand the Current War on Terrorist Financing,"*Studies in Conflict and Terrorism* 27, no. 3 (May/June 2004), 169–185.

15 Jennifer Windsor, "Promoting Democratization Can Combat Terrorism," *Washington Quarterly* 26, no. 3 (Summer 2003), 43–58.

16 United Nations Integrated Regional Information Networks, "Famine, Not Fanaticism, Poses Greatest Terror Threat in Sahel," October 14, 2004. Also see James A. Piazza, "Rooted in Poverty? Terrorism, Poor Economic Development, and Social Cleavages," *Terrorism and Political Violence* 18, no. 1 (2006), 159–177.

17 Robert Pape, *Dying to Win: The Strategic Logic of Suicide Terrorism* (New York: Random House, 2005).

18 Pew Global Attitudes Project, available at<http://pewglobal.org/reports/>.

19 Marc Sageman, *Understanding Terror Networks* (Philadelphia: University of Pennsylvania Press, 2004).

20 International Crisis Group, "Counterterrorism in Somalia: Losing Hearts and Minds?" *Africa Report*, no. 95, July 11, 2005.

21 United States Office of Director of National Intelligence, "Summary of High Value Terrorist Detainee Program," September 6, 2006, available at <www.dni.gov/announcements/content/TheHighValue Detainee Program.pdf>.

22 International Crisis Group, "Counterterrorism in Somalia." See also International Crisis Group, "Somalia's Islamists," *Africa Report*, no. 100, December 12, 2005.

23 International Crisis Group, "Somalia's Islamists."

24 Sunguta West, "Hardline Islamist Militia Group Shabbab Emerges in Somalia," *Terrorism Focus* 3, no. 31 (August 8, 2006).

25 U.S. Office of Director of National Intelligence, *Country Reports on Terrorism 2005*.

26 U.S. Department of State, "Summary of High Value Terrorist Detainee Program."

27 International Crisis Group, "Somalia's Islamists."

28 Reuters, "Mystery Plane Fuels Somalia War Fears," July 26, 2006.

29 Tobias Hagmann, "Beyond Clannishness and Colonialism: Understanding Political Disorder in Ethiopia's Somali Region, 1991–2004," *Journal of Modern African Studies* 43, no. 4 (2005), 509–536.

30 Ruth Iyob, "Shifting Terrain: Dissidence versus Terrorism in Eritrea," in *Terrorism in the Horn of Africa*, United States Institute of Peace *Special Report*, no. 113, January 2004.

31 International Crisis Group, "Somalia's Islamists." See also William Rosenau, "Al Qaida Recruitment Trends in Kenya and Tanzania," *Studies in Conflict and Terrorism* 28, no. 1 (January 2005), 1–10. See also Jeffrey

Haynes, "Islamic Militancy in East Africa," *Third World Quarterly* 26, no. 8 (2005), 1321–1339.

32 Godwin Rapando Murunga, "Conflict in Somalia and Crime in Kenya: Understanding the Trans-Terroritiality of Crime," *African and Asian Studies* 4, no. 1–2 (March 2005). See also David C. Sperling, "Islam and the Religious Dimension of Conflict in Kenya," undated manuscript, available at <http://payson.tulane.edu/conflict/Cs%20St/SPERLFIN5.html>.

33 Barbara G. Brents and Deo S. Mshigeni, "Terrorism in Context: Race, Religion, Party, and Violent Conflict in Zanzibar," *The American Sociologist* 35, no. 2 (Summer 2004), 60–74. Also, Suzette Heald, "State, Law, and Vigilantism in Northern Tanzania," *African Affairs* 105, no. 419 (December 22, 2005), 265–283. See also Felicitas Becker, "Rural Islamism During the 'War on Terror': A Tanzanian Case Study," *African Affairs* 105, no. 421 (August 2, 2006), 583–603.

34 International Crisis Group, "Islamism in North Africa I: The Legacies of History," *Middle East/North Africa Briefing*, no. 12, April 20, 2004.

35 Alison Pargeter, "The Islamist Movement in Morocco," *Terrorism Monitor* 3, no. 10 (May 19, 2005).

36 Alison Pargeter and Ahmed Al-Baddawy, "North Africa's Radical Diaspora in Europe Shift Focus to Iraq War," *Jane's Intelligence Review*, April 1, 2006.

37 David Ing, "Moroccan Islamist Group Linked to Madrid Bombs," *Jane's Intelligence Review*, April 1, 2004.

38 Reuters, "Morocco Cell 'Equipped for Huge Attack,'" August 25, 2006.

39 Andrew Black, "The Importance of the Western Sahara to Maghrebi Security," *Terrorism Monitor* 4, no. 8 (April 20, 2006).

40 International Crisis Group, "Islamist Terrorism in the Sahel: Fact or Fiction?" *Africa Report*, no. 92, March 31, 2005.

41 Ibid.

42 Raffi Khatchadourian, "Pursuing Terrorists in the Great Desert," *The Village Voice*, January 31, 2006.

43 Pargeter and Al-Baddawy, "North Africa's Radical Diaspora."

44 *Jane's Intelligence Review*, "JTIC Briefing: Al-Qaeda-GSPC Alliance—Spin or Substance?" September 21, 2006.

45 Andrew Black, "The Reconstituted Al-Qaeda Threat in the Maghreb," *Jamestown Terrorism Monitor* 5, no. 2 (February 1, 2007).

46 Jane's Sentinel Security Assessments, "Tunisia: Country Summary," June 3, 2004.

47 See "Tunisia: The Next Militant Hotspot?" STRATFOR.com, January 4, 2007, available at <www.stratfor.com/products/premium/read_article.php?id=282570>, and Jane's Terrorism and Insurgency Centre, "Tunisia's Terrorist Scare," January 18, 2007.

48 *Jane's Intelligence Review*, "Counter-terrorism Successes Force Algerian Militants to Evolve," June 1, 2006.

49 International Crisis Group, "Islamism in North Africa IV: The Islamist Challenge in Mauritania: Threat or Scapegoat?" *Middle East/North Africa Report*, no. 41, May 11, 2005. See also *Jane's Intelligence Review*, "Mauritania Teeters on the Brink of Civil War," April 1, 2005.

50 Alison Pargeter, "LIFG: An Organization in Eclipse," *Terrorism Monitor* 3,

no. 21 (November 3, 2005); Alison Pargeter, "Militant Groups Pose Security Challenge for Libyan Regime," *Jane's Intelligence Review*, August 1, 2005; Moshe Terdman, "The Libyan Islamic Fighting Group," The Project for the Research of Islamist Movements Occasional Paper 3, no. 2 (June 2005).

51   International Crisis Group, "Islamism in North Africa II: Egypt's Opportunity," *Middle East/North Africa Briefing*, no. 13, April 20, 2004.

52   Sarah Gauch, "Extremism Rises Among Egypt's Poor Bedouin," *The Christian Science Monitor*, May 24, 2006. See also Chris Zambelis, "Egypt Attacks May Indicate Emerging Sinai Bedouin Insurgency," *Terrorism Focus* 3, no. 19 (May 17, 2006).

53   Max Taylor and Mohamed Elbushra, "Hassan al-Turabi, Osama bin Laden, and al Qaeda in Sudan," *Terrorism and Political Violence* 18, no. 3 (September 2006), 449–464. See also Alex de Waal and A.H. Abdel Salam, "Islamism, State Power, and Jihad in Sudan," in *Islamism and Its Enemies in the Horn of Africa*, ed. Alex de Waal (London: Hurst and Company, 2004), 71–113.

54   *Africa Confidential* 47, no. 19 (September 22, 2006).

55   Peter Lewis, "Islam, Protest, and Conflict in Nigeria," Center for Strategic and International Studies *Africa Notes*, no. 10, December 2002. See also John Paden, "Islam and Democratic Federalism in Nigeria," Center for Strategic and International Studies *Africa Notes*, no. 8, March 2002.

56   Tayler, "Worse Than Iraq?"

57   Stephen Schwartz, "Islamic Extremism on the Rise in Nigeria," *Terrorism Monitor* 3, no. 20 (October 21, 2005). See also United Nations Integrated Regional Information Network News, "Nigeria: Muslim Fundamentalist Uprising Raises Fears of Terrorism," October 14, 2005. See also *Daily Champion* (Nigeria), "Ijaw Militants Deny Al-Qaeda Link," March 13, 2006.

58   Andrew Clark, "Imperialism, Independence, and Islam in Senegal and Mali," *Africa Today* 46, no. 3–4 (Summer/Autumn 1999).

59   David Dickson, "Political Islam in Sub-Saharan Africa," U.S. Institute of Peace *Special Report*, no. 140, May 2005.

60   *Jane's Islamic Affairs Analyst*, "How the Lebanese Conflict Affects West Africa," September 1, 2006.

61   D. Fleming, "Islamic Militancy in Southern Africa," *Jane's Terrorism and Security Monitor*, November 1, 2004.

62   Kurt Shillinger, "Al-Qaida in Southern Africa: The Emergence of a New Front in the War on Terrorism," *Armed Forces Journal International* 143 (February 2006).

63   Ibid.

64   United States Department of the Treasury, "Treasury Targets Al Qaida Facilitators in South Africa," press release, January 26, 2007.

65   Anneli Botha, "PAGAD: A Case Study of Radical Islam in South Africa," *Terrorism Monitor* 3, no. 17 (September 8, 2005). See also Keith Gottschalk, "Vigilantism v. the State," Institute for Security Studies Occasional Paper no. 99, February 2005.

66   Shillinger, "Al-Qaida in Southern Africa."

67   Fleming, "Islamic Militancy."

68   International Crisis Group, "A Strategy for Ending Northern Uganda's Crisis," *Africa Briefing*, no. 35, January 11, 2006.

69 United Nations Integrated Regional Information Network, "Uganda: IRIN Special Report on the ADF Rebellion," December 8, 1999. See also United Nations Department of Political Affairs, "All Known Ugandan Rebel Camps in Eastern Congo Captured, Says MONUC," December 28, 2005.

70 Project for the Research of Islamist Movements, "Islamization in Rwanda: A Possible Breeding Ground for Radical Islam?" *Islam in Africa Newsletter* 1, no. 2, June 2006.

71 Although an Islamist leader and businessman named Ahmed Abdallah Mohamed Sambi was elected President of the Comoros Islands in May 2006, there are no concerns that his party is linked to terrorism, and it continues to cooperate with the United States to combat extremism. See Moshe Terdman, "Will the Comoros Islands Become an Islamic State?" *Islam in Africa Newsletter* 1, no. 1 (May 2006).

72 Quintan Wiktorowicz, "Anatomy of the Salafi Movement," *Studies in Conflict and Terrorism* 29, no. 3 (2006), 207–239.

73 International Crisis Group, "Islamism in North Africa I: The Legacies of History," Middle East/North Africa Briefing, no. 12, April 20, 2004.

74 Osama bin Laden has also seized on this notion and included it in recent audio messages. See Associated Press, "Purported bin Laden Tape Describes 'War on Islam,'" April 23, 2006.

75 For instance, see Andre Le Sage, "Stateless Justice in Somalia: Formal and Informal Rule of Law Initiatives," *Centre for Humanitarian Dialogue*, July 2005. See also Johannes Harnischfeger, "Sharia and Control Over Territory: Conflicts Between 'Settlers' and 'Indigenes' in Nigeria," *African Affairs* 103, no. 412 (2004), 431–452.

76 For instance, see Benjamin Soares, "Islam in Mali in the Neoliberal Era," *African Affairs* 1, no. 5 (December 2005).

77 Jonathan Benthall, "Humanitarianism and Islam After 11 September," in *Humanitarian Action and the Global War on Terror: A Review of Trends and Issues*, ODI-HPG Report 14, ed. Joanna Macrae and Adele Harmer (London: Overseas Development Institute, 2003), 39.

78 Evan Kohlmann, "The Role of Islamic Charities in International Terrorist Recruitment and Financing," Working Paper, Danish Institute for International Studies, 2006.

79 Nicholas Howenstein, "Islamist Networks: The Case of Tablighi Jamaat," United States Institute of Peace Briefing, October 2006.

80 "A Muslim Missionary Group Draws New Scrutiny in U.S.," *The New York Times*, July 14, 2003.

81 Daniel Chirot, "Could There Be Muslim-Christian Wars in West Africa?" Muslim World E-Bulletin, U.S. Institute of Peace, May 2005, available at <www.usip.org/muslimworld/bulletin/2005/may.html>.

Chapter Two: The African Union Role in Global Counterterrorism

1 Among its various provisions, Security Council (SC) Resolution 1373 instituted a system for states to report on their progress in implementing the requirements of the resolution, set up a technical assistance group to support national efforts, and established the Counter-Terrorism Committee to monitor its implementation. It was soon followed by Resolution 1377 of November 12, 2001, which invited states that required

help in drafting counterterrorism legislation and establishing an implementation machinery to request assistance.

2   The Special Security Council meeting of March 6, 2003, between the Security Council and some 65 regional and subregional organizations was in some ways an acknowledgment of the potential importance of regional organizations in the counterterrorism campaign. The meeting stressed the need to further involve regional organizations in the implementation of SC Resolution 1373 and other international initiatives.

3   The unwillingness of the U.S. Congress to fund serious engagement by other parts of the U.S. Government has been noted and has left the Pentagon as the major player in U.S. counterterrorism efforts in Africa. For instance, see the International Crisis Group's recent report, "Islamist Terrorism in the Sahel: Fact or Fiction?" *Africa Report*, no. 92, March 2005, which raises this concern with respect to the U.S. initiatives in the Sahel and suggests that a more effective counterterrorism policy there "needs to address the threat in the broadest terms, with more development than military aid and greater U.S.-European collaboration."

4   See Stefan Mair, "Terrorism in Africa: On the Danger of Further Attacks in Sub-Saharan Africa," *African Security Review* 12, no. 1 (2003).

5   See, for example, the International Crisis Group, "Islamist Terrorism in the Sahel," and P. Berman, "The Philosopher of Islamic Terror," *The New York Times*, March 23, 2003, 1.

6   See Mair, "Terrorism in Africa."

7   See, for example, statement of Edward Royce, "Fighting Terrorism in Africa," hearing before the Subcommittee on Africa, Committee on International Relations, House of Representatives, April 1, 2004, in which he quoted General James Jones, USMC, then-Commander, U.S. European Command, that

> much of Africa, unfortunately, is hospitable ground to terrorist groups, as the continent has very vast and very remote areas, and it has a number of weak governments and weak security services as well. For the past 2 decades, Wahabbist charities have supported a growing number of *madrassa*s throughout Africa. This mostly Gulf State–sponsored phenomenon, unfortunately, is often aimed at radicalizing Islam in Africa. . . . Africa, indeed, with resource-strapped governments, is unable often to effectively control their (sic) territories, and this has been, frankly, described as the "soft underbelly of the war on terror."

> Also see statement of Karl Wycoff, Associate Coordinator for Press, Policy Programs, and Plans for Counterterrorism, U.S. Department of State, at the same hearings, noting that proximity to the Arab Peninsula and the failed state of Somalia contribute to make the Horn of Africa "the most at risk." Wycoff, testimony, "Fighting Terrorism in Africa," Subcommittee on Africa, Committee on International Relations, U.S. House of Representatives, April 1, 2004, available at <http://www.state.gov/s/ct/rls/rm/2004/31077.htm>.

8   See, generally, Esther Pan, *Africa: Terror Havens*, Council on Foreign Relations Backgrounder, December 30, 2003, available at <http://www.cfr.org/publication/7716/africa.html>. Experts warn that any African

nation with a combustible mix of a weak central government, widespread poverty, and an increasingly politicized Muslim population is at risk of being a haven for international terrorists. See also Douglas Farah, *Blood From Stones: The Secret Financial Network of Terror* (New York: Broadway Books, 2004); Matt Levitt, "Hizballah's African Activities Remain Undisrupted," *RUSI/Jane's Homeland Security Monitor*, March 1, 2004; Lansana Gberie, *War and Peace in Sierra Leone: Diamonds, Corruption, and the Lebanese Connection,* The Diamonds and Human Security Project, Occasional Paper 6, January 2003.

9   For an overview of the trends and pattern of terrorism in Africa, see U.S. Department of State, *Patterns of Global Terrorism—2004*, April 2005, available at <http://www.state.gov/s/ct/rls/c14813.htm>.

10   See, for example, R.W. Johnson, "Tracking Terror Through Africa: Mugabe, Qaddafi, and Al Qaeda," *The National Interest*, no. 75 (Spring 2004), discussing alleged connections between President Robert Mugabe of Zimbabwe and al Qaeda through Libyan President Muammar Qaddafi, and the existence of Muslim networks on the east coast of Africa, possibly involving Malawi, South Africa, and Zimbabwe and relationships with Ayman al-Zawahiri.

11   S. E. Rice, "The Africa Battle," *AAPS Newsletter* (January–April 2002), 6.

12   In the International Crisis Group's "Islamist Terrorism in the Sahel," the argument is made that a heavy-handed approach to fighting terrorism in the Sahel, the region bordering the Sahara comprised of Mauritania, Mali, Niger, and Chad, would risk fueling exactly what it aims to prevent—a rise of Islamist militancy—and suggests broader Western support with equal emphasis on the economic, social, and political components to complement the military, along the lines proposed in the Trans-Saharan Counterterrorism Initiative.

13   The context in which insurgents such as the LRA use violence and the nature and scope of that violence are remarkably different from the nightclub bombings in Bali, for instance, and it does not help the counterterrorism cause to lump the two together.

14   See, for example, Tony Blair's attempt to join ranks with mainstream Islam and attribute the London attacks on an extremist, "evil" ideology that is repugnant to mainstream Islam: "What we are confronting here is an evil ideology. It is not a clash of civilizations—all civilized people, Muslim or other, feel revulsion at it. But it is a global struggle and it is a battle of ideas, hearts and minds, both within Islam and outside it." "Blair Says 'Evil Ideology' Must Be Faced Directly," *The New York Times*, July 16, 2005.

15   Ibid. "This is the battle that must be won, a battle not just about terrorist methods, but their views. Not just about their barbaric acts, but their barbaric ideas. Not only what they do, but what they think and the thinking they would impose on others."

16   The African Union formally succeeded the Organization of African Unity in July 2002, but the idea of transforming the OAU to the AU was officially endorsed by the Summit of Heads of State and Government in 2001, just a few months before September 11.

17   See, generally, Mark Malan, "The Post-9/11 Security Agenda and Peacekeeping in Africa," *African Security Review* 11, no. 3 (2002), 57.

18 See OAU resolution AHG/Res. 213 (XXVIII), adopted in 1992.

19 For example, the summit meeting on October 17, 2001, in Dakar, Senegal, was called at the initiative of President Abdoulaye Wade, to consider a practical approach to fighting terrorism in Africa and ways in which Africa could contribute more meaningfully to the new global campaign against terrorism.

20 OAU Convention on the Prevention and Combating of Terrorism, adopted by the 35th Ordinary Session of the Assembly of Heads of Sate and Government in Algiers, Algeria, in July 1999, Decision AHG/Dec.132 (XXXV). The convention entered into force 30 days after Ghana deposited the required 15th instrument of ratification, as provided by article 20.

21 For example, the Heads of State and Government adopted the Dakar Declaration Against Terrorism, in which African leaders reiterated their strong conviction of the necessity to make Africa a continent where every act, or any support, of terrorism must be outlawed and condemned without any consideration to political, philosophical, ideological, racial, ethnic, religious, or other factors.

22 An example is the Communiqué of the Central Organ of the Mechanism for Conflict Prevention, Management, and Resolution of November 11, 2001, which expressed Africa's support for resolution 1373 and the political will to implement the resolution as well as relevant international instruments to combat terrorism.

23 See Stephen Ellis and David Killingray, "Africa After September 11, 2001," *African Affairs* 101 (2002), 5–8, contending that although the votes of over 50 UN members cannot be discounted, the impact of September 11 on Africa was likely to be minimal because the continent is of limited strategic interest to the West, and it plays a small role in world politics.

24 Article 2 of the convention calls on member states to review their national laws and establish criminal offenses for terrorist acts as defined in article 1.

25 In articles 4 and 5, state parties agree to cooperate and extend to each other the best possible assistance.

26 See articles 17 and 5(3) (4).

27 Article 6.

28 Articles 14–18.

29 The convention makes no reference to the obligations of financial institutions and the specific measures to be undertaken. The plan of action deals with the suppression of financing of terrorism in greater detail but does not address the need for an implementation mechanism.

30 The Peace and Security Council shall be responsible for harmonizing and coordinating continental efforts in the prevention and combating of terrorism.

31 Needless to mention, the African Union is deliberating the need for additional instruments on, for example, suppressing the financing of terrorism, intensifying and accelerating the exchange of operational information on the activities and movements of terrorist persons or networks, intercepting forged or falsified travel documents, and so forth. Nevertheless, by most estimates, the existing instruments cover most of the contemporary issues.

32   Article 6 of the protocol provides that regional mechanisms shall play a complementary role in the implementation of the protocol and the convention and, among other activities, establish contact points at the regional level, liaise with the commission in developing counterterrorism measures, promote regional cooperation in the implementation of the protocol and the convention, and report regularly to the commission on measures taken at the regional level to prevent and combat terrorist acts.

33   The self-determination exception represents Africa's traditional position in defense of the use of force in the struggle against colonialism and apartheid, and reflects its experience in the 1960s when many liberation movements in Africa were labeled as terrorists, much to the chagrin of African leaders. See, for example, the discussion of the political struggle between RENAMO and the government of Mozambique in Alex Vines, *RENAMO Terrorism in Mozambique* (Bloomington and Indianapolis: Indiana University Press, 1991). See also P. Johnson and D. Martin, eds., *Apartheid Terrorism: The Destabilization Report* (Bloomington and Indianapolis: Indiana University Press, 1989); and E. S. Efrat, "Characteristics of Terrorist Movements in Africa," in *International Terrorism: National, Regional, and Global Perspectives*, ed. Y. Alexander (New York: Praeger Publishers, 1976), 194–208.

34   See paragraph 10 (e) of the plan of action.

35   There is a growing consensus within the UN that terrorism constitutes "criminal acts intended or calculated to provoke a state of terror in the general public, a group of persons, or particular persons for political purposes" and that such acts are in "any circumstances unjustifiable, whatever the considerations of a political, philosophical, ideological, racial, ethnic, religious or any other nature that may be invoked to justify them." See, for example, operative paragraph 2 of the resolution of the General Assembly A/RES/51/210, adopted on December 17, 1996, by the 88th Plenary Meeting.

36   See, for example, C. Walter, 13, referrring to the debate on Article 2 of the Draft Comprehensive Convention Against Terrorism, submitted by India in 2000.

37   See, for example, the 12 conventions adopted by the United Nations on terrorism-related issues since 1963.

38   The commission's counterterrorism desk is manned by one staff member of fairly low to middle rank. Technically, he is a consultant, not a permanent staff of the unit.

39   For a description of U.S. counterterrorism initiatives in Africa, see Karl Wycoff, testimony; also, see chapter seven of this book, "U.S. Support for African Counterterrorism Efforts," by Andre Le Sage, for further details.

40   See E. Royce's statement, quoting General James Jones.

41   See, for example, David Payne's testimony before the House Committee on International Relations, Subcommittee on Africa, April 1, 2004, that "severe poverty, extreme frustration, with the feeling of being left out and forgotten by the rest of the world, and in particular, the West are among the factors that create conditions that contribute to terrorism. . . . We

fight terrorism by paying attention to people, the poor and the uneducated." See also the statement by Mr. Wycoff at the same hearings acknowledging the need to pay attention to development issues. Regrettably, Mr. Wycoff did not offer any specific strategies to deal with these development and other issues, compared to the military and security dimensions. The nonmilitary initiatives that he mentions seem limited to public relations—promoting discussions, seminars, and travel by foreign policymakers "to explore Islam in America, to explore U.S. values, traditions, and American society as part of our effort to expand multicultural understanding"—and do not indicate what the United States can or will do differently in response to some of these reactions.

42 Princeton Lyman, testimony before House Committee on International Relations, Subcommittee on Africa, April 1, 2004.

43 See *Report of the Meeting of Experts to Consider Modalities for the Implementation of the AU Plan of Action on the Prevention and Combating of Terrorism in Africa*, Addis Ababa, Ethiopia, October 28–29, 2003.

Chapter Three: The Role of the Inter-Governmental Authority on Development in Preventing and Combating Terrorism

1 For a comprehensive analysis of the effects of the Sudanese civil war, see Monica Kathina Juma, "Sudan," in *Dealing With Conflicts in Africa: The United Nations and Regional Organizations*, ed. Jane Boulden (New York: Palgrave Macmillan, 2003), 189–190.

2 Owing to uncertainty in Somalia, the Transitional Federal Government was constituted and sworn in in Kenya, and has only partially returned to the towns of Baydhowa and Jowhar rather than to Mogadishu, which is still insecure and hostage to various warlords and militia groups. See International Crisis Group, "Counter-Terrorism in Somalia: Losing Hearts and Minds?" *Africa Report*, no. 95, July 11, 2005, 1–4.

3 The peace process is handicapped by the divergent approaches of the parties regarding the implementation of the April 2002 Decision on the Boundary Commission. See African Union, *Report of the Chairperson of the (AU) Commission on Conflict Situations in Africa*, EX.CL/191 (VII), presented to the AU Summit in Sirte, July 2005, 2; for the causes of the conflict see Leenco Leta, "The Ethiopia-Eritrea War," in Boulden, *Dealing With Conflicts in Africa*, 153–184.

4 For instance, the Oromos, widely believed to constitute at least 40 percent of Ethiopia's population, seek self determination and formed the Oromo Liberation Front to wage war against Addis Ababa. See Siegfried Pausewang, Kjetil Tronvoll, and Lovise Aalen (eds.), *Ethiopia Since the Derg: A Decade of Democratic Pretension and Performance* (London: Zed Books, 2002).

5 For the scale and impact of the war in northern Uganda, see International Crisis Group, "Northern Uganda: Understanding and Solving the Conflict," *Africa Report*, no. 77, April 14, 2004.

6 Human Rights Watch, *Failing the Internally Displaced: The UNDP Displaced Persons Program in Kenya* (New York: Human Rights Watch/Africa, 1997).

7 The idea was to focus on nonpolitical or security issues that were not controversial; hence, its mandate is confined to areas of mitigation of the effects of drought and desertification.

8   International Peace Academy, *The Infrastructure of Peace: Assessing the Peace-building Capacity of African Institutions*, report to Ford Foundation, 2002, 20.

9   This change is reflected in the amendment of its charter, signed in 1996, which outlined a broader agenda and altered the structures of the organization. See IGAD Implementation Plan of Action of 1996, available at <http://www.issafrica.org/AF/RegOrg/unity_to_ union/pdfs/ igad/AgreementEstab.pdf>.

10   The vision of IGAD focuses on the "promotion of regional cooperation in order to achieve sustainable development, peace, and security in the region." See IGAD Strategy, October 2003, available at <http:// www.igad.org/docs/igad_strategy.pdf>, para. 2.

11   For the debate and theorization on conflict cycle, see World Bank, *Breaking the Conflict Trap: Civil War and Development Policy* (Washington, DC: World Bank, May 2003).

12   It has been argued that the collapse of the Somali state gave a new impetus for the Somali Islamic Union (al Ittihad al Islami) to extend its organizational network to Ethiopia and Northern Kenya. See Medhane Tadesse, *Al-Ittihad Political Islam and Black Economy in Somalia* (Addis Ababa: Meag Printing, 2002).

13   See Karl Wycoff, statement to the Second Session of the Hearing on Fighting Terrorism in Africa Before the Subcommittee on Africa, Committee on International Relations, House of Representatives (108th Congress), April 1, 2004, available at <http://wwwc.house.gov/international_ relations/108/wyc040104.htm>.

14   Sudan is on the U.S. list of countries sponsoring terrorism. Discussions with the United States to rescind the designation have been stalled by the Darfur crisis.

15   An attack on a stadium in Mogadishu during an address by the prime minister on May 12, 2005, was a reminder of the vulnerability of these countries. While no group claimed responsibility for the attack, international security agents monitoring events in Somalia since the launch of the global war on terror are exploring possible terrorist links to the attack. See Mark Agutu, "Rude Homecoming Awaits Exiles," *Daily Nation*, May 13, 2005.

16   Sudan has been on the U.S. Foreign Terrorist Organizations List since 1995 following the botched attempt on the life of President Hosni Mubarak of Egypt.

17   All IGAD countries have signed and ratified the Algiers Convention, which entered into force in 2002.

18   This particular clause has prompted considerable controversy in the United Nations as it was intended by the Arab sponsors to allegedly exempt Palestinian groups that use terrorist tactics.

19   IGAD Implementation Plan of Action, 11.

20   See Introduction to the Draft Implementation Plan to Counter Terrorism in the IGAD Region, available at <http://www.iss.co.za/af/RegOrg/ unity_to_union/pdfs/igad/confjun03plan.pdf>.

21   IGAD Implementation Plan for the Prevention and Combating of Terrorism, June 2003.

22   See Communiqué of the 9th Summit of the Assembly of Heads of State

and Government of IGAD, Dakar, October 17, 2001.

23 IGAD Implementation Plan for the Prevention and Combating of Terrorism, 3.

24 All IGAD countries have national mechanisms for dealing with small arms and light weapons in line with the Nairobi Declaration (2000) to which they are signatories. This declaration has been reinforced further by the Nairobi Protocol for the Prevention, Control, and Reduction of Small Arms and Light Weapons in the Great Lakes region and the Horn of Africa, signed in April 2004.

25 CEWARN was created outside the IGAD framework and is run as a semi-autonomous outfit.

26 All IGAD states are members of Interpol, which facilitates police coordination in combating global crime, provides national police with a secure global communications system, collects crime information and maintains a database, provides operational support services, and runs a number of anti-terrorism programs through its regional bureaus. See "Horn of Africa Nations Pledge to Fight Terrorism," *The Times of India,* January 24, 2004, available at <http://timesofindia.indiatimes.com/articleshow/442804.cms>.

27 This training was sponsored by the commonwealth and organized in Kenya. See also address of the Hon. Danson Mungatana, Assistant Minister, during the opening of the Second Conference on Prevention and Combating Terrorism in the IGAD Region, October 18–20, 2004.

28 At the Oslo meeting in April, the donors pledged some US$4.1 billion while the Sudan government is expected to put up some US$6 billion for the reconstruction of Sudan. If these pledges translate into resources, the interim administration would be on the way to jump-starting the rehabilitation and reconstruction of this country, which was embroiled in Africa's longest civil war.

29 See Communiqué of the IGAD Heads of State and Government on Somalia, in Abuja, Nigeria, January 31, 2005. This was the first time that IGAD had supported a military operation.

30 See SaferAfrica, "Africa's Peace and Security Agenda: Progress Made and Way Forward," report of the *Ukumbi* Policy Forum held in Pretoria, South Africa, July 19, 2005.

31 John Prendergast and Philip Roessler, "Can a Leopard Change Its Spots? Sudan's Evolving Relationship With Terrorism," in *Terrorism in the Horn of Africa,* United States Institute of Peace Special Report no. 113, January 2004.

32 See David Shinn, "Fighting Terrorism in East Africa and the Horn," *Foreign Service Journal* 81 (September 2004).

33 Wycoff, testimony.

34 Gilbert Khadiagala, "Kenya: Haven or Helpless Victim of Terrorism,"in *Terrorism in the Horn of Africa.*

35 Kenya has two critical bills that await passage by parliament: the Suppression of Terrorism Bill (2003), which was rejected by parliament for its potential to violate the bill of rights, and the Witness Protection Bill (2004) to protect witnesses in terrorism cases.

36 See "State Dropped Two Charges Against Terror Suspects," *East African Standard,* May 11, 2005.

37 The abuse of travel documents is evidenced by the discovery that two of

the suspected London bombers, who are originally from Somalia, traveled to the United Kingdom on Kenyan passports. See Derek Otieno, "UK Bombing Suspects Had Kenyan Passports," *Daily Nation,* July 27, 2005.

38 Mungatana, address.

39 Ruth Iyob, "Shifting Terrain: Dissidence versus Terrorism in Eritrea," in *Terrorism in the Horn of Africa.*

40 Central Intelligence Agency, *The World Fact Book,* available at <https://www.cia.gov/cia/publications/factbook/index.html>.

41 See J. Stephen Morrison, "Africa and the War on Global Terrorism," testimony before the House International Relations Committee Subcommittee on Africa.

42 Stefan Mair, "Terrorism in Africa: On the Danger of Further Attack in Sub-Saharan Africa," *African Security Review* 12, no. 1 (2003).

43 In a study of the changing tactics of the Mungiki gangs in Nairobi, Peter Mwangi Kagwanja illustrates how militia groups identify with, and borrow tactics (including the beheading and displaying of mutilated bodies of victims) from, fundamentalist groups operating in Afghanistan and/or Iraq. See Peter Mwangi Kagwanja, "Facing Mount Kenya or Facing Mecca? The Mungiki, Ethnic Violence and the Politics of the Moi Succession in Kenya, 1987–2002," *African Affairs* 102 (2003), 25–49.

44 In an incident in July 2005, a series of raids by marauding gunmen left over 90 dead and thousands wounded and displaced in the Marsabit district of Kenya. While such attacks are explained in terms of tribal rivalry and competition for scarce resources owing to widespread poverty and longstanding neglect of the area, mention is also made of the conflict in the border region where the Oromo secessionists have managed to seek sanctuary and sometimes attacked populations in Kenya and Ethiopia in the absence of proper patrolling. See Mathew Ngugi Kihuithia, "Why Marsabit Killings Constituted Genocide," *East African,* July 27, 2005.

45 Mair, "Terrorism in Africa," 2.

46 Shinn, "Fighting Terrorism," 36–42.

47 Some of these policy recommendations have been implemented. For instance, the United States set aside some $100 million annually for the Trans-Sahara Counterterrorism Initiative (a followup to the Pan-Sahel Initiative) to be launched in summer 2005.

48 Johnnie Carson, "Shaping U.S. Policy on Africa: Pillars of a New Strategy," Institute for National Strategic Studies *Strategic Forum* no. 210, National Defense University Press, September 2004.

49 See International Crisis Group, "Counter-Terrorism in Somalia," 17.

50 In an argument that has resonance to this situation, in which the international action ended up supporting and bolstering the capacity of negative forces, Rakiya Omaar and Alex De Waal argued that neutral humanitarian action is impossible and could be counterproductive. See Rakiya Omaar and Alex De Waal, *Humanitarianism Unbound? Current Dilemmas Facing Multi-Mandate Relief Operations in Political Emergencies* (London: African Rights, 1994).

51 International Crisis Group, "Counter-Terrorism in Somalia," 18.

52 See also Tadesse, *Al-Ittihad Political Islam,* 185.

53 Peter Kagwanja, "Responding to Terrorism in East Africa," presentation at the Conference on Terrorism and Counter-Terrorism in Africa, Centre for International Political Studies, University of Pretoria, March 23, 2004.

Chapter Four: Counterterrorism Measures in the East African Community

1 David H. Shinn, "Fighting Terrorism in East Africa and the Horn," *Foreign Service Journal* 81 (September 2004), 38.

2 Karanja Mbugua, "East Africa: A Haven or Hapless Victim of International Terrorism?" *Conflict Trends*, no. 3 (2004); Gilbert Khadiagala, "Kenya: Haven or Helpless Victim of Terrorism," in *Terrorism in the Horn of Africa*, Special Report of a U.S. Institute of Peace workshop on Assessing Terrorism in the Horn of Africa: Threats and Responses, Washington, DC, May 28, 2003.

3 Eight of the hijackers belonged to the Popular Front for the Liberation of Palestine and two were from Germany's Baader-Meinhof gang.

4 Khadiagala, "Kenya."

5 Karl Wycoff, Associate Coordinator of the U.S. Office of the Coordinator for Counterterrorism, testimony before the House International Relations Committee, Subcommittee on Africa, April 1, 2004, available at <http://www.state.gov/s/ct/rls/rm/2004/31077.htm>; and Peter Mwangi Kagwanja, "Responding to Terrorism in East Africa," presentation at the Conference on Terrorism and Counter-Terrorism in Africa, Center for International Political Studies, University of Pretoria, March 23, 2004.

6 Charles Cobb, Jr., "Hints of Military Action Cause Puzzlement, Worry," allAfrica.com, December 23, 2001.

7 East Africa Counterterrorism Initiative Conference, U.S. Department of State, available at <http://www.state.gov/s/ct/rls/rm/2004/31731.htm>. Participants at the conference "Examining the 'Bastions' of Terror: Governance and Policy in Yemen and the Horn of Africa," held November 4–6, 2004, at the Belfer Center for Science and International Affairs at Harvard University, concluded that these cells need to be found and eradicated through concerted diplomatic, intelligence, law enforcement, and military cooperation and coordination.

8 Muriithi Mutiga, "How Terrorist Attack Was Planned and Executed," *The East African Standard* (Nairobi), November 27, 2004.

9 David H. Shinn, "Terrorism in East Africa and the Horn: An Overview," *Journal of Conflict Studies* 23, no. 2 (Fall 2003). Muslims comprise over 10 percent of Kenya's population, 16 percent of Uganda's, and 35 percent of Tanzania's. Zanzibar's population is 99 percent Muslim.

10 Mutiga, "How Terrorist Attack Was Planned and Executed."

11 Matthew A. Levitt, "The Political Economy of Middle East Terrorism," *Middle East Review of International Affairs* 6, no. 4 (December 2002).

12 While Kenya revoked al-Haramain's registration in 1998, Tanzania ordered it in 2004 to cease its operations in the country.

13 Shinn, "Fighting Terrorism in East Africa and the Horn," 39.

14 Roni Singer, "Nairobi's 'Little Kibbutz' Gets Together in Attack Aftermath," *Haaretz*, April 2, 2005.

15   Chege Maina, "How the Kenya Government Invites Terrorist Attacks," *eXpression Today*, no. 24 (2003).

16   *Transparency International Newsletter*, March 2002, available at <http://www.transparency.org/publications/newsletter/editions>.

17   Shinn, "Fighting Terrorism in East Africa and the Horn," 38.

18   Mbugua, "East Africa."

19   East African Community (EAC) Web site, <www.eac.int>.

20   EAC, *The Second East African Community Development Strategy, 2001–2005*, Arusha, April 24, 2001.

21   *The East African Standard* (Nairobi), November 12, 2004.

22   Fred Nabea, "The Unsettling Questions of Security in the EAC Countries," *The East African Standard*, February 12, 2005.

23   Mutiga, "How Terrorist Attack Was Planned and Executed."

24   A leading Kenyan security analyst has dismissed the antiterrorism unit as virtually nonexistent. "It is just an extravagant title for a squad we would wish to have in future, and not any genuine elite anti-terror response unit presently in existence." The officers currently deployed in the unit "operate from wooden prefabs . . . with no training or technical capability worthy of the unit's name." See Ambrose Murunga, "Pitfalls Michuki Must Avoid," *Daily Nation*, February 19, 2005.

25   Michelle Kagari, "Anti-terror Bill an Affront to Human Rights," *The Daily Nation*, November 18, 2003.

26   Solomy B. Bossa and Titus Mulindwa, "The Anti-Terrorism Act, 2002 (Uganda): Human Rights Concerns and Implications," International Commission of Jurists Legal Resource Center, available at <http://www.icj.org/news.php3?id_article=3517&lang=en>.

27   Solomy B. Bossa is a judge on the East African Court of Justice; Titus Mulindwa is the principal legal officer for Banks Supervision, Bank of Uganda.

28   Kagari, "Anti-terror Bill an Affront to Human Rights."

29   Nasser Kigwangallah, "Lawyer Criticizes Anti-Terrorism Law," IPPMedia.com, March 13, 2005.

30   BBC News, "East African Leaders Condemn Terrorism," January 10, 2002, available at <http://news.bbc.co.uk/1/hi/world/africa/1752463.stm>.

31   EAPCCO was founded in Kampala, Uganda, during the first meeting of East Africa police chiefs in February 1998 and is composed of Burundi, Djibouti, Ethiopia, Eritrea, Kenya, Rwanda, Seychelles, Sudan, Tanzania, and Uganda. The body came into force in August 2002 and is recognized by Interpol as its affiliate. Interpol also organizes regional police coordination in Southern Africa, Central Africa, and West Africa.

32   On January 5, 2005, Kenya ratified the Protocol against the Illicit Manufacturing of and Trafficking in Firearms, Their Parts and Components and Ammunition, supplementing the United Nations Convention against Transnational Organized Crime.

33   William Pope, U.S. Deputy Coordinator for Counterterrorism, remarks delivered at the East Africa Counterterrorism Initiative Conference, April 21, 2004, Kampala, Uganda, available at <http://www.state.gov/s/ct/rls/rm/2004/31731.htm>.

34   Ibid.

35   African Union Declaration of the Second High-Level Inter-Governmental Meeting on the Prevention and Combating of Terrorism in Africa (II), Rev. 2.

36   Shinn, "Fighting Terrorism in East Africa and the Horn," 42.

37   Jim Lobe, "Terror War Diverting Attention From Roots of Insecurity," *Inter Press Service* (Johannesburg), January 12, 2005.

38   Wycoff, testimony.

39   Transparency International, "Global Corruption Report 2003," available at <http://www.globalcorruptionreport.org/download/gcr2003/22_East_Africa (Mwenda).pdf>.

40   Jennifer Bakyawa, "Uganda Aid 'Serves and Fuels War On Terror,'" *PANOS* (London), November 16, 2004. See also Christian Aid, "The Politics of Poverty: Aid in the New Cold War," May 10, 2004, available at <http://www.christian-aid.org.uk/indepth/404caweek/index.htm>, which criticizes Western donor countries for using "aid . . . to serve in the global 'War on Terror,'" rather than addressing the real needs of poor people.

41   Ibid.

42   Ibid.

43   Matthew Green, "U.S. Fear of Horn of Africa Radicals Overblown-Expert," *Reuters*, February 7, 2005; and Alex De Waal, ed., *Islamism and Its Enemies in the Horn of Africa* (Bloomington: Indiana University Press, 2004).

44   Alisha Ryu, "U.S. General Sees Progress in Fighting Terror in East Africa," *Voice of America*, July 13, 2004, available at <http://www.globalsecurity.org/security/library/news/2004/07/sec-040713-21f0e0e7.htm>.

45   Bossa and Mulindwa, "The Anti-Terrorism Act, 2002 (Uganda)."

46   See Amnesty International, *Kenya: The Impact of "Anti-terrorism" Operations on Human Rights*, March 23, 2005.

47   "Terrorism Must Be Addressed in Parallel with Poverty, Underdevelopment, Inequality, General Assembly Told, as General Debate Concludes," 56th General Assembly, GA/9971, November 16, 2001.

Chapter Five: Terrorism Threats and Responses in the Southern African Development Community Region

1   For a brief history of SADCC and SADC, see Margaret Lee, *SADCC: The Political Economy of Development in Southern Africa* (Nashville, TN: Winston–Derek, 1989); and Ibbo Mandaza and A. Tostensen, *Southern Africa in Search of a Common Future: From the Conference to the Community* (Gabarone, Botswana: SADC, 1994).

2   Christopher Landsberg and Mwesiga Baregu, "Introduction," in *From Cape to Congo: Southern Africa's Evolving Security Challenges*, ed. Mwesiga Baregu and Christopher Landsberg (Boulder, CO: Lynne Reinner, 2003), 2–3.

3   For a comprehensive view of security, see Sola Akinrade, "Democracy and Security in Africa," *Journal of Contemporary African Studies* 17, no. 2 (1999), 217–244.

4   See Joseph Hanlon, *Apartheid's Second Front: South Africa's War Against Its Neighbors* (New York: Penguin, 1986), and Gilbert M. Khadiagala,

Allies in Diversity: The Frontline States in Southern African Security (Athens, OH: Ohio University Press, 1994).

5   Brian Kagoro, *The Zimbabwe We Want: The Politics of Change* (Harare: Mwengo, 2005).

6   Michael Rifer, "SADC and Terrorism: Where Is the Regional Strategy?" *African Security Review* 14, no. 1 (2005).

7   Anneli Botha, "Introduction," in *Terrorism in the SADC Region: An Historical Perspective and Regional Counter-Measures,* ed. Anneli Botha (Pretoria: Institute for Security Studies, Monograph Series, no. 113, March 2005).

8   Samuel Huntington, "The Clash of Civilizations?" *Foreign Affairs* (Summer 1993).

9   Anneli Botha, "The Threat of Terrorism in Southern Africa," in *Terrorism in the SADC Region,* 22–23.

10 Assis Malaquias, "Ethnicity and Conflict in Angola: Prospects for Reconciliation," in *Angola's War Economy: The Role of Oil and Diamonds,* ed. Jakkie Cilliers and Christian Dietrich (Pretoria: Institute for Security Studies, 2000).

11 Botha, "The Threat of Terrorism in Southern Africa," 40.

12 Reynolds L. Richter, "'Uncivil Society?' The Rise of PAGAD as a Response to the Experiences of Progressive Islamic Political Movements in South Africa During the Transition to Democracy," unpublished paper, December 1999.

13 William Zartman, ed., *Collapsed States: The Disintegration and Restoration of Legitimate Authority* (Boulder, CO: Lynne Reinner, 1995).

14 David Smith et al., *States and Sovereignty in the Global Economy* (London: Routledge, 1999). See also Zartman, *Collapsed States.*

15 Botha, "The Threat of Terrorism in Southern Africa," 54.

16 Kenny Kapinga et al., "Towards a SADC Counter-Terrorism Strategy," in *Terrorism in the SADC Region,* 76–102.

17 Ibid., 80–81.

18 Botha, "The Threat of Terrorism in Southern Africa," 24.

19 See Kurt Shillinger, "Al-Qaida in Southern Africa: The Emergence of a New Front in the War on Terrorism," *Armed Forces Journal International* 143 (February 2006).

20 Rifer, "SADC and Terrorism."

Chapter Six: Economic Community of West African States Counterterrorism Efforts

1   Particularly noteworthy is the "youth problem" in the subregion: the emergence of a large pool of unemployed, marginalized, and increasingly alienated youth, some demobilized from recent conflicts in Liberia, Sierra Leone, and Côte d'Ivoire.

2   IGAD is probably ahead of any other subregion in the development of a counterterrorism strategy. Since 2002, IGAD has sponsored a series of meetings and conferences designed to forge a regional framework for addressing issues of terrorism. It has been repeatedly asserted that the problems of IGAD countries with terrorism predate September 11. See *Report on IGAD Conference on the Prevention and Combating of Terrorism,* Addis Ababa, June 24–27, 2003, as well as other IGAD reports cited in this study.

3   Of course, these variables are not inconsistent with "terrorism" (on the contrary), and many acts undertaken in the course of these conflicts may qualify as "terrorist."

4   For instance, "Nigeria's Most Wanted Terrorists: The Al-Qaeda Connection," *Tell*, no. 26 (April 26, 2004), 20–26, referring to an uprising by the pro-Taliban *Ahl Ul Sunnah Wal Ja ma'ah* in Yobe state in December 2003. Until this incident (according to the paper), "the federal government [of Nigeria] has persistently denied the existence of an Al-Qaeda cell or terrorist groups in the country."

5   While cases of international terrorism have been rare, the subregion has been known for egregious instances of domestic terrorism by nonstate armed groups (most notoriously the Revolutionary United Front) in the context of the conflicts in Sierra Leone, Liberia, and Côte d'Ivoire. There have also been cases of violence associated with religious fundamentalism in northern Nigeria and the ongoing conflicts in the Niger delta.

6   See ECOWAS Protocol Relating to the Mechanism for Conflict Prevention, Management, Resolution, Peacekeeping, and Security, December 1999, Article 3 (d).

7   ECOWAS, Protocol on Democracy and Good Governance Supplementary to the Protocol Relating to the Mechanism for Conflict Prevention, Management, Resolution, Peacekeeping, and Security, December 1999, Article 24 (1).

8   Ibid., article 24 (2).

9   See "ECOWAS experts adopt anti-corruption protocols, ponder terrorism," Panapress.com, October 25, 2001, available at <http://www.panapress.com/newslatf.asp?code=eng021247&dte=25/10/2001>.

10   Namely Benin, Burkina Faso, Côte d'Ivoire, Guinea-Bissau, Mali, and Senegal.

11   The central bank for WAEMU states.

12   Interview with General Charles Okae, Abuja, June 1, 2005.

13   Christine Agboton-Johnson, Adedeji Ebo, and Laura Mazal, *Small Arms Control in Ghana, Nigeria, and Senegal*, International Alert, March 2004.

14   Côte d'Ivoire, The Gambia, Guinea-Bissau, Liberia, Niger, and Sierra Leone are among the ECOWAS states that have signed but not ratified the convention.

15   It should be noted that some of the training being offered under these programs (such as detection of explosives and training for law enforcement officials) requires a hands-on approach and is best organized within a national rather than regional framework.

16   "U.S. Turns Horn of Africa Into a Military Hub," *The New York Times*, November 17, 2002, and "German and Spanish Navies Take on Major Role Near Horn of Africa," *The New York Times*, December 15, 2002.

17   The AU itself suffers from similar capacity constraints, though perhaps not on the same scale as that of ECOWAS. See *Report of the Meeting of Experts to Consider Modalities for the Implementation of the AU Plan of Action on the Prevention and Combating of Terrorism in Africa*, Addis Ababa, October 28–29, 2003.

18   Amnesty International, *Kenya: The Impact of "Anti-terrorism" Operations on Human Rights*, March 23, 2005.

19   Hence, article 3 of the Algiers Convention contains the controversial and potentially contradictory stipulation that: "(i) Notwithstanding the provisions of article 1 (above-mentioned definition), the struggle waged by peoples in accordance with the principles of international law for their liberation or self-determination, including armed struggle against colonialism, occupation, aggression and domination by foreign forces shall not be considered as terrorist acts. (ii) Political, philosophical, ideological, racial, ethnic, religious or other motives shall not be justifiable defence against a terrorist act."

20   Africa Center for Strategic Studies, *North and West Africa Counterterrorism Topical Seminar: Program Highlights*, Bamako, Mali, October 12–17, 2003, 17, available at <http://www.africacenter.org/iDuneDownload.dll?GetFile?AppId=100&FileID=297207&Anchor=&ext=.pdf>.

21   Jessica Almquist, *Which Justice for Perpetrators of Acts of Terrorism? The Need for Guidelines*, Working Paper 5, *Fundacion par alas Relaciones Internacionales y el Dialogo Exterior* (FRIDE), March 2005.

22   Kenya's anti-terrorism bill is a case in point. Although the bill has been suspended pending further public discussion, critics of the counterterrorism offensive in Kenya have detailed extensive abuses of human rights. Amnesty International, *Kenya*.

23   In particular, the stress on intelligence should be seen in this light, since intelligence agencies are among the most weakly controlled African security institutions.

24   The UN Policy Working Group thus aptly warns that

> the rubric of counterterrorism can be used to justify acts in support of political agendas, such as the consolidation of political power, elimination of political opponents, inhibition of legitimate dissent . . . labeling opponents or adversaries as terrorists offers a time-tested technique to de-legitimise and demonise them. The United Nations should beware of offering . . . a blanket or automatic endorsement of all measures taken in the name of counterterrorism.

Report of the Policy Working Group on the United Nations and Terrorism, Annex to A/57/273, S/2002, 873, available at <http: //www. global security/library/report/2002/un-wrkng-grp-terrorism-intro.htm>.

25   It is understood that the U.S. Government has already offered assistance in the establishment of such a center, though ECOWAS for a variety of reasons has been slow to take up the offer.

26   It is possible that several regional centers (rather than just one) may be established or affiliated with ECOWAS to execute or facilitate functions, including a focal point for gathering and sharing data; a regional center dedicated to the study of terrorism and its causes, working closely with both the UN Counter-Terrorism Center and the AU's office in Algiers; and a regional training and technical assistance center.

27   IGAD's experience in the utilization of aid suggests that existing limits in absorptive capacity associated with the very constraints identified here

may in turn affect the ability of countries to utilize external assistance even when it is made available. See *Report of the Second Conference on the Prevention and Combating of Terrorism in the IGAD Region*, Mombasa, October 18–20, 2004, 5–6.

28   A good example of such collaboration is the role of the Institute for Security Studies of South Africa in facilitating the 2003 IGAD Counterterrorism Conference in Addis Ababa, Ethiopia.

29   A Draft Implementation Plan to Counter Terrorism in the IGAD Region was tabled at the first conference in Addis Ababa in June 2003 and approved at the 10th annual IGAD Summit in Kampala in October. As a prelude to the Mombasa meeting, the IGAD commissioned an assessment report, "Terrorism in the IGAD Region: Vulnerability and Countermeasures." In Mombasa, working groups fleshed out the strategic vision of the Implementation Plan with a set of solid proposals (see IGAD, *Report of the Second Conference on the Prevention and Combating of Terrorism in the IGAD Region*, Mombasa, Kenya, October 18–20, 2004). The IGAD strategy clearly identifies the various components of the plan and defines a clear role for the IGAD Secretariat.

30   Mutual Assistance in Criminal Matters and on Extradition, signed in Dakar, Senegal, on July 29, 1992, and Abuja, Nigeria, on August 6, 1994.

31   See, for instance, "How Nigeria's (sic) Fuels Cross-border Crimes, by Immigration Chief," *The Guardian*, June 1, 2005, in which the Comptroller of the Nigeria Immigration Service, William Park, alleges that the free-movement protocol had undermined Nigeria's national security and fueled cross-border crime.

32   I say "within ECOWAS" because much of the focus on border controls as they relate specifically to terrorism in the subregion has focused on the critical (largely unpatrolled) frontiers between the Sahelian countries and North Africa.

33   The Africa Center for Strategic Studies counterterrorism seminar in Mali in 2003 demonstrated that such courses can change the perceptions of senior security and political officials (as I learned during the course of my interviews at ECOWAS), particularly if they bring together regions with different experiences and perceptions of terrorism (as in the case of this particular workshop).

34   Organization for Economic Cooperation and Development, Development Assistance Committee (DAC), "Development Cooperation Responses to Terrorism and Development," December 3, 2001; Stephen Ellis and David Killingray, "Africa After 11 September 2001," *African Affairs* 101 (2002), 5.

35   See, for instance, the discussions in the Legal Committee of the 58th General Assembly, 7th and 8th Meetings, October 17, 2003, especially the contribution by South African representative Albert Hoffman. These concerns are broadly endorsed by the United Nations, *A More Secure World: Our Shared Responsibility*, Report of the Secretary-General's High-Level Panel on Threats, Challenges, and Change (New York: United Nations, 2004).

36   Almquist, *Which Justice for Perpetrators of Acts of Terrorism?*

37   United Nations, *A More Secure World.*

38   Ibid., 23. In the words of the panel:

> In describing how to meet the challenge of prevention, we begin with development because it is the indispensable foundation for a collective security system that takes prevention seriously. It serves multiple functions. It helps to combat the poverty, infectious disease, and environmental degradation that kill millions and threaten human security. It is vital in helping states prevent or reverse the erosion of State capacity, which is crucial for meeting almost every class of threat. And it is part of the long-term strategy for preventing civil war, and for addressing the environments in which both terrorism and organized crime flourish.

39   Kofi Annan, "A Global Strategy for Fighting Terrorism," keynote address to the Closing Plenary of the International Summit on Democracy, Terrorism, and Security, Madrid, March 10, 2005.

Chapter Seven: U.S. Support for African Counterterrorism Efforts

1   Organization of African Unity Convention on the Prevention and Combating of Terrorism, 1999, article 1, paragraph 3 (see appendix one).

2   Plan of Action of the AU High-Level Inter-Governmental Meeting on the Prevention and Combating of Terrorism in Africa, September 11–14, 2005 (see appendix two).

3   Modalities for the Functioning of the African Center for the Study and Research on Terrorism, July 2005 (see appendix four).

4   Michael Rifer, "SADC and Terrorism," *African Security Review* 14, no. 1 (2005).

5   "SADC to Establish Counter-Terrorism Unit," *New Era* (Namibia), December 6, 2006.

6   For instance, see Kenny Kapinga, "The Current and Future Role of SARPCCO," unpublished and undated manuscript. Also, Interpol Terrorism Fact Sheet TE/01, available at <www.interpol.int>.

7   Information received from African Center for the Study and Research on Terrorism, updated through September 2006.

8   This is limited here to funding through Child Survival and Health Programs Fund, Development Assistance, Greater Horn of Africa Initiative, Migration and Refugee Assistance, Peacekeeping Operations, Public Law 480, and Transitional Initiatives.

ABOUT THE AUTHORS

Eboe Hutchful, a Ghanaian political scientist, is Professor of African Studies at Wayne State University and Executive Director of African Security Dialogue and Research, a nongovernmental organization in Accra, Ghana, involved in research and advocacy in civil-military relations and security sector governance. Professor Hutchful also taught at several other universities in Africa and North America, including the University of Toronto, the University of Port Harcourt, and the University of Ghana. His research has focused on militarism, the politics of economic reform, and the environment. He is the author and co-editor of several books and numerous journal articles, including *The Military and Militarism in Africa* (Codesria, 1998) with Abdoulaye Bathily; and *Ghana's Adjustment Experience: The Paradox of Reform* (United Nations Research Institute for Social Development, 2002). Fluent in English and Akan and proficient in French, he obtained his PhD and MA in Political Science from the University of Toronto and his BA from the University of Ghana.

Monica Kathina Juma is a Senior Analyst working on the African Union–New Economic Partnership for African Development Program at SaferAfrica in Pretoria, South Africa. She also serves as a resource person for the South African Army College in Pretoria and the Staff College and National Defence College in Nairobi, Kenya. Previously, Dr. Juma was a Research Associate at the International Peace Academy in 2001 where she directed a project that assessed the capacities of African institutions to respond to crisis and conflict in Africa. She was a lecturer from 1991 to 1999 in the Department of Political Science at Moi University, where she developed and taught courses and seminars in governance and African politics. During this time, she helped establish the Centre for Refugee Studies. She is a member of the International Academic Advisory Group to the United Nations High Commissioner for Refugees and is the author of numerous publications including, as co-editor, *Eroding Local Capacity: International Humanitarian Action in Africa* (African Nordic Institute, 2002). Dr. Juma graduated with a BA and an MA in Government and Public Administration from the University of Nairobi. She also earned a Certificate in Forced Migration and a DPhil, both from the Oxford University, where she was a Commonwealth Fellow and a Wingate Scholar. Dr. Juma has participated in previous Africa Center events.

Andre Le Sage is Assistant Professor and Academic Chair for Terrorism and Counterterrorism at the Africa Center for Strategic Studies. Previously, Dr. Le Sage worked across the Horn of Africa, East Africa, and Central Africa with the United Nations, *Médecins Sans Frontières*, and other organizations. He was Political Adviser to the Somalia National Reconciliation Conference and has worked with other peace processes and negotiations efforts in Africa and Southeast Asia. His research and publications have focused on militia-faction politics, Islamic movements, and counterterrorism efforts in Somalia, particularly Mogadishu. He holds an MA in International Relations from Yale University and a PhD from Cambridge University's Faculty of Social and Political Science.

Julius Nyang'oro is currently Professor and Chairperson of African and Afro-American Studies at the University of North Carolina at Chapel Hill, where he has been a faculty member since 1990. He is a consultant for the Civil Society Task Force, MWENGO, and previously served in a variety of positions, including as a visiting professor and Head of the Political Science Unit at the University of Asmara in 1996–1997. Dr. Nyang'oro was also the Executive Director of the Institute for Comparative Studies of Africa and Afro-America and an instructor and coordinator for the UNITAS program at the University of North Carolina at Chapel Hill, and he taught at the Salzburg Seminar in Austria (1998). Dr. Nyang'oro has over 10 years of experience in international consultancies in Africa dealing with democratization, civil society, and human rights with projects in Addis Ababa, Dar es Salaam, Harare, Johannesburg, Nairobi, Bujumbura, Lilongwe, and Arusha. He is a member of several professional organizations, including the African Studies Association, the African Association of Political Studies, the International Studies Association, and the American Political Science Association. He has also served on many committees and boards, including several at the University of North Carolina, the African Studies Association Task Force on Sustainable Development in Africa, the Editorial Board of the American Review of Politics, and the Current Issues Committee of the African Studies Association. He is the author of more than 50 articles and chapters on civil society, democratic development, state building, and political economy, and has also authored and edited several books. Dr. Nyang'oro earned his JD from Duke University, a PhD and an MA in Political Science from Miami University of Ohio, and a BA in Political Science from the University of Dar es Salaam. He has participated in previous Africa Center events.

Wafula Okumu was at the time of writing with McMaster University's Center for Peace Studies. He has held teaching posts at Prescott College, Mississippi University for Women, Chapman University, and United Nations University. He also served as a conflict analyst for the African Union (AU), where he drafted the Memorandum of Understanding between the AU and Regional Mechanisms on conflict prevention, management, and resolution, and was a member of the teams that drafted the Protocol on Relations between the AU and Regional Economic Communities, set up the African Mission in Burundi, and drafted the Common African Defense and Security Policy. He has done consultancy work with a number of international organizations and research organizations on governance, peace, security, and humanitarian matters in Africa. While serving as an Academic Program Associate at the United Nations University, Tokyo, he coordinated international courses on peacekeeping and on the United Nations. His research and publications have been on a variety of topics, including child soldiers in Africa, human rights in Somalia and South Africa, peace and conflicts in Africa, the African Union, and humanitarian assistance in Africa. His most recent publication is a co-edited volume (with Paul Kaiser) entitled *Democratic Transitions in East Africa* (Ashgate, 2004). Dr. Okumu completed his undergraduate studies in Government and Sociology from the University of Nairobi and graduate studies in Political Science at Atlanta University. He also holds an International Diploma in Humanitarian Assistance from the City University of New York.

Ibrahim Wani is Chief of the Research and Right to Development Branch in the Office of the High Commissioner for Human Rights (OHCHR) in Geneva. Prior to his current position, he was the Regional Representative of the Office of the High Commissioner for Human Rights in Addis Ababa, Ethiopia, in which capacity he represented OHCHR at the African Union and other African regional and subregional organizations and managed OHCHR's programs and activities in the region. Preceding his service with the United Nations, Mr. Wani had an illustrious career in academia, international development, and public service. His academic career included service on the law faculties at the University of Virginia and University of Missouri. Mr. Wani also worked at the World Bank, where he served in various capacities in Africa and at the bank's headquarters in Washington, DC. He started his professional career in his native Uganda as a foreign service officer and subsequently as the legal officer in the Permanent Mission of Uganda at the United Nations in New York. Mr. Wani is a lawyer by training and received his law degree from Makerere University and LLM and SJD degrees from the University of Virginia Law School.

ABOUT THE
AFRICA CENTER
FOR STRATEGIC STUDIES

ACSS Vision

The Africa Center for Strategic Studies (ACSS) supports the development of U.S. strategic policy toward Africa by providing a variety of academic programs, fostering awareness of and dialogue on U.S. strategic priorities and African security issues, building networks of African military and civilian leaders, assisting U.S. policymakers in formulating effective African policy, and articulating African perspectives to U.S. policymakers.

ACSS Mission

The Africa Center for Strategic Studies supports the efforts of the Department of Defense and other U.S. agencies to counter ideological support for terrorism, foster regional cooperation on security issues, promote democracy, and assist African nations in improving their security and strengthening their defense establishments by promoting good governance, security sector professionalism, and democratic civil-military relations. ACSS also endeavors to foster the development of long-term, mutually beneficial relations between the United States and African countries by its open and frank consultations and seminars.

ACSS Goals

The goals of the Africa Center for Strategic Studies are to:

- promote military professionalism and democratic civil-military relationships in the security sector of African countries
- convey African views on the causes, scope, and ramifications of key security challenges to appropriate U.S. policymakers and help define options for addressing these issues

- explain U.S. policy perspectives to African leaders; build understanding of, and support for, the war on terror
- promote regional cooperation, capacity building, and information sharing among individuals and organizations with an interest in African security issues
- foster cooperative programs with European allies, other partner countries, and relevant international, regional, and civil society organizations
- use technology as a tool to support education programs, communicate with ACSS audiences, and collaborate with relevant U.S. Government entities
- build and maintain relationships of trust among African, U.S., European, and international civilian and military professionals with a common vision for a stable and peaceful Africa
- increase collaboration with other regional centers to maximize consistency of message and program effectiveness.

INDEX

221